The Good Granny Cookbook

Traditional favourites for modern families

Jane Fearnley-Whittingstall

With a foreword by Hugh Fearnley-Whittingstall
Illustrated by Alex Fox

First published in 2007 by
Short Books.
3-A Exmouth House
EC1R 0JH
10 9 8 7 6 5 4 3 2 1

This paperback edition published in 2009

A CIP catalogue record for this book
is available from the British Library.

Illustration Copyright ©
Alex Fox

ISBN 978-1-906021-66-5

Printed in Italy by L.E.G.O Spa

Design: Georgia Vaux

Every effort has been made to contact copyright holders for use of
material in this book, and the publishers would welcome any errors or
omissions being brought to their attention.

With happy memories of my mother and grandmothers and their delicious food

Contents.

Foreword. 8

Introduction. 10

Chapter 1. Breakfast 21

Chapter 2. Sunday Lunch 39

Chapter 3. Monday Left-overs 59

Chapter 4. Mid-week Meals 75

Chapter 5. Fish on Friday 99

Chapter 6. Saturday Stews 111

Chapter 7. Vegetable Dishes and Salads ... 131

Chapter 8. Teatime 161

Chapter 9. Soups, Starters and Savouries 187

Chapter 10. Puddings 221

Chapter 11. Treats and Sweets 269

Index. 280

Foreword.

Hugh Fearnley-Whittingstall

Obviously I'm biased, but I do think my Mum (or perhaps I should call her the granny of my children, to disguise the shameless nepotism) is rather brilliant. Underpinning her last book, *The Good Granny Guide*, with all its practical tips and witty insights about Grannydom, was a big and important truth: that the role of Grannies and Grandpas in family life is both privileged and vital, because grandparents can, and sometimes must, do things for their grandchildren that their parents cannot do.

Well this book, to me, encapsulates a truth at least as important: that food and family are inextricably linked, and that families that don't make time for the sharing of food, between the generations, will not thrive as they might. Her argument is simple: good family food is one of the fundamentals of a good family life, and like other timeless family values, it is only right and proper to hand down the wisdom through the generations. There is no better way to do that than to share with your family, and cook with them, the very recipes you yourself have loved, since your own childhood – the foods that made you, whenever you ate them, feel loved by those who fed you.

To some that may sound unduly idealistic, quaint or old-fashioned, or just plain mad. And it may well seem wholly unachievable, in a modern world where fast-food chains, big supermarkets and huge global food brands are bombarding us constantly with their corporate messages. But it is of course this onslaught of the mass-produced and the mediocre that makes real home cooking – like Granny used to do it – more important than ever.

As it happens, I've just eaten a slice of delicious lemon drizzle cake (for Granny's recipe, see page 176), with a cup of tea, at the kitchen table, with my family. Oscar and Chloe got back from school about half an hour ago, and so I took a break from my work. Now Oscar is watching cricket on the telly, and Chloe and Freddy are playing on the lawn. I'm back at my desk (obviously). I have to admit that I didn't actually make the cake, and neither did my wife. It was home-made, however, with Freddy's assistance, by our nanny, Claire. Such is modern life.

In my defence, I did collect some strawberries with Oscar in the greenhouse this morning before school. And he had them for breakfast with pancakes, made by Marie. And last weekend, at my parent's house, Oscar helped Granny Jane make a fish pie (see page 104). And Freddy helped Grandpa pick some asparagus – if you can call picking spears that are not yet ready, and sticking them up your nose, "helping".

The point is that ours is a household where food, the cooking of food, and the sharing of recipes in between the generations (in both directions, I hasten to add) is part of the fabric of the family. And I can honestly say that this is in no way a consequence of my career choice – although the reverse may well be the case. My sister and I learned to cook, literally, at our mother's knee – and sometimes while sitting on our grannies' laps.

Our two grannies were accomplished cooks, and my recollections of both of them are generously sprinkled with sweet treats and memorable meals. With Little Granny – my father's mother – the stand-out moment was a simple slice of hot granary toast, generously spread with bramble jam, after a chilly autumn walk on the beach at Worthing. I've no idea whether the jam was home-made. It may have been Tiptree, or Robertson's. But I remember her telling me that I didn't have to worry – there would be no prickles in it.

Big Granny loved to cook, and when she came to stay, she often used to help us make meringues. And I hope I will be forgiven for saying that they were always better when she made them with us than when mum did. In the end it was her son – my uncle Peter – who revealed the family secret. Not one ounce of caster sugar per egg white, as so many recipes will tell you, but two. As you will see on page 256 – the secret is now safe with Granny Jane.

I am delighted to be introducing this book for many reasons, some of them obvious. For Mum to have captured so many of the tastes – and smells, and textures, and warm feelings – of my own childhood, is a huge treat for me, and for future generations of my family. But that's only to be expected. What's remarkable is that she's produced a book that I know will chime with all her readers, and offer inspiration to a whole new generation of home cooks.

She's done it not only through a wonderful collection of rightly loved recipes, but also by including funny and touching recollections about food and family eating from friends, and friends of friends. The result is a lovely glow in the tummy, for everybody to share.

I honestly think anyone who spends time with this book will come to love it as much I do. Well, almost.

Introduction.

For some ha'e meat that canna eat,
And some nae meat that want it.
But we hae meat and we can eat,
And may the Lord be thankit.
ROBERT BURNS

The purpose of this book is to celebrate traditional British home cooking "like Grandma used to make," and to encourage another generation to give it a try. Cooks of my own generation remember with pleasure the robust, comforting food of our childhood. It is no-nonsense food, easy to prepare and has a distinctive style. A cousin describes it succinctly. Her mother, she says, left her and her siblings "with a legacy that includes wonderful food memories, a reverence for quality ingredients, an abhorrence of waste and... barely a recipe among us."

Many recipes were not passed directly, in writing, from mother to daughter, because they were taken for granted. They have been rescued and recreated here from many different sources.

As a granny, I look back at the food cooked by my grandmothers and my mother. Equally, I look forward to the meals I shall be preparing next week or next month for my children and grandchildren. It gives me pleasure to introduce them to Mum's chicken pie, or Granny's fudge sauce, hoping these dishes will become part of their own culinary repertoire when they grow up.

The power of food to unlock memories adds to the pleasure of cooking and eating food we enjoyed as children. In Marcel Proust's *Remembrance of Things Past* the narrator was inspired by such an experience, when he dipped his cake in a cup of lime tea. "As soon as I had recognized the taste of the piece of Madeleine soaked in the lime-blossom *tisane* which my aunt used to give me (although I did not yet know and must long postpone the discovery of why this memory made me so happy) immediately the old grey house upon the street, where her room was, rose up like a stage set..." Proust goes on to describe in vivid detail and not inconsiderable length the house, the town streets and the country lanes of his childhood. A recipe for Madeleines can be found on page 175.

Our memories, triggered by certain dishes, go beyond the appearance, smell and taste of the food, to include the way it was served: the table-cloth with a neat darn near one edge and a cluster of tiny rust spots at the centre; the pattern of Chinese birds strutting round the rim of Granny's tea cups; the glass cake plate with a stem like a goblet.

Often such memories extend to the rituals of preparing food. Perhaps you helped your grandmother or mother peel potatoes, chop onions and sieve soup. Or you sprinkled flour on to the pastry board from the tin with holes in its lid, and were given your own scrap of pastry to make a little man with currants for eyes, nose and mouth, and currant buttons down his front. Your arms ached as you struggled to cream the butter and sugar for a cake, and you were then rewarded by being allowed to lick the bowl.

My own early memories of home cooking date from the years after World War II when many food items were still rationed. As far as rationing was concerned, we got off lightly. We lived in London but most of our school holidays were spent with our maternal grandparents in Wiltshire. They had a large garden and a farm. The sources of our food were all around us, in neat, weed-free vegetable rows, under fruit cages draped with black cotton nets, on the trees in the orchard, and in the chicken run. The pigs were in their sty, the litter of sausage-like pink baby piglets declared by the pig-man who tended them to be "the prettiest little things ever born." Future mutton and beef grazed the fields and the cows moved twice a day from meadow to farmyard with their full, low-slung udders swaying from side to side. In the dairy we watched the milk run through a separator, and had a go at turning the handle of the churn, making cream into butter.

In good weather my brothers and cousins and I spent most of our time outdoors, in the garden and on the farm. Back in the kitchen, we "helped" by slapping the butter with ridged wooden bats to get rid of any water and air pockets, and rolling nuggets of butter between two bats to make elegant balls with a criss-cross pattern. The butter balls were dropped into cold water until it was time to pile them on a small glass dish for the breakfast or tea table.

The kitchen was the destination of all raw ingredients from the farm and garden. It was the largest room in the house if you included the scullery where vegetables were washed and peeled, and the larder with its marble shelves. I suppose my grandmother sometimes visited the kitchen, but I never saw her there, although we spent a great deal of time pestering the cook, Mrs Malone, when it was too wet or cold to go out. Our excuse for visiting the kitchen was to collect outer leaves of cabbages to feed our rabbits and scrounge a carrot and some spent tea-leaves to make their coats glossy.

I don't think Mrs Malone had ever been married, but cooks were always "Mrs". She was known to us all as Loney. Her streaky grey hair was screwed into a bun and she wore a large white apron over a striped dress with the sleeves neatly rolled up to the elbow, exposing lean, strong fore-arms – nothing like plump Mrs Bun the Baker's Wife in the Happy Families pack of cards, although, like Mrs Bun, Loney often wielded a rolling pin. She was a brilliant cook and must have been as precious to my grandparents as Anatole was to Aunt Dahlia in P.G. Wodehouse's Bertie Wooster stories. Luckily Loney was less temperamental than Anatole. She seemed not to mind us hanging around in her kitchen, sticking our fingers in mixing bowls for a taste. But her invariable answer to "What's for lunch?" (or tea or supper) was, "bread and look-at-it."

Loney was one of those instinctive cooks who never referred to a cookery book or wrote down a recipe. When asked, for example, how much sugar she put into a particular dish, she would reply, "Oh, just enough." Nevertheless, my mother and her sisters were able, by trial and error, to recreate a few of her recipes, and some are included in this book.

The kitchen was more fun than the dining room, where formality reigned. A friend, Alison, remembers, of her own childhood, "You never helped yourself, but sat waiting until you caught Grandma's eye. She then asked you what you would like, and it was passed to you. Meal times were very formal, and grace was always said before the meal. One day my grandfather was saying grace and my grandmother said, 'Speak up, John, I can't hear,' to which he replied, 'It is not you I am speaking to, Elizabeth.'"

I don't remember Grace being said in the dining room at Hazelbury except when the vicar came to lunch, when we were often caught unawares, earning a little admonishing frown from our grandmother. In the nursery, however, every meal started with "For what we are about to receive…" and ended with "Thank-God-for-my-good-lunch-please-may-I-get-down." In both dining room and nursery, we were expected to observe basic table manners, sitting up straight, keeping our elbows off the table, not speaking with our mouths full and not kicking the table leg.

At term-time weekends we had Sunday lunch with our other, London grandparents. Their small flat in Putney was on the fifth floor, with views up and down the River Thames. My father belonged to a rowing club just across the river and liked to go sculling on Sunday mornings. My brother and I spent the time beach-combing along the tide line and playing ducks and drakes with smooth, flat pebbles. By lunchtime we were always starving. During the week Granny bustled around in her green WVS uniform, doing meals on wheels, but on Sunday she cooked for us, producing, from her tiny kitchen, wonderful roasts with all the trimmings, and my all-time favourite pudding, vanilla ice cream with fudge sauce made from condensed milk. Offers to help in the kitchen were always refused, but after lunch we dried up while she washed.

At home, on the other hand, our help in the kitchen was taken for granted. My mother adored food and loved cooking; it would never have occurred to her that helping prepare food was a chore; to her the whole process was a delight. We inherited this attitude and, I hope, have passed it on to our children and grandchildren.

But cooking did not come easily to all of my mother's contemporaries. One heeded her own mother's advice, "Darling, never learn to cook, and then you won't have to." But along came the war, and she did have to. Some women never managed to learn. A friend put it down, in the case of her own mother, to "a combination of a wartime Scottish girlhood, eating institutional food first at school then in the Wrens, then early married life without much money and still on rations… Oddly enough she really enjoyed good food – it's just that she couldn't create it herself, and her wartime upbringing ran too deep ever to be properly eradicated." Nevertheless, her grandchildren remember fondly baking cakes with her.

My mother, and others like her, turned, for their knowledge, to the few cookery books that were available: *Mrs Beeton*, of course, and from 1956, *The Constance Spry Cookery Book*. "Connie was the Bible," a friend explained, "My godmother had Constance Spry on her bedside table and read nothing else to my knowledge." Other friends have shown me their mothers' kitchen notebooks, full of recipes, handwritten or cut out from newspapers and pasted in. Inherited cookbooks with worn-out spines fall open at favourite pages, splattered with fat or chocolate, and, in one case, still redolent of 1960s cigarette fumes. My mother's bedtime reading included Ambrose Heath's *Good Food* and *Good Savouries* and the useful *Plats du Jour* by Patience Gray and Primrose Boyd. When TV cooks Philip Harben and Fanny Craddock came on the scene, she enjoyed their programmes as entertainment rather than looking to them for serious instruction. Plus ça change.

A few rare and gifted cooks needed no books but cooked by instinct. My mother's sister Ray was one of them; "She cooked four meals a day using only fresh ingredients, and rarely consulted a recipe." Her daughter Prue wrote, "Certainly, to my knowledge, she never wrote one down. Each of us, though, has managed to continue with at least one speciality that we all recognize as hers. My oldest sister has followed my mother's tradition of making marmalade; a unique, strong, even harsh, chunky version. Another sister makes a dynamite Summer Pudding using blackcurrants picked from her garden; The youngest has a great way with potatoes. And my brother makes her curries and kedgerees. The closest I've come to emulating one of her distinctive creations is in her recipe for chocolate sauce, which she dictated to me a few years ago at my children's request."

Ray's chocolate sauce, and some of her other recipes are in this book, together with other cherished family recipes that have, by great good luck, been written down at some stage.

Our mothers and grandmothers achieved their results without the benefit of freezers, microwaves, food processors, blenders, or even dishwashers, and, in the absence of mechanical aids, an extra pair of hands was always welcome. As a result, we absorbed much of their knowledge effortlessly, just by being in the kitchen.

The kitchens of my two grandmothers could not have been more different. My London Granny cooked in a room where there was hardly space to swing a cat. There was a small electric cooker, a smaller fridge, a work table with a white enamel surface and a marbled lino floor. On the window sill there was always a large glass jar salvaged from the local sweet shop, no longer filled with bull's-eyes or gobstoppers, but with Granny's home-made potato crisps.

Our country grandmother Ginny's, or rather Loney's, kitchen was vast. An enormous Esse range with several ovens gobbled up coke and occupied the whole of one wall. Light poured in from leaded windows on two sides and between them were dressers and cupboards with work-tops of scrubbed pine, like the sturdy table in the centre of the room. There was a separate slate-shelved walk-in larder, and vegetables were prepared in the scullery, in shallow rectangular sinks with grooved wooden draining boards. There, bunches of carrots with feathery green tops still attached, and cabbages the size of footballs, mined and tunnelled by pale green Cabbage White caterpillars waited to be dealt with. In summer my brother was seldom seen without a butterfly net, and therefore remained on fairly good terms with the gardener in spite of our raids on the fruit cage.

The two kitchens had one thing in common: both were spotlessly clean and orderly: a place for everything and everything in its place. Compared to these models of tidiness my mother's kitchen was chaotic. Mum, adept at multi-tasking, liked to read while she stirred a sauce or waited for milk to come to the boil. She always had more than one book on the go, so there might be several on the kitchen table, her place marked with a spill charred from lighting the gas, or, if nothing else came to hand, the outside leaf of a leek. Novels jostled for space with recipe books, half-drunk mugs of tea, half-eaten biscuits, and pots of cooked vegetables waiting to be sieved into soup.

Like all good meals, ours began with shopping. I used to pass one of the first ever supermarkets in London daily, on the way home from school, and, seduced by the prospect of Green Shield Stamps, I urged Mum to use it, but she was slow to take advantage of its convenient one-stop shopping facilities. She and my London grandmother stayed loyal to their suppliers and trusted them to provide ingredients of the best quality. We shopped in what we called "the village," a row of shops a short walk from home, in an otherwise residential area. It consisted of a chemist, a grocer, a greengrocer, a fishmonger, a butcher, a baker (but no candlestick maker) and a newsagent. Milk was delivered daily to our doorstep, and errand boys on bicycles delivered meat and bread to people who lived further away from the shops, or didn't want to walk back with laden shopping bags. The boys whistled tunefully, and as they pedalled past you would hear snatches of "Put another nickel in" or "How much is that doggie in the window?"

Mum enjoyed talking to the shopkeepers and their assistants, and they would say things like, "I saved a bit of calf's liver specially for you," and "We'll have the first strawberries in tomorrow, shall I put a pound on one side?" They probably said the same to all their customers, but it made her feel good.

In the 1950s, Britain was still emerging from the austerity of wartime and postwar food rationing, and far fewer ingredients were available than there would be when I became a housewife a decade later. There were no exotic, imported veg – no peppers, no aubergines, no avocados. As far as fruit was concerned, we took oranges and lemons for granted, along with home-grown orchard fruits and soft fruits, and bananas soon became ever-present in the fruit bowl, but grapes and pineapples were luxuries, only bought for special occasions.

You ate what was in season, and what you lost in variety and choice, you gained from the anticipation that came with the annual cycle of farming and market gardening. In winter you could look forward to purple sprouting broccoli, and a month or two later to asparagus, then strawberries and raspberries followed by the glut of vegetables and fruit in late summer and early autumn.

Seasonality led to cooking sessions to fill the store cupboard with neat rows of bottled fruit, jars of jam and chutney, and crocks of salted beans. Marmalade was made in February when bitter Seville oranges were cheap. Plums, greengages, damsons, raspberries and blackberries were bottled or made into jam when they were at their most plentiful and cheapest. When my country grandmother's hens were laying well, we brought eggs home to preserve in isinglass in a big earthenware crock.

My mother, like others of her generation, had a habit of frugality, inherited from the days of rationing. She enjoyed making a little meat, fish or butter go a long way, and I don't think the food suffered as a result, except perhaps from the practice of using "top of milk" instead of cream. Some of our favourite staples, like shepherd's pie, risotto, and fish pie owe their existence to the necessity to use up every scrap.

Menus tended to follow the same weekly pattern, starting with the Sunday roast joint. What was left would be used on Monday to make croquettes, stovies or savoury pancakes – or of course shepherd's pie. Midweek meals were quick and easy dishes like toad-in-the-hole, grilled cutlets or fried liver and bacon, cheese and onion tart, or eggs in cheese sauce. Friday was always fish, sometimes yielding leftovers to make fishcakes or a risotto on Saturday. There was something comforting about knowing roughly what to expect, just as, at school, we felt lighthearted on Wednesday mornings because there would be treacle tart for lunch.

Most women took more trouble over everyday food than they do today, partly because there were no short cuts (no ready meals, no pre-washed, chopped and packaged vegetables, no modern kitchen gadgets), so taking trouble was the only way to achieve anything but the most basic meal. They also had more time, since fewer women went out to work. Our parents' and grandparents' diet was higher in carbohydrates than would be recommended today. But people burnt up calories by walking or cycling to work or school (there were far fewer cars), and taking part in games and sports at school and at weekends. In the days when the majority of houses and flats had no central heating, hearty meals in winter provided fuel to keep warm.

In the 1960s everything changed. We had never had it so good. New technology and a booming economy brought us American-style dream kitchens full of labour-saving devices. Feminism freed women to go to work, and many preferred slaving over a hot typewriter or a hot factory bench to slaving over a hot stove, and were able to come home to the benefits of frozen meals and pressure cookers.

Now we have arrived at a time when both women and men relish spending at least part of their life in the slow lane, and that applies particularly to the way they cook. The difference is that for us, it is not compulsory to cook the methodical hand-wrought way, as it was for our parents and grandparents. With modern kitchen gadgets and machinery, we can cook food like Grandma used to make in half the time it took her. With that in mind, I have adapted some traditional recipes to take advantage of labour-saving methods.

I found, when testing dishes that were untried in my family for thirty years or so, that tastes change from one generation to the next. My parents and grandparents were wary of herbs and spices, and only flirted nervously with garlic, just rubbing half a cut clove around the salad bowl or tucking a sliver or two up against the bone of a leg of lamb. I have therefore adapted some old favourites, beefing up the herbs and spices in line with modern ideas about flavour.

These days it no longer suits most people to eat stodgy puddings and sugary cakes, although some of us have a nostalgic yearning for them and others a sweet tooth that will not be denied. In order to appeal to a new generation, I have made some recipes lighter and less sweet than they were when I was a child.

The recipes are arranged as far as possible by meals, because that is how we tend to think about food: "What shall we have for supper?" "What shall I cook when the family comes to lunch on Saturday?" "Shall I do them a cooked breakfast for a special treat?" But many dishes are multi-purpose (kedgeree, for instance, could be served at breakfast, lunch or supper), and there are extra chapters for recipes that don't fit easily into the weekly routine of family cooking, such as puddings and special treats.

On a practical note, I recommend all cooks to use a timer with a good, loud ping to alert you when to take a dish out of the oven. Then you need never know the anguish of finding your masterpiece reduced to cinders.

This book offers a trip down memory lane for my generation and, for my children's generation, practical ideas for everyday, easy home cooking for hungry, active families. It also sets out to pass on traditional recipes to the next generation before they are forgotten. Cooking with children is immensely rewarding. It is shared fun, and introduces them to the deep creative satisfaction of preparing, cooking and serving food to family and friends. Not a bad legacy.

Jane Fearnley-Whittingstall
June 2007

The Recipes.

Chapter 1.

Breakfast.

15 Recipes

*We had our breakfasts — whatever happens in a house — robbery or murder,
it doesn't matter, you must have your breakfast.*
THE MOONSTONE BY WILKIE COLLINS

*I always remember what a great feature was made of the breakfasts at my
grandfather's (the Earl of St Germans) house parties at Port Eliot
(in Cornwall, 1870)… There would be a choice of fish, fried eggs,
and crisp bacon, a variety of egg dishes, omelets, and sizzling
sausages and bacon… On a side table… [were] delicious home-smoked hams,
pressed meats, one of the large raised pies for which Mrs Vaughan (the cook)
was justly famous, consisting of cold game and galantine, with aspic jelly.
The guests drank either tea or coffee, and there were the invariable
accompaniments of home-made rolls (piping hot) and stillroom preserves
of apple and quince jelly; and always piled bowls of rich Cornish cream.
The meal usually finished with a fruit course of grapes or hothouse
peaches and nectarines.*
MEMORIES OF THREE REIGNS BY ETHEL, LADY RAGLAN, 1928

On a more intimate scale is a scene from P.G. Wodehouse, where Bertie
Wooster, wearing a startling silk dressing gown, is shaking out his immac-
ulately ironed copy of *The Times*, waiting for Jeeves to come shimmering in
from the kitchen carrying on a silver tray a pair of perfectly grilled kippers.

In the late 1940s my country grandparents who were themselves products
of the Edwardian era, still went in for elaborate breakfasts, although not on
the scale described by Lady Raglan. Those breakfasts of my childhood are
firmly embedded in my memory, and, although few families go in for the full

English any more, except perhaps at special weekends, many traditional breakfast dishes are perfect for brunch, lunch or supper.

My brother Peter and I were often first into the dining room at breakfast time, with ravenous appetites, having been up since 6 o'clock to herd the cows from their field to the farmyard for milking. The long dining table was covered with a white damask cloth and often laid for eight or more, including assorted aunts, uncles and cousins. On it were two kinds of marmalade, one dark and thick cut, the other pale, with thin strips of rind; honey-in-the-comb dripping on to its dish; a jar of pale, grainy, set honey from our grandmother's bees; home-made jam; and a pot of Marmite. There was a plate of oatcakes and toast in silver racks. The toast was always made with white bread, something my grandchildren only get at Granny and Grandpa's, and consider a great treat. They refer to two racks I bring out when they visit as toast racquets.

We helped ourselves from the sideboard to porridge or cereals: corn flakes, puffed wheat (slogan: "Shot from Guns"), or grapenuts. We wrote our names on the surface of our porridge in runny honey dripped from a spoon. Some things don't change. "My grandchildren are Swiss," an old friend told me, "but, thanks to my edifying influence, they are hooked on porridge for breakfast, with names dribbled over with imported Golden Syrup – try writing Zacharias in syrup."

Porridge is good with jam, too, or demerara sugar. My grandmother, an early health food freak, used to spoil her porridge by sprinkling wheatgerm on it. Real Scots are said to put nothing on theirs except salt, and to eat it standing up, wearing a kilt and sporran, like the muscular chap tossing the caber on the Scotts Porage Oats packet.

Porridge is immensely comforting before setting out for work or to school on a cold winter morning, and addicts love it all the year round, its slow-burning nutritious qualities taking you through till lunch. It can be made quickly and easily, using milk or water or half of each, or cooking it the Scottish way, with one cup of steel-cut oats to three cups of water and a pinch of salt. Simply bring the water and salt to the boil in an uncovered saucepan (preferably non-stick; porridge is difficult to clean off), add the oats and simmer uncovered, stirring often, for about 10 minutes or until the porridge has thickened to your taste, then eat it immediately.

At breakfast with our country grandparents there was always a moment of excitement when we lifted the lids off a row of covered dishes keeping warm on a wide hotplate, to reveal what Loney had cooked that morning. There was always bacon and fried bread and eggs, fried, poached or scrambled; wild mushrooms and grilled tomatoes sometimes appeared, and fish featured once a week, in the form of kippers, fish cakes, herrings in oatmeal, or kedgeree.

Breakfast at my London grandparents' flat was less exciting: cornflakes followed by a boiled egg and toast, and a glass of milk. I stayed there only a few times. The atmosphere was uneasy, probably because my grandmother knew nothing about looking after children. On one visit she washed my hair in Lux soap flakes and it stood on end like Struwelpeter's for the rest of the day.

Fruit: Although it was well known that fruit is good for you, and gets the day off to a good start, fruit juice only appeared on hotel breakfast menus, never at home. Half a grapefruit was an occasional treat, but appeared more often as a starter at dinner, with a glacé cherry in the middle, than at breakfast. It was only welcome if someone else had taken the trouble to cut the flesh loose and detach each segment from its membrane. Elizabeth Craig, whose book *Cooking with Elizabeth Craig* (1932) lay spattered with fat and egg yolk on my mother's kitchen shelf, wrote, "If grapefruit be served, have it at each place with pointed spoon on the side before announcing breakfast." My father went through a phase of having stewed prunes for breakfast every day, albeit with an air of martyrdom, but fruit was not part of the children's routine.

Lady Jekyll, in *Kitchen Essays* (1921-2) suggests, alongside more traditional breakfast dishes, "Bananas, skinned and halved across, and again lengthwise, and served frizzling from a buttered sauté pan on fried toast, with perhaps a dash of orange juice added, an excellent and wholesome food for the young." A crispy rasher of streaky bacon might go well with this.

Devilled Kidneys.
2 helpings

This archetypal Edwardian breakfast dish is more easily appreciated at lunch or supper, and provides an excellent chance to convert eaters who are squeamish about offal. Once it appeared at lunch in my grandparents' house. When the butler presented the dish to him, my grandfather said, "What's this?" poking at it with the serving spoon. "Kidneys, Sir," was the reply. My grandfather, who liked to be sure all the produce came from his own farm, said "Where do they come from?" "They are your own kidneys, Sir."

1 TABLESPOON SUNFLOWER OIL
4 LAMBS' KIDNEYS
1 SMALL GLASS (25ML) OF SHERRY
1 DESSERTSPOON BALSAMIC VINEGAR
1 TEASPOON REDCURRANT JELLY
1 TEASPOON WORCESTERSHIRE SAUCE
1 TEASPOON ENGLISH MUSTARD
CAYENNE PEPPER
1 TABLESPOON DOUBLE CREAM
SALT AND GROUND BLACK PEPPER
CHOPPED PARSLEY

Heat the oil in a frying pan. Add the kidneys and cook them for one minute, turning them occasionally. Pour in the sherry, let it bubble for a moment, then add the vinegar and redcurrant jelly, stirring to dissolve. Add the Worcestershire sauce, the mustard, a pinch of cayenne, a pinch of salt and a generous amount of black pepper. Stir, then add the cream and let it bubble for a minute or two. If you like it really hot, add more cayenne and pepper. Sprinkle the parsley over the kidneys and eat them with triangles of fried bread or, for a main dish, rice or mashed potatoes.

Drop or Dropped Scones, or Scotch Pancakes.

Amanda Hornby

*My first cooking was dropped scones for my brother, cooked on a
Sunday afternoon after gardening. They should be eaten slightly warm
so that the butter half melts. As they were cooked we put them between
the layers of a damp tea towel to keep the steam in and keep them soft.*
ALISON MCMAHON

*You can drop them to make the children's initials,
or 3 scones joined to look like Mickey Mouse heads.*
SANDRA SMITH-GORDON

This variation on the pancake theme makes smaller, thicker cakes, somewhere
between a pancake and a crumpet.

225G/8OZ PLAIN FLOUR
1 TEASPOON BICARBONATE OF SODA
2 TEASPOONS CREAM OF TARTAR
PINCH OF SALT
1 ROUNDED TABLESPOON CASTER SUGAR
2 SMALL EGGS
150ML/ ¼ PINT MILK

Sift the dry ingredients into a bowl. Beat the eggs and pour them in. Mix to a
smooth batter, adding the milk gradually. Drop tablespoonfuls on to a well-
heated griddle or frying pan. When the surface bubbles turn over and cook the
other side. Serve warm with butter and honey or jam.

Note: The cream of tartar makes the scones rise with a structure of vertical air
holes, rather like a scaled-down crumpet. It doesn't matter if you leave it out;
they will simply be more pancake-y.

Pick and Mix Fry-up.

Visitors to Britain who have only breakfasted at the average hotel will wonder what the fuss is all about. It's not easy to deliver the full English with each component perfectly cooked, and many catering establishments fail. But when it works, it's hard to beat for breakfast, lunch or supper. It's a question of the quality of ingredients and timing. In the average domestic kitchen, four people is the most you can cater for successfully.

One for each person of some or all of the following:

RASHER OF BACK BACON

PORK SAUSAGE

SLICE OF BLACK PUDDING

TOMATO

1 MEDIUM OR ½ LARGE FIELD MUSHROOM

COOKED POTATOES

FRIED BREAD

EGG

Put a large dish in a slow oven to get hot. Start with the components which take longest to cook. In a large frying pan, heat enough fat or sunflower oil to just cover the surface. Put in the sausages and tomatoes, turning them as they cook on each side. After five minutes add the bacon and mushrooms. If the pan is too small, cook them in another pan on an adjacent burner. Remove the sausages, tomatoes and bacon when they are cooked, and put them in the dish in the oven to keep warm. Fry the black pudding, potatoes and/or bread in the fat from the sausages and bacon. Finally, fry the eggs.

Kedgeree.

6-8 helpings

In my youth, dances used sometimes to end with a breakfast of kedgeree. The smoky, fishy aroma began percolating into the ballroom at about 2am. More recently it has become our regular Saturday lunch dish, served piping hot with lots of leafy salad on the side. People argue about what goes into the definitive kedge. Most agree that the basic ingredients are smoked haddock, hard-boiled eggs, rice and butter, and I was brought up on a purist version which added nothing else, so that is the recipe I give here. Beauty needs no adornment. But the original dish was Anglo-Indian, so those who add spice with onions, curry powder, turmeric and even garlic (for breakfast?) have logic on their side. Others like to posh up their kedgeree by making it with salmon, or even smoked salmon and stirring in cream at the end.

900G/2LB SMOKED HADDOCK FILLETS

A BAY LEAF

A BUNCH OF PARSLEY

250ML/9 FL OZ MILK

250ML/9 FL OZ WATER

3 HARD-BOILED (9 MINUTES) EGGS

225G/8OZ BASMATI RICE

115G/4OZ BUTTER

SALT AND FRESHLY GROUND BLACK PEPPER

Put the haddock in a shallow dish with the bay leaf and parsley stalks (keep the leaves to garnish the kedgeree) and just cover it with the milk and water, mixed. If necessary, add a little more water. Cover with foil and put in a moderate oven until just cooked; check after 10 minutes. The flesh should be opaque and the flakes should separate easily.

Meanwhile, boil and shell the eggs.

Wash the rice and put it in a large saucepan. Strain off the liquid the haddock was cooked in and add it to the rice. Bring it to the boil, stir, cover and simmer without stirring until the rice is tender, about 12 minutes. Drain off any surplus liquid.

Meanwhile, skin and roughly flake the fish and roughly chop the hard-boiled eggs. Chop the parsley.

Melt the butter over gentle heat in a saucepan big enough to hold the finished dish. Now is the time, if you're adding extra flavourings, to soften the chopped onion in the butter and cook the spices for a few minutes to release their flavour. Add the rice, haddock and eggs to the butter, stir gently until heated through, scatter the chopped parsley over and eat hot.

Pancakes.

Pancakes are our grandchildren's regular Saturday breakfast treat.

300ML/ ½ PINT MILK
2 EGGS
20G/½ OZ CASTER SUGAR
PINCH OF SALT
115G/4OZ PLAIN FLOUR
55G/2 OZ MELTED BUTTER
SUNFLOWER OIL

Make the batter the easy way, in a blender. Put in the milk, eggs, sugar and salt and whiz for a few seconds. Add the flour and whiz again till the mixture is smooth. Put the batter in a jug or bowl and leave it to rest for 30 minutes. Just before cooking the pancakes, stir in the melted butter.

Heat a frying pan and add just enough sunflower oil to cover the surface, then quickly wipe off the surplus with kitchen paper. When it's smoking hot, pour in about half a ladle of batter and immediately tip the pan to and fro so the batter thinly covers the whole surface. After a few seconds, when the uppermost surface of the pancake looks dry, turn it over, gently easing a palette knife under it.

Squeeze lemon juice over the pancake and sprinkle it with sugar, before rolling it up or folding it into quarters.

Variations: Spread the pancake with maple syrup, jam or chocolate spread.

Hot Cross Buns.

(Traditionally eaten on Good Friday.)
Makes 12 buns

If you have no daughters,
give them to your sons.
One a penny two a penny,
hot cross buns.

If you have never cooked with yeast before, don't be afraid to have a go at it. It's not difficult and it's exciting when the dough rises according to plan.

200ML/ ⅓ PINT MILK
50G/2OZ CASTER SUGAR
1 LEVEL TABLESPOON DRIED YEAST
450G/1LB STRONG PLAIN FLOUR
½ TEASPOON SALT
1 HEAPED TEASPOON MIXED SPICE
1 SMALL TO MEDIUM EGG, BEATEN
50G/2OZ MELTED BUTTER
115G/4OZ RAISINS
50G/2OZ CHOPPED MIXED PEEL

Warm the milk to hand-hot. Stir in a teaspoon of the sugar, sprinkle in the dried yeast and leave for about 10 minutes until it froths.

Meanwhile, sift the flour, salt, the remaining sugar and spice into a warm mixing bowl. Make a well in the centre and stir in the yeast liquid, egg, melted butter, raisins and peel. Mix everything together to form a soft dough and knead it on a floured surface until it is smooth. Shape it into a round, replace it in the bowl, cover with a cloth and leave in a warm place to rise. It should take 40 to 50 minutes.

When the dough has doubled in size, set the oven at 220°C, and line one or more baking trays with parchment. Turn the dough on to a floured surface, knead it lightly and divide it into 12 pieces. Shape them into slightly flattened rounds and put them on the lined baking trays.

Cover with a cloth and leave in a warm place to prove for 20 minutes or until the buns look puffy. Slash the top of each bun with a sharp knife, to form a cross. Brush them with milk and bake in the oven for 15-20 minutes.

Variation: If you leave out the spices, these buns are teacakes. In the days when trains had dining cars with waiter service, toasted teacakes were always on the Great Western Railway's teatime menu, served with butter and jam in little glass dishes. A delicious reward for going through the agony of catching a train with my mother.

Loney's Oatcakes.
Makes 12 2 ¹/₂-inch cakes

These were always served at breakfast for my Scottish grandfather, to be eaten with thick, pale, grainy honey from my grandmother's bees, but they are also good with marmalade, jam and, for lunch or supper, cheese.

225G/8 OZ MEDIUM OATMEAL
115G/4 OZ PLAIN FLOUR
1 TEASPOON BAKING POWER
PINCH OF SALT
85G/3 OZ BUTTER OR LARD

Set the oven at 180°C. Line a baking tray with parchment.

Mix all the dry ingredients in a bowl. Make a well in the centre, pour in the melted butter or lard and mix with your hands, adding enough water to make a stiff dough. Scatter some oatmeal on a pastry board or work surface to stop the dough sticking. Roll out the dough about 3mm/¹/₈ in thick and cut out rounds with a 6¹/₂cm/2¹/₂in plain cutter. Bake the oatcakes on a baking tray lined with parchment for about 40 minutes, until they are very light brown. Cool them on a wire rack.

Armand 2001 Marmalade.

Making marmalade is much more than providing an essential breakfast accompaniment. It's a valuable and enriching therapy for the overworked, exhausted executive. I learned the following recipe from my mother in the early 1950s. She had eleven grandchildren and six great-grandchildren. We shared much discussion and humour over the making of our marmalade.

TOM ROBERTS

10 SEVILLE ORANGES

2 LEMONS

2 GRAPEFRUIT

4.5 LITRES/8 PINTS WATER

3.6KG/8LB GRANULATED SUGAR

This will make about 23lb of marmalade (about 25 jars), which should provide plenty for the family, friends and the church bazaar. If you want to try less, halve the above quantities.

You need a pan of 45-50cm/18-20in diameter to hold 6.75 litres/12 pints.

Cut the oranges, lemons and grapefruit in half and squeeze out the juice. Pour the juice into the pan. Save the pips and bits of pith in a separate bowl. Cut the peel into quarters, and add these and the water to the pan. Place the pips and pith into a square of muslin and tie the muslin into a bag with string. Immerse the bag in the pan and tie it to the handle. Heat the mixture and simmer for two hours. Leave it to cool, preferably overnight.

Next day wash the jam jars and allow them to dry. Put the sugar in a large ovenproof dish and warm it in the oven.

Take the peel quarters out of the pan and cut them into slices. Unless you want chunky marmalade, it's important to make them really thin. Place the cut peel back into the pan. Extract the muslin bag and place it in a separate bowl. Now bring the mixture up to simmering point.

Place 4 saucers in the freezer. Take the warm sugar out of the oven and add it to the fruit mixture. Stir it slowly with a wooden spoon until all the sugar has dissolved. Turn the heat up, take the bag of pips and squeeze it over the pan to extract as much pectin as you can. Stir it in with a whisk.

Boil the mixture vigorously for 20 minutes, take a frozen saucer and using a wooden spoon pour a small sample on to the saucer to test for set. Tip the saucer at a slight angle. If the marmalade runs down slowly, showing legs or creases, then it's ready to set. You may need to test several times. Keep washing the saucers and putting them back into the freezer. When the mixture reaches setting point, put the jam jars in a warm oven for about 5 minutes. Turn the heat off under the marmalade. Take the jam jars out of the oven and, using a jug, pour the marmalade into the jars. Place wax seals into each jar while the marmalade is still hot, and cover.

Tip: The longer you boil the marmalade, the darker it gets. When you make your first batch you may be nervous about getting it to set, so you will tend to make darker marmalade. You gain confidence with experience.

You can vary the basic recipe according to your taste by substituting a sweet orange for one or both of the grapefruit.

Cinnamon Toast.
For 4

Our daughter Sophy brought this recipe home when she was an au pair in New York in the 1980s. Her American employer taught her how to make it for the boys she was looking after, and now it's a favourite with her own boys.

4 SLICES OF WHITE BREAD
BUTTER (SOFT)
2 TABLESPOONS CASTER SUGAR
1 TEASPOON GROUND CINNAMON

Mix the sugar with the cinnamon. Toast the bread and cut off the crusts. Butter the toast and sprinkle thickly with the sugar/cinnamon mixture. Put under a moderate grill or into the oven until the sugar has melted and turned golden brown. Cut into strips.

Eggs.

Go to work on an egg
1960s ADVERTISING SLOGAN

*My English granny had a maid called Kate, a sweet spinster, who told me once
that when her father had an egg for breakfast, he would put a dab of egg yolk on
the front of all his children's clothes, just before they went to school, to make it
look as though they were rich enough to all have an egg for breakfast.*
ALISON McMAHON

*Every Easter we wrapped eggs in various coloured ribbons and boiled them
for 10 minutes – the dye from the ribbons made the most perfect patterns
and we produced many masterpieces. Sadly the ribbons of today are too
superior and the dye does not come out.*
MERLE BARRINGTON

For decades eggs were frowned on, as contributing too much chloresterol to the diet, but recently their reputation has been restored and they are once more recognized as providing nourishment in an extraordinarily compact package.

Daily breakfast eggs may not be part of the average household's routine, but an egg slipped on top of a plateful of bubble and squeak or Welsh rabbit "turns a snack into a meal."

Whether you like your eggs poached, fried, boiled or cooked some other way, there are right and wrong ways of doing it.

Poached Eggs.

An egg that is not new-laid will not poach without breaking. A man writes that for
this reason he always, when he wants an egg in a teashop, asks to have it poached.
GOOD THINGS IN ENGLAND BY FLORENCE WHITE

For perfect poaching, break the (new-laid) egg into a cup or small bowl. Bring a saucepan of water to the boil. Turn down the heat so the water is barely simmering and stir the water to make a whirlpool. Gently slide the egg from the cup into the centre of the whirlpool. After 3 minutes lift the egg out with a slotted spoon. Some cooks think the egg white hardens quicker if vinegar is added to the water – a tablespoon of vinegar to two pints of water.

Fried Eggs.

If you are making a full English breakfast, the eggs are best fried in fat left over from frying the bacon. Otherwise, fry them in butter rather than oil. The fat should be hot enough to start cooking the egg white immediately, so that it does not spread all over the frying pan. In a large pan you can cook several eggs at the same time. Tilt the pan and spoon the hot fat over the eggs to cook them on top.

Oeufs en Cocotte.

My mother used to make these as a change from boiled, poached, fried or scrambled, allowing, for each person, one egg, a tablespoon of double cream, butter, salt and pepper. Grease the cocotte dishes with butter and put them in a roasting tin. Spoon into each cocotte enough cream to cover the base. Break an egg into each. Season and dot with small pieces of butter. Place the tin in a moderate oven and pour in hot water till it comes halfway up the sides of the cocottes. Bake for 6 to 8 minutes, until the whites are just set.

Boiled Egg with Marmite Soldiers.

Marmite has the power to evoke memories. Expat Brits long for it, dreaming at night of the familiar fat brown jar with the yellow label.

Marmite soldiers to dip in the yolk of a boiled egg can be of white bread or brown, toasted or not, buttered, spread sparingly with the magic substance, and cut into fingers.

Everyone knows how long they like their eggs boiled. Four minutes suits most, yielding a soft yolk with no risk of a transparent white.

Scrambled Eggs.

One scrambled egg will serve three people if the egg is mixed with more milk than usual, and a heaped tablespoonful of very fine breadcrumbs is added.
A WARTIME MAGAZINE

The wheeze of adding water or milk to make a few eggs go further was useful in times of wartime deprivation when eggs were a scarce commodity, but there is no longer any excuse for it. Scrambled eggs are the best-ever, all-purpose, instant dish, for breakfast, lunch, high tea or supper and have become a pleasure to cook since the invention of the non-stick saucepan.

Allow 3 eggs for two people, 5 eggs for three, and so on. Melt a generous lump of butter in a saucepan. Break the eggs into a bowl and whisk with a fork to mix the whites and yolks together. Season with salt and pepper and pour the eggs into the saucepan. Cook them over gentle heat, stirring all the time, scraping the eggs from the bottom and sides of the pan as they cook. Remove from the heat just before they are the consistency you like, and continue stirring. Serve on hot buttered toast.

Scrambled eggs can be turned into a more substantial dish for lunch or supper by adding chopped smoked salmon or ham or mushrooms sliced and cooked in a little cream, asparagus tips or grated cheese.

Eggy Bread, or French Toast.

A versatile standby popular with students fending for themselves, eggy bread also has a history in some families. One grandmother remembers it served with maple syrup when a great aunt arrived from Canada. Another says "we always had it at Granny's – it was part of the ritual." I have seen recipes for eggy bread which include milk, cream, peanut butter, raspberries, or ham and cheese; to my mind they are missing the point which is that eggy bread is just about as simple as cooking gets.

For each person:

ONE EGG

ONE THICKISH SLICE OF BREAD

SALT

PEPPER

FAT OR OIL FOR FRYING

In a shallow dish or deep plate large enough for at least one slice of bread to lie flat, whisk up the egg(s) with a pinch of salt and a few twists of freshly ground black pepper.

Lay the bread in the egg, turning it so the egg can soak into both sides. Heat a frying pan, add about 1 tablespoon of oil and fry the bread until golden brown on each side, turning it over once. If you are having bacon rashers with the eggy bread, you can cook them first and fry the bread in bacon fat.

Chapter 2.

Sunday
Lunch.

9 Recipes

*Our Sunday lunches were beef, pork and lamb or mutton in weekly rotation,
put in the oven before we all went to church. I seem to remember it as rather
grey looking meat. The mutton was always riddled with fat, which I hated.
I would drop it under the table unseen, except by a sharp-eyed brother who
would say in a loud voice, 'I can see Alison!'*
ALISON MCMAHON

*A young neighbour of Sir William's was invited to lunch at Windlestone and
arrived in justifiable trepidation. Sir William was charming, until at lunch the
butler, House, wheeled in a covered trolley. When he lifted the cover to reveal a
large and excellent loin of lamb, Sir William shouted, 'Not bloody lamb again!',
seized it and threw it out of the window. House, who had evidently experienced
this before, meekly wheeled out the empty trolley. The family and guests lunched
off vegetables while the young guest reflected that all he had heard of Sir
William appeared to be well-founded."*
ANTHONY EDEN BY R RHODES JAMES 1986

One of the perennial problems for all cooks is how to vary the menu enough
to keep the family happy and interested. A friend's grandmother, faced with
deciding yet again whether to order beef or mutton from the butcher, sighed,
"Oh, if only God would invent a new animal." In my family the monotony of
alternate sheep, ox and pig was relieved by rabbit, hare and game birds and
in the days of wartime and postwar rationing, these were sometimes the
only available source of meat. Another friend remembers the food in her
grandparents' house in Scotland as relentlessly plain. "The only things I
remember vividly were unbelievably disgusting to a small child – a rabbit,
shot that morning and skinned in the kitchen, which upset me, undercooked

and apparently swimming in its own blood (come to think of it, it now sounds highly fashionable!" She was undergoing temporary exile from her parents' house in Iran in that dour Scottish household, and yearned for food cooked by Georgie, the Persian giant who presided over her mother's kitchen. Georgie's several wives made delicious chapattis on a brazier in the yard, where he kept tethered a sheep called Rahmat. "The sheep was always called Rahmat, even though every year, just before Noh Ruz – the Persian New Year, in the spring – he would go away to the hills for a holiday with his relations. My sisters and I would kiss him goodbye and then we would eat a lot of mutton, and then he would come back looking much, much younger and with no horns."

Whether the meat comes from a familiar four-legged friend, or from the local butcher, the Sunday lunch ritual is still a powerful force in holding families together: the one meal of the week when everyone makes an effort to be at home; Mum's chance to feed up schoolchildren and students who she imagines alternately starving and bingeing on junk food once they're out from under her wing; the children's chance to take on fuel for the week ahead, and squabble, amiably let's hope, with their siblings; and Dad's chance to pose as a figure of authority. When my father died a friend wrote that her most vivid memory of him was at Sunday lunch, brandishing the carving knife and fork, and beaming. "Wackington hoggin!" he would cry as he attacked the joint. Another friend remembers that her own father always surreptitiously dropped the best morsels to his waiting spaniel.

Sunday lunch was not always idyllic. Some people remember it as more penance than pleasure, with grey, gristly meat and congealing fat, watery cabbage and potatoes with hard, grey eyes. Puddings of stodgy suet with lumpy custard were not much better, and there was no question of leaving anything on your plate. "I don't like it," or "I'm not hungry" were not considered valid excuses. But for those of us whose food was chosen and cooked with skill as well as love, the rich flavours and contrasting textures linger in our grateful memories, inspiring us to cook memorable meals for the next generation.

The archetypal Sunday lunch is roast beef and Yorkshire pudding, and success is pretty well guaranteed provided the beef is pink and not grey, the roast potatoes are golden brown and crunchy outside and fluffy inside, and the Yorkshire pud is crisp and full of air.

Yorkshire pudding: In the past I have occasionally tried to get away with dishing up roast beef without the Yorkshire pud. It was not popular, but the truth was, my Yorkshire puddings (little individual ones, not a big rectangle like the ones my mother made) didn't always rise, and I was nervous. Now I know how to get it right every time (touch wood).

The secrets of success are, (1) use half milk, half water rather than all milk, (2) let the batter rest for half an hour, (3) have the oil or fat really hot before you put the batter in. The beef joint which the Yorkshire pudding is to accompany should be allowed to rest (there seems to be a lot of resting involved in preparing Sunday lunch, but not for the cook) before it is carved. When you take the meat out, turn the oven up to 220°C, pour 2 tablespoons of olive oil into the Yorkshire pudding tin, and put it in the oven to heat for at least 5 minutes. You can tell when it is hot enough by dropping a little batter into the tin. If it sizzles, it is hot enough, if not, it needs a few more minutes before the batter goes in.

If you follow these rules, after 20 or 25 minutes, the pudding will be puffed up and golden brown.

Rescue remedy: If it doesn't work out quite like that, try using self-raising flour instead of plain next time, or adding a teaspoon of baking powder.

Pork crackling: When roast pork was on the menu, I sometimes had trouble with crackling, or rather, the lack of it. Now I have crack[l]ed the problem.

There are three essentials. (1) Make sure the skin is properly scored. If the butcher has done a poor job, do it again with a Stanley knife. (2) Rub salt into the skin, getting it well down into the cracks. Do not add oil. (3) Roast at a high heat (220°C) for at least the first 20 minutes, then turn the heat down to 160°C for the rest of the cooking time.

Rescue remedy: If by any chance the crackling is still not blistery and golden when the meat is ready, if you have an in-oven grill, turn it on high and give the crackling a quick blast. Watch it like a hawk, or it will turn to black ashes. Otherwise, while the meat is resting, turn the oven up, cut off the crackling all in one piece and cook it in the top of the oven for a little longer.

For the best ever roast potatoes see page 154.

Mira's Rack of Lamb with Herby Mustard Crust.

Serves 6

A rack of lamb is a row of cutlets all in one piece. Our friend Mira Osmond cooked this succulent dish for us one summer evening, and kindly let me have the recipe. The only difficult part is the timing: the lamb must be pink.

2 TABLESPOONS OF ROSEMARY LEAVES
3 GARLIC CLOVES, CRUSHED
1½ TABLESPOONS OF MALDON SALT
2 TABLESPOONS DIJON MUSTARD
1 TABLESPOON BALSAMIC VINEGAR
3 RACKS OF LAMB

Put the rosemary, garlic and salt in the small bowl of a food processor and whiz until the rosemary is very finely chopped. Add the mustard and vinegar and whiz until the mixture is thoroughly amalgamated.

Spread the mixture over the outside (the outer curve) of each lamb rack. Put the racks in a roasting tin with the rubs curving downwards and leave to rest for 1 hour.

Heat the oven to 220°C and roast the lamb for 20 minutes if you like the meat rare, or 25 minutes if you like it just pink. Leave it to rest, covered loosely with foil, for 15 minutes before carving.

Gammon with Parsley Sauce.

To cook a whole ham is a major undertaking, needing, just for a start, a massive pan to cook it in. A gammon is a little more manageable, but you don't have to buy a whole one; a 1.8kg/4lb corner of gammon is ideal for the average family, leaving plenty of meat to eat cold or *rechauffé*. Serve it with spinach, then you can sing, "with a roly, poly, gammon and spinach/ Heigh-ho says Antony Rowley."

GAMMON JOINT WEIGHING ABOUT 1.8KG/4LB
1 LARGE ONION, 1 LEEK, 2 LARGE CARROTS
PARSLEY, THYME, BAY LEAF
10 BLACK PEPPERCORNS
2 TABLESPOONS OF DIJON MUSTARD
2 TABLESPOONS SOFT BROWN SUGAR
ABOUT 20 CLOVES

Put the gammon in a large saucepan with the vegetables. Add enough cold water to just cover the meat. Bring to the boil, skimming any scum that forms, then simmer very gently for 1 hour 40 minutes. Remove the gammon from the stock and put it in a roasting tin. Cut away the skin, leaving a good layer of fat. Score the fat, cutting through it almost to the lean mean beneath, in a cross-cross, diamond pattern. Mix the sugar and mustard together and rub them all over the surface. Stick a clove in the centre of each diamond.

Roast in a hot oven for 30 minutes. Remove and rest for at least 10 minutes before carving.

Parsley sauce: This is a classic sauce which has suffered from too often being made with the usual basic white sauce ingredients of butter (or margarine), flour and milk, with the flour insufficiently cooked to take away its raw taste, and the milk not properly stirred in, producing a depressingly lumpy result. This recipe is based on a properly flavoured béchamel sauce, which makes all the difference.

1 CARROT

½ ONION

1 CELERY STICK

500ML/18 FL OZ WHOLE MILK

A BAY LEAF

50G/1¾ OZ BUTTER

50G/1¾ OZ PLAIN FLOUR

A LARGE BUNCH OF PARSLEY, FINELY CHOPPED

SALT AND PEPPER FOR SEASONING

Grate the carrot, onion, and celery stick and put them in a saucepan with the milk and bay leaf. Bring the milk to the boil and take it off the heat. Leave it to infuse for an hour, then strain it.

Melt the butter in a saucepan, stir in the flour and cook gently for a few minutes but do not let the mixture brown. Add the milk gradually, stirring until the sauce is smooth. Simmer it gently for 5 minutes. If necessary thin it with stock from the gammon. Stir in the parsley and season with salt and pepper.

Variations: Egg sauce is good with boiled chicken or steamed or baked fish: leave out the parsley but add two chopped hard-boiled eggs and a tablespoon of chopped chives. For onion sauce to have with mutton, finely chop two onions, cook them gently in butter until soft, then stir into the béchamel sauce.

Boiled Beef and Carrots with Diana's Dumplings.

Serves 8

This wonderful winter warmer makes a change from roast meat. My mother always used salt beef, but fresh meat is also excellent, cooked at the slowest of simmers, specially if you are in any doubt about its tenderness. If you want to use salt beef, order it a week in advance from your butcher. Our friend Diana makes the lightest, fluffiest dumplings to go with rich beef casseroles for her shooting lunches. When I asked her for her secret, she told me she used the recipe off the Atora suet packet.

For the beef:
A PIECE OF SALT SILVERSIDE, TOPSIDE OR
BRISKET WEIGHING 2 KG/4LB 8OZ OR MORE
3 STICKS OF CELERY, CHOPPED
PARSLEY, THYME, 2 BAY LEAVES
10 BLACK PEPPERCORNS
6 ONIONS, PEELED
6 CARROTS, PEELED AND CUT IN QUARTERS LENGTHWAYS
2 TURNIPS, DICED INTO 2IN SQUARES
LEEKS, CLEANED AND CUT INTO 5CM LENGTHS

Put the beef in a saucepan large enough to hold all the vegetables as well, and cover it with cold water. Add the celery, a good bunch of parsley stalks and 4 or 5 sprigs of thyme and the bay leaves and peppercorns. Bring slowly to the boil, skimming off any scum that rises to the surface. Simmer very gently for 2 hours. Add the onions and simmer for another ½ hour. Add the carrots, turnips and leeks. Make the dumplings (see below). After another ½ hour, if the vegetables are cooked, remove the meat and vegetables to a serving dish. Let the stock simmer more vigorously, drop the dumplings in, and cook them for 15 to 20 minutes. If you want them fluffy all through, cover the pan. If crispy on top, leave the lid off.

Herb dumplings: This is the Atora suet recipe with my own variation of added herbs.

175G/6OZ SELF-RAISING FLOUR
85G/3OZ SUET
PINCH SALT
2 TABLESPOONS CHOPPED PARSLEY

Mix all the ingredients in a bowl, then add enough cold water to make a workable dough. Knead the dough until it is elastic, and chill it for 15 minutes. Shape the dough into balls the size of walnuts.

Variations: Add grainy mustard or grated horseradish to the dumplings, or vary the herbs. For a change, serve the boiled beef without dumplings, with lentils and salsa verde.

Boeuf à La Mode.
Serves 8-10

My mother used to make this dish of cold beef and vegetables in a rich jellied sauce for family lunches in the summer. She served it with a green salad, heeding Elizabeth David's advice, "do not, I beseech you, succumb to the English custom of serving hot vegetables with cold meat. In the first place their presence on the plate will melt the jelly and nullify the whole idea of the dish and, in the second place, they are totally out of keeping. You already have meat, carrots and a wine-flavoured jelly... nothing else is needed." Start a day or two before you need the dish. Don't be put off by the calf's feet in the ingredients. They provide the gelling agent, and are available from good butchers. If they are not available, use 4 pig's trotters instead.

BUTTER OR OIL
2 ONIONS, SLICED
A 1.8-2.25KG/4-5LB PIECE OF SILVERSIDE, TOP RUMP OR TOPSIDE OF BEEF
FLARE FAT OR 8 RASHERS OF FATTY STREAKY BACON
A SMALL GLASS OF BRANDY
300ML/ ½ PINT RED WINE
2 CALF'S FEET (ASK THE BUTCHER TO SPLIT THEM)
900G/2LB CARROTS
2 GARLIC CLOVES, CRUSHED
2 BAY LEAVES, 6 STEMS OF PARSLEY, 2 SPRIGS OF THYME AND A PIECE OF
ORANGE PEEL
SALT AND PEPPER
MEAT STOCK OR WATER

When you buy the meat ask the butcher to tie it in a sausage shape, and tie a piece of flare fat over it. Failing this, you can yourself tie on rashers of streaky bacon, with as much fat on them as you can get.

In a large frying pan, heat some oil and cook the onions until they begin to colour. Remove the onions, put the meat in and brown it well all over.

Heat the brandy, pour it over the beef, setting it alight as you do so. Put the beef in a large casserole or high-sided, lidded roasting tin with just enough space for the other ingredients. Put the onions around the meat.

Deglaze the frying pan with the wine, and pour it over the beef. Rinse the calf's feet in cold water and tuck them, with 2 of the carrots, the garlic and herbs, around the meat. Season with salt and pepper and add enough hot stock or water just to cover the meat.

Cover tightly with two layers of greaseproof paper or foil, then the lid of the pot.

Simmer very gently on top of the stove or in the oven at 150°C for 4½ hours.

Cook the rest of the carrots separately until just tender.

When the beef is cooked, remove it from the stock, cover it and put it in a cool place. When it is cold, put it in the fridge. Strain the stock through muslin into a bowl and put it in the fridge overnight. By morning it should be jellified, with some fat on top. Remove the fat and heat the jelly until it is just melted. If by any chance it has not jelled, boil it fiercely to reduce it by one-third or so. That should do the trick.

Carefully slice the beef and arrange it on a deep serving dish with the carrots. When the stock is cold but not yet set, pour it over the beef and carrots, and put it in the fridge so that the winey, meaty, herby jelly can set.

Shoulder or Leg of Lamb à La Boulangère.

Serves 6

On their way to church on Sundays, French housewives used to take their joint round to the baker's to be cooked in his oven after the bread came out. Cooked this way, with the juices from the meat permeating a bed of vegetables, it is succulent and full of flavour. Our parents routinely served the traditional English accompaniments, mint sauce and redcurrant jelly, with roast lamb, but it would be disrespectful to the French to have them with lamb cooked this way. An Italian salsa verde, a punchy green, herby sauce which we have taken to serving with lamb, would go well.

A SHOULDER OR LEG OF LAMB, AT LEAST 1.5-2KG

3 CLOVES OF GARLIC

ROSEMARY

ABOUT 1KG/2LB 4OZ POTATOES (EXACTLY HOW MANY DEPENDS HOW MANY
PEOPLE YOU ARE FEEDING)

3 OR 4 ONIONS

OLIVE OIL

SALT AND PEPPER

ABOUT 500ML STOCK

Set the oven at 220°C.

With the point of a sharp knife make incisions in the lamb and stick a sliver of garlic and a few rosemary needles in each incision. Cut the onions and potatoes into slices about the thickness of a £1 coin (this can be done in a food processor or using a mandoline).

Grease a large roasting tin with olive oil and lay some sprigs of rosemary and any remaining garlic on the bottom. Put the lamb in the middle and spread the potatoes and onions around it, a layer of potatoes, a layer of onions, and a top layer of potatoes, adding salt and pepper to each layer. Rub olive oil over the lamb and pour enough stock over the potatoes to moisten but not swamp them.

Bake in a hot oven for 25 minutes. Reduce the heat to 160°C and bake for a further 15 minutes per 500g/lb. If the potatoes are browning too fast, cover them with foil. With this timing the lamb should be pink (not grey) and the vegetables tender and infused with the unctuous fat and juices of the meat. Rest the meat for 15 minutes before carving. If necessary you can turn up the oven to crisp and brown the potatoes while the lamb is resting.

Salsa verde: You'll need a good handful of flat-leaved parsley; a bunch of chives; 4 or 5 mint leaves and/or basil leaves; 2 garlic cloves, crushed; 2 teaspoons of rinsed capers; 5 anchovy fillets; a squeeze of lemon; and olive oil. Roughly chop the herbs. Put them in the small bowl of a food processor with the anchovies, garlic and capers and whiz until the mixture is finely chopped. Add the lemon juice and whiz again, then dribble in enough olive oil to make a thick, spoonable sauce. Make it at the last minute and it will taste very fresh and herby.

Variations: Adding other root vegetables to the lamb makes it a one-pot meal: carrots, parsnips, leeks, celeriac, or all of these. Instead of sliced potatoes, you can use whole new potatoes.

The salsa verde can be varied according to what herbs you have in the garden or on the windowsill. It is excellent with fish (add dill and tarragon instead of mint and basil) and boiled beef or tongue (add horseradish and/ or mustard).

Steak and Kidney Pudding.
Serves 6

Kate and Sidney, in Cockney rhyming slang, is as majestic, in the deep mid-winter, as a sirloin of beef, leg of mutton or loin of pork. In order to achieve a rich, dark gravy, it's worth the small extra effort of cooking the meat before it goes into the pudding.

1KG/2LB 4OZ BEEF SKIRT, SHIN OR CHUCK
6 LAMBS' KIDNEYS
55G/2OZ PLAIN FLOUR
SALT AND PEPPER
FAT OR OIL FOR FRYING
1 GLASS OF RED WINE
2 MEDIUM ONIONS
1 TABLESPOON OF TOMATO KETCHUP, 1 TEASPOON OF ENGLISH MUSTARD
ABOUT 500ML/18 FL OZ OF STOCK

Trim the beef and cut it into large cubes. Quarter the kidneys, discarding the white cores. Season the flour with salt and pepper and turn the meat in it until coated all over. Heat the fat or oil in a large frying pan and brown the meat well on all sides. Do this in batches so the meat browns but does not cook. Transfer the meat to a large saucepan. Over the heat, pour the red wine into the frying pan to deglaze it, and pour over the meat.

Heat more fat or oil in the pan and cook the onions until softened. Add them to the meat. Add the ketchup and mustard and enough stock just to cover the meat. Stir gently to mix everything, heat to simmering point and simmer very gently for about 1½ hours. If you want to make the sauce thicker, mash a tablespoon of flour with a tablespoon of butter (this mixture is called *beurre manié*) and stir it in, a few little pieces at a time.

This pudding or pie filling can now, if you like, be kept in the fridge for a day or two, or frozen until needed.

Suet crust

Suet crust: As I have said, don't be afraid of suet; it's easy to use and makes for the best bit.

500G/1LB 2OZ SELF-RAISING FLOUR
250G/9OZ SHREDDED BEEF SUET
PINCH OF SALT
WATER

Mix the flour, suet and salt in a bowl and gradually add enough cold water to make a workable dough. Keep one-third of the dough for the top of the pudding. Roll out the rest on a floured surface to about 1cm/³⁄₈in thick. Grease a pudding basin large enough to hold the meat and line it with the rolled suet crust. Put in the meat and gravy. Roll out the lid, wet the edges of the lining and put on the lid, pressing it together with the edges of lining, to seal it. Fold a piece of foil or double layer of greaseproof paper with a generous pleat to allow the crust to rise, and tie it over the top of the basin.

Put a saucer upside down in a saucepan large enough to hold the pudding basin. Fold a long strip of foil, put it under the basin, and, holding the two ends, lower the basin into the saucepan. Pour in boiling water to two-thirds up the sides of the basin, cover and simmer for 2 hours. Check from time to time that the water has not boiled away, and top up with more boiling water if needed.

Use the strip of foil to lift the pudding out of the saucepan. Remove the foil or greaseproof covering. Run a palette knife around the edge to loosen the pudding. Put a deep plate over the basin, and invert it to turn out the pudding. It may need a tap and a shake to dislodge it. The faint-hearted can serve the pudding without turning it out of the basin.

Variations: Traditionally, oysters were sometimes added to the beef filling. You could also add quartered mushrooms. The same filling makes an excellent pie covered with puff or short-crust pastry.

Tarragon-Roasted Chicken.

Serves 4

For many families chicken is a weekly event, but it was not always so. Even an "old boiler" was a treat, and roast chicken was in the luxury class. Strenuous efforts were made to upgrade the boiler. The Senior family's Sunday lunch was sometimes "Boily Roast Chicken," the bird being gently simmered with stock vegetables for 40 minutes before being roasted. A dry method "to make an old bird tender" is described in *The Constance Spry Cookery Book*. The hen is cooked very gently, with no liquid added, in a hermetically sealed pan for half an hour to tenderise its flesh before roasting.

Nowadays an old boiler is hard to come by, but a good-sized organic chicken is full of flavour and tender enough to roast. Fanatical as I am about bread sauce, I am willing to forgo it occasionally for the buttery, herby, garlicky scent and taste of chicken roasted with its natural partner, tarragon.

AN ORGANIC CHICKEN WEIGHING ABOUT 1.5KG/3LB 5OZ

55G/2OZ BUTTER, SOFTENED

A BUNCH OF TARRAGON

2 CLOVES OF GARLIC, CRUSHED

SALT AND PEPPER

Set the oven at 190°C. Put the butter in a mortar, add a tablespoonful of tarragon leaves, the crushed garlic, a good pinch of salt and a few turns of ground black pepper. Mash it all together with a pestle. Loosen the skin over the chicken's breast on each side by working your fingers under it, making space between the skin and meat. With a spoon, push one-third of the butter mixture under the skin on each side. From outside the skin, using your fingers, massage the butter to spread it evenly over the breast. Put the rest of the butter and any tarragon that is left, inside the bird.

Roast the chicken in the oven. After about 45 minutes, test for doneness by sticking a skewer into the thigh. If clear, not pink, juice comes out, it is done. Rest it for at least 10 minutes before carving. The juices in the roasting tin should be sauce enough, but if they need loosening and scraping, add a splash of white wine and a splash of water and simmer while the bird is resting.

Gerda's Chicken.

Gerda Barlow
Serves 6

For many decades, coronation chicken from the big pink book (*The Constance Spry Cookery Book*) was the basis of every family celebration in summer time. The dish was originally devised for a luncheon to celebrate Queen Elizabeth II's coronation in June 1953, and became something of a cliché. Cold, cooked chicken, boned and sliced, was coated with mayonnaise flavoured with curry and apricot purée. A number of other ingredients added subtlety, but that was the gist of it. My busy generation reduced the recipe to Hellmann's mayo with a spoonful of curry and another of apricot jam. It passed the taste test, though not with flying colours.

Recently, Gerda Barlow, my friend and neighbour, came to my rescue with her own version of cold curried chicken, which I give here. For more guests, increase the amount of chicken but use the same quantity of sauce.

150ML/¼ PINT SINGLE CREAM
150ML/¼ PINT PLAIN YOGHURT
150ML/¼ PINT MAYONNAISE
1 OR MORE TEASPOONS MADRAS CURRY POWDER OR PASTE
1 TABLESPOON MANGO CHUTNEY
2 EATING APPLES
1 GREEN PEPPER
2 CELERY STICKS
2 TEASPOONS FINELY CHOPPED ONION
A 1.3-1.8KG/3-4LB CHICKEN, COOKED AND CUT INTO BITE SIZED PIECES
55G/2OZ TOASTED ALMONDS
SALT AND PEPPER

Put the cream, yoghurt, mayonnaise, curry powder and chutney in a large bowl and mix well. Season, taste and adjust with more curry powder and/or chutney if needed. Peel, core and dice the apples; deseed and dice the pepper; dice the celery. Add these, along with the onion and chicken, to the mayonnaise, mix and turn on to a serving dish. Scatter the almonds on top.

Big Granny's Chicken and Ham Pie.

Serves 6

*The children have fond memories of a strange china blackbird with its beak
sticking up that she used to put in the middle of pies, to hold up the pastry
and let the air out. I wish I'd saved that.*

JAN DALLEY

There are just a few dishes that can compete with a roast joint for the
honoured place at the centre of Sunday Lunch, and this pie is one of them.
My mother used to make it to be eaten hot in the winter or cold in the summer.
She was known as Big Granny to distinguish her from my husband's mother,
Little Granny.

350G/12OZ COOKED CHICKEN CUT IN FAIRLY UNIFORM, BITE-SIZED PIECES
275G/9OZ HAM, ROUGHLY DICED
55G/2OZ BUTTER
1 ONION, CHOPPED
175G/6OZ MUSHROOMS, SLICED
55G/1½OZ FLOUR
200ML/⅓ PINT MILK
150ML/6FL OZ GLASS OF WHITE WINE
200ML/⅓ PINT CHICKEN STOCK
1 LARGE BUNCH OF FRESH TARRAGON, CHOPPED
200ML/⅓ PINT CREAM
SALT AND PEPPER
A PACKET OF FLAKY OR PUFF PASTRY

Set the oven at 190°C. Mix the chicken and ham together in a large bowl. In a
saucepan melt the butter and soften the onion. Add the mushrooms and cook
gently for 5 minutes. Remove the mushrooms and onions and add them to the
chicken and ham. Add the flour to the butter and cook for a few minutes, but
do not let it brown. Add the milk and stir until smooth. Add the wine and
enough stock to bring the sauce to a creamy consistency. Stir in the cream
and tarragon, season with salt and pepper and add the sauce to the chicken

mixture. Stir and put it in a 850ml/1½ pint pie dish.

Roll out the pastry. Cut a 1cm/⅜in wide strip to cover the rim of the dish. Brush the rim with water and press the strip around the rim. Brush water over the strip. Cover the pie with pastry, trim off the surplus and press around the rim to seal. Make a hole in the centre of the pie to let out steam, and if you like, use pastry remnants to decorate the top. Brush the pastry with beaten egg. Bake the pie for 20 to 30 minutes, until golden brown.

Chapter 3.

Monday
Left-overs.

13 Recipes

And what they did not eat that night
The Queen next morning fried.
<small>WHEN GOOD KING ARTHUR RULED THIS LAND, ANON.</small>

We ate endless stews and mince in various versions. I remember an old green
mincer, the kind that clamps on to the edge of the table with big screws;
Mum used to mince the remains of the Sunday roast for Monday supper.
I remember the wriggly worms of overcooked minced beef and fat coming
out, very disgusting actually.
<small>JAN DALLEY</small>

The most remarkable thing about my mother is that for 30 years she served the
family nothing but leftovers. The original meal has never been found.
<small>CALVIN TRILLIN</small>

Cold meat and salad, perhaps with a baked potato, often featured on Mondays, and seemed unexciting, not being supplemented, as it might be now, with salami or terrine from the local deli. There was no local deli in those days. But the frugal habit of making a little meat go a long way often produced delicious results. Some of our best-loved comfort food consisted of left-overs in one form or another, and delicious sauces compensated for sparse meat rations.

Many of these dishes are devised to use what is left of the Sunday joint. Others are not just for Mondays, but are good on any day of the week and some, for example the recipes for cold turkey, have a seasonal slant.

Bubble and Squeak (English).
Colcannon (Irish).

Quantities are very approximate. It just depends on what you have left over. We often cook extra cabbage and potato for lunch or dinner, with bubble and squeak next day in mind.

Fairly dry mash and undercooked greens make the best bubble and squeak. The addition of garlic and herbs is unorthodox, but times and tastes have changed. Use whatever fresh herbs you have in the garden or on the kitchen windowsill.

FAT OR OIL FOR FRYING
1 ONION, SLICED
1 GARLIC CLOVE, CHOPPED FINE
1 OR 2 TABLESPOONS OF CHOPPED, MIXED, FRESH HERBS
COOKED SAVOY CABBAGE OR OTHER GREENS, SHREDDED OR CHOPPED
A MORE OR LESS EQUAL QUANTITY OF MASHED POTATO
1 EGG, BEATEN
SALT AND PEPPER

Fry the onion until it is soft and turning brown. Fry the garlic for a moment. Add the onion, garlic and herbs to the greens and potato and beaten egg, season with salt and pepper. Mix all together. Heat the fat or oil in a frying pan and put in large spoonfuls of bubble and squeak, flattening them with a spoon or spatula. Turn them to brown on both sides. Serve piping hot with Worcestershire sauce or tomato ketchup.

Variations: Add diced, cooked bacon to the mixture, or crumble crispy streaky bacon over. Add fried slices of cooked beef or lamb.

Curried Chicken or Lamb.

This bears no resemblance to an authentic Indian curry of the kind you might get from your local take-away, but it is nevertheless a spicy, comforting lunch or supper dish.

1 TABLESPOON OF SUNFLOWER OIL
1 LARGE OR 2 SMALL ONIONS, SLICED
1 LARGE CARROT, CUBED
1 LARGE POTATO, CUBED
CURRY POWDER OR PASTE (MADRAS IF YOU LIKE A HOT, KNOCK-YOUR-SOCKS-OFF CURRY, "MILD" OR "MEDIUM" IF YOU ARE A WIMP, LIKE ME)
1 TABLESPOON OF TOMATO PURÉE
1 TABLESPOON APRICOT JAM
STOCK OR WATER
COOKED LAMB OR CHICKEN CUT INTO BITE-SIZED PIECES
2 TABLESPOONS THICK CREAM OR GREEK YOGHURT
SALT AND PEPPER
225G/8OZ BASMATI RICE
POPPADUMS

In a saucepan, fry the onions, carrot and potato for about five minutes, till they begin to brown. Add the curry powder or paste, modifying the amount recommended on the packet or jar to suit your own tastes, and cook for a few minutes. Add the tomato purée, the jam and enough stock or water to just cover the vegetables. Stir well, bring to the boil and simmer gently.

Meanwhile, put a large saucepan of salted water on to boil for the rice, and rinse the rice in cold water. When the curry has been simmering for 20 minutes, put the rice into the water and boil it with the lid off. Add the meat to the curry, stir it and continue to simmer. Just before serving, season and stir in the cream or yoghurt.

Test the rice after it has been cooking for 10 minutes. If it is done, drain it and put it back in the saucepan with a clean tea-cloth over it to absorb any steam. Put the poppadums in a hot oven or under the grill until they puff up and blister.

Serve with mango chutney and lime pickle, and, if you like, some of these: sliced bananas, raw onion rings, skinned and sliced tomatoes, yoghurt to cool things down a bit.

Variations: Curried, hard-boiled eggs, very comforting. Or use more vegetables, but no meat.

Devilled Turkey or Chicken.

Better the Devil you know… This is a great way to eat left-over turkey at Christmas and just as good with chicken or pheasant. This version of devil sauce is my Aunt Joyce's and could not be easier to make.

55G/2OZ BUTTER
1 DESSERTSPOON ENGLISH MUSTARD
1 TABLESPOON SOFT BROWN SUGAR
1 DESSERTSPOON WORCESTERSHIRE SAUCE
COOKED CHICKEN OR TURKEY IN LARGE PIECES

Mix all the devil ingredients together, score the surface of the cooked chicken or turkey pieces, spread with the devil sauce, put in a shallow ovenproof dish and brown in the oven for 12 minutes. Eat with mash.

Pork and Beans.

This is a dish to throw together when you have the remains of a pork joint and have picked off all the crackling when nobody was looking. It is related to chilli con carne, which first hit us in the sixties. If there is not enough meat, add a couple of sausages cooked and cut into chunks.

COOKED PORK

2 TABLESPOONS OLIVE OIL

1 ONION, CHOPPED

2 GARLIC CLOVES, FINELY CHOPPED

4 TABLESPOONS CHOPPED HERBS (ROSEMARY, THYME, PARSLEY)

1 TEASPOON CHILLI POWDER

1 x 400G/14OZ TIN ITALIAN PLUM TOMATOES, CHOPPED

2 x 400G/14OZ TINS BORLOTTI BEANS, DRAINED AND RINSED

SALT AND PEPPER

Cut the pork into bite-sized pieces. Over a gently heat, cook the onion gently in the olive oil until it is soft and translucent. Add the garlic, herbs and chilli powder and stir until well mixed. Add the tomatoes, beans and pork and heat, stirring occasionally until the pork is heated through. Adjust the seasoning.

Variations: You can also used tinned cannellini beans, or cannellini and borlotti mixed.

Hugh's TV Chicken Dinner.

From The River Cottage Cook Book

To be eaten wearing your slippers and watching television.

2-3 THICK RASHERS OF STREAKY BACON, CUT INTO SMALL DICE
OLIVE OIL
1 ONION, CHOPPED
1 GARLIC CLOVE, CHOPPED
115-200G/4-7OZ FRESH OR FROZEN PEAS
LEFTOVER CHICKEN, CHOPPED FAIRLY SMALL
A FEW TABLESPOONS OF DOUBLE CREAM
SALT AND FRESHLY GROUND BLACK PEPPER
THE PASTA OF YOUR CHOICE
FRESHLY GRATED PARMESAN CHEESE TO SERVE

In a heavy-based frying pan, fry the bacon in a little olive oil until just crisp. Turn the heat down, add the onion and garlic and sweat until soft but not coloured. Add the peas and a splash of water and allow to bubble for a couple of minutes. When the pan is almost dry again, add the chicken and heat through. Pour in the cream and season well with salt and pepper.

Let it bubble until the cream has reduced a little and the sauce has a nice coating consistency. Serve tossed with your chosen pasta, with plenty of freshly grated Parmesan.

Shepherd's Pie.

Serves 4

What truly constitutes shepherd's pie and how does it differ from cottage pie? Is it made with raw or cooked meat? Is the meat lamb or beef, or can it be either? Most people are convinced they know the true answer, and you are unlikely to convince them they are wrong. This is how we make it in my family.

1 LARGE ONION

THE REMAINS OF A ROAST LEG OR SHOULDER OF LAMB, CUT OFF THE BONE
AND ANY GRISTLE AND FAT DISCARDED, ABOUT 450G/1LB

2 MEDIUM CARROTS, FINELY DICED

1 GARLIC CLOVE, CRUSHED

OLIVE OIL

½ A GLASS OF RED WINE

1 TABLESPOON OF TOMATO KETCHUP

2 TEASPOONS OF WORCESTERSHIRE SAUCE

ANY LEFTOVER GRAVY

STOCK

450G/1LB POTATOES

30G/1OZ BUTTER

MILK

SALT AND PEPPER

Set the oven at 200ºC. Grease a pie dish.

Peel and roughly cut up the onion, put it in a food processor and pulse to chop finely. Add the meat and pulse again until it is the texture of coarse mince. In a small sauté pan, cook the carrots and garlic gently in a little of the oil. In a large frying pan, brown the meat and onion mixture in the rest of the olive oil. Add the wine, ketchup, Worcestershire sauce, gravy and enough stock to stop the meat drying out. Simmer gently, stirring occasionally, for 15 minutes. Meanwhile, boil the potatoes and mash them with butter and milk. Add the carrots to the meat and season with salt and pepper. Put the mixture in a pie dish and cover with the mash. With a fork, draw furrows on the surface of the mash, first long-ways, then across. Bake in the oven for 20 minutes or until brown on top.

Variation: "Shepherd's pie always HAD to have sultanas in it for my children." (Diana Royden)

Rissoles.

My mother called these flat, shallow-fried savoury cakes rissoles, but Constance Spry insists that proper rissoles are enclosed in pastry and deep fried. What a palaver. Both methods are good vehicles for left-overs; ours are less glamorous, but a good deal less complicated to make, and still taste good.

ABOUT 450G/1LB OF MINCED COOKED CHICKEN, TURKEY,
PHEASANT, GAMMON, LAMB, PORK OR BEEF
ABOUT 225G/8OZ MASHED POTATO
1 ONION, FINELY CHOPPED
1 EGG, BEATEN
2 TABLESPOONS FRESH PARSLEY, CHOPPED
SALT AND PEPPER
FLOUR
BUTTER

Put the meat and potato in a mixing bowl. Cook the onion gently in butter until soft, and add it to the meat mixture with the egg, parsley and seasoning. Mix thoroughly. On a floured surface, with floured hands, form the mixture into patties about the size of fishcakes. Fry the rissoles in butter, first on one side, then the other, until brown and hot all through. Serve with home-made tomato sauce (page 93) or salsa verde (page 51).

Red Flannel Hash.

The eyes of anyone who remembers World War II and the years of rationing that followed mist over at the mention of corned beef. It came in tins with rounded corners, which you opened by winding a thin strip of tin round a key, which was quite hard to achieve without cutting your hand. The contents of the tin, once extracted, were either sliced to make fritters, or shredded to make hash. My cousin George also remembers a fried egg on a slab of corned beef for supper when he was a child.

In *Lady Maclean's Cookbook* (1965) there is a facsimile hand-written recipe for corned-beef hash from the Countess of Hardwicke, who adds a note at the end of the recipe: "can buy tins of Corn Beef Hash at Fortnum & Mason." Left-over cooked salt beef (as in Boiled Beef and Carrots) is a good substitute.

Recipes vary: most include tomatoes and Lady Hardwicke's includes green peppers and half a pint of sour cream, but I prefer this American New England version for its re-instatement of the poor, maligned beetroot.

A 340G/12OZ TIN OF CORNED BEEF OR 340G/12OZ COOKED SALT BEEF
2 ONIONS
ABOUT 750G/1.5LB COOKED POTATOES (OR WHATEVER YOU HAVE LEFT OVER)
450G/1LB COOKED BEETROOT (NOT SOUSED IN VINEGAR)
FAT OR OIL FOR FRYING
2 TABLESPOONS WORCESTERSHIRE SAUCE
3 TABLESPOONS CHOPPED PARSLEY
6 POACHED EGGS (OPTIONAL)

Shred the beef; roughly chop the potatoes and beetroot into 1-2cm/½ - ¾in cubes. Slice the onions and fry them in fat or oil in a large frying pan until they are beginning to brown. Add the beef, beetroots and potatoes and continue to fry until everything is heated through, adding more oil if necessary, and turning so that the mixture browns on both sides. Stir in the Worcestershire sauce, sprinkle the parsley over and serve with mustard and tomato ketchup or Worcestershire sauce, and, if you like, a poached egg on top of each helping.

Savoury Pancakes.

Using the recipe on page 29 but leaving out the sugar, make as many pancakes as you need. Any surplus to requirements can be frozen.

Filling:

A SMALL ONION, FINELY CHOPPED

40G / 1½ OZ BUTTER

A CLOVE OF GARLIC, FINELY CHOPPED

THREE OR FOUR MEDIUM MUSHROOMS, CHOPPED

1 HEAPED TABLESPOON OF FLOUR

ABOUT 200ML / ⅓ PINT MILK

COOKED CHICKEN, MINCED OR CHOPPED FINE

2 TABLESPOONS GRATED CHEDDAR CHEESE

Cook the onion gently in the butter until soft. Add the garlic and mushrooms and cook for 5 more minutes. Stir in the flour and cook for 2 more minutes, but do not let the flour brown. Add milk gradually, stirring all the time, until the sauce is smooth, thick and creamy. Take off the heat and stir in the chicken. Spread some of the filling over each pancake. Roll the pancakes up and place in a shallow, fireproof dish. Sprinkle the cheese over them and bake in a fairly hot oven for 15 minutes.

Variations: More ideas for fillings: spinach (fresh or frozen) in cheese sauce; thin slices of ham in parsley sauce; mushrooms with garlic, cream and parsley; smoked haddock; smoked salmon.

Stovies.

Serves 2

A sort of deconstructed Scottish shepherd's pie, stovies featured for supper every Thursday at my husband's boarding school. The dish played a sinister role in a séance held by a group of boys one Monday evening. By moving a glass across a table they managed to call up the spirit of a Greek slave who spelt out his name: Logs Lemaby. The boys, knowing that Monday invariably meant macaroni cheese, decided to test the spirit's power of prophecy. "Oh spirit," they asked, "what's for supper tonight?" The glass moved laboriously to and fro spelling out: "S...T...O...V...I...E...S" Ten minutes later they went down to supper where, as usual, they were served macaroni cheese. Not all spirits can foretell the future.

1 TABLESPOON DRIPPING OR OIL
450G/1LB POTATOES, PEELED AND SLICED
1 LARGE ONION, SLICED
175G/6OZ OR MORE OF COLD ROAST BEEF OR LAMB, DICED
STOCK OR WATER
SALT AND PEPPER

In a large, shallow saucepan, melt the dripping or oil. Add the potatoes, onion and meat. Add enough stock or water to just cover the meat and potatoes. Season generously with salt and pepper. Cover and cook for 30 minutes or until the potatoes are cooked and the stock or water has been absorbed.

Turkey Tonnato.

sometimes make the classic Italian dish vitello tonnato for summer lunch parties. This more everyday dish uses the same delicious tuna mayonnaise sauce with slices of cold turkey. A turkey is not just for Christmas – it gives a celebratory air to any gathering, at Easter, for example, and invariably generates left-overs.

ENOUGH SLICES OF COLD TURKEY FOR THE NUMBER OF
PEOPLE YOU ARE FEEDING
2 YOLKS OF EGG
SALT
300ML/½ PINT OLIVE OIL
JUICE OF HALF A LEMON
115G/4OZ TIN OF TUNA IN OIL
LIGHT CHICKEN STOCK
SALT AND FRESHLY GROUND BLACK PEPPER
2 TABLESPOONS CAPERS

Make a stiff mayonnaise with the egg yolks and olive oil, adding just enough lemon juice to make it sharp. Sieve or liquidize the tuna and stir it gradually into the mayonnaise. Thin the sauce with a little stock until it is of pouring consistency. Taste and season. Pour the sauce over the turkey slices and leave for a few hours in a cool place, for the turkey to absorb it. Rinse the capers and scatter them over the dish before serving.

Variation: The tuna mayonnaise is also good with cold chicken or hard-boiled eggs.

Rob's Turkeyburgers.

Post-Christmas, when some of the turkey has been devilled and grilled, and some has been "tonnato", what is left can be burgered and frozen, to be eaten when you are no longer suffering from turkey fatigue.

ABOUT 450G/1LB COOKED TURKEY
225G/8OZ COOKED HAM
1 LARGE ONION
2 TABLESPOONS CHOPPED PARSLEY
SALT AND PEPPER
2 EGGS, BEATEN
FLOUR

Roughly cut up the turkey, ham and onion. Put the onion into a food processor and pulse till chopped fine. Add the turkey and ham and pulse until it is the texture of coarse mince.

Turn the mixture into a bowl, add the parsley and season with salt and lots of freshly ground black pepper. Add the eggs and mix thoroughly. On a floured board, with floured hands, shape the mixture into burgers. Freeze them on a tray in a single layer and, when frozen, put them in plastic bags or boxes and return them to the freezer until needed.

Ham and Leek Parcels.

Serves 4

This is a versatile recipe. Vegetables, in this case leeks, are wrapped in thin slices of ham or gammon, and heated in cheese sauce. Nostalgia for grilled gammon steaks with pineapple, which invariably featured on steak house menus in the 1960s, can be assuaged by wrapping the ham around pineapple chunks.

4 THICK OR 8 THIN LEEKS

25G/¾ OZ BUTTER

1 TABLESPOON FLOUR

300ML/½ PINT MILK

55G/2OZ GRATED STRONG CHEDDAR CHEESE

1 TEASPOON MUSTARD

SALT AND PEPPER

1 TABLESPOON CREAM

8 THIN SLICES OF HAM OR GAMMON

Set the oven to 210°C. Grease a gratin dish.

Discard the outer leaves of the leeks, clean them thoroughly and cut them in half long-ways. Simmer them gently in water or stock until they are just tender. While they are cooking make the cheese sauce. In a saucepan melt the butter, stir in the flour and cook for a few moments. Add the milk gradually, stirring all the time until the sauce is thickened and smooth. Add the cheese and mustard and stir until the cheese has melted. Season to taste and stir in the cream.

Season the leeks and wrap one half in each slice of ham (two halves if the leeks are thin). Lay them in the gratin dish, pour the cheese sauce over and heat in the oven until the sauce is brown and bubbling.

Chapter 4.

Mid-week
Meals.

19 Recipes

Weekday lunches in the school holidays were very much a matter of re-fuelling. We would rush in from the garden or farm, impatient to stoke up and be outside again. "Not so fast. Go and wash your hands and brush your hair." We skittered off and, after a brief encounter with soap, water and comb, were back in the dining room, skidding to a halt with palms outstretched for inspection.

Our patience was sorely tried by grown-up admonishments to sit up straight, take your elbows off the table, don't eat with your mouth open, or talk with it full, use your knife and fork.

Grown-ups ate so slowly. We were not allowed to go until they had finished, and we watched in agony as our grandmother lifted her fork halfway to her mouth then put it down again to ask us, "Well, what have you been up to all morning?" There were two possible answers. One was, "Mucking about," the other, "Biking up and down." We were not going to let on that we had been catching the bantams and throwing them in the air to see if they would fly, or "borrowing" the penknife from our grandfather's desk to make notches on our home-made bows and arrows. Finally our grandmother laid her pudding spoon and fork down side by side on her plate. "Please-may-we-get-down," we gabbled in unison, and off we went.

Although we wolfed down our food, we enjoyed it, with the exception of spinach, cabbage (even prepared by the wonderful Loney, it was often overcooked and watery), and mashed swedes. At Hazelbury, lunch always consisted of a hot dish, usually meat, but sometimes fish, eggs or macaroni cheese, with two vegetables, followed by pudding.

For us children, lunch was our main meal. We didn't stay up for dinner. Instead, having stoked up on bread and cake at teatime, we had a minimalist supper in the nursery of cereals or bread and milk, following long-established tradition. In 1833 Thomas Carlyle described how, "On fine evenings I was wont to carry forth my supper (breadcrumbs boiled in milk) and eat it out-of-doors… many a sunset have I [watched], looking at the distant western mountains, [as I] consumed, not without relish, my evening meal." In our version of bread and milk, hot milk was poured over bread cut into cubes, and sprinkled generously with demerara sugar.

At home in London, my mother was the cook and during the week she concentrated on feeding the breadwinner in the evening. My father would return from the office to a three-course dinner, although the third course might be cheese and fruit rather than pudding. Weekday lunch, when Dad was at work, was a more modest affair. It might be thick, aromatic vegetable soup, cauliflower cheese or ham and salad.

My mother's main dishes for dinner midweek were mostly quick and easy to make. My father's favourite mixed grill would appear once a week, and there was often a slow-cooked chicken, which provided enough meat for two meals and rich stock for soup or risotto. But meat did not always feature, and egg and cheese dishes were popular with us children. Popular with the bank manager too, no doubt. The success of dishes which include cheese depends on the strength and quality of the cheese, and although I sometimes encountered something called "processed cheese" in friends' houses, it never appeared in ours. For cooking as well as eating in its own right, my mother bought the equivalent of today's "Mature" or "Extra Strong" Cheddar from the local grocer, always tasting a slither before deciding to buy. A wedge was then severed from the huge block with a garotting wire, and neatly parcelled up in greaseproof paper. I still follow my mother's example and buy cheese from a shop or counter where you are encouraged to taste before buying.

At home, we usually helped in the kitchen, not because my mother demanded it, but because it was fun and companionable to be there. Also, in term time, I liked to pick her brains about my homework. While she peeled potatoes and I washed spinach or grated cheese, turning the wheel on a little Mouli grater, I would collect her ideas on "Character is Fate – discuss with reference to Thomas Hardy's *The Mayor of Casterbridge*," then go upstairs and write them down. It took several Parents' Meetings for my English teacher to discover that Mum supplied the ideas for most of my essays.

Cheese Pudding.

Serves 4

From The Dictionary of Daily Wants, 1859

Of many recipes combining cheese, bread, eggs and milk, this is one of the best; it is as good as a "proper" cheese soufflé. Most of the recipes in *The Dictionary* are frugal and nourishing, but lacking in glamour; this, however, is a winner.

250G/9OZ FRESH WHITE BREADCRUMBS
280G/10OZ GRATED MATURE CHEDDAR CHEESE OR HALF LANCASHIRE,
HALF CHEDDAR
600ML/1 PINT MILK
50G/1¾ OZ BUTTER
4 EGGS
SALT, PEPPER
1 GOOD TEASPOON ENGLISH MUSTARD

Grease a 20cm/8in soufflé dish.

Mix the breadcrumbs and cheese in a bowl. In a saucepan, heat the milk and butter until the butter melts; pour it over the breadcrumbs and stir. Whisk the eggs with the salt, pepper and mustard. Stir them into the breadcrumb mixture, and pour into the prepared dish. Leave to stand for 1 hour.

One hour before you plan to eat, set the oven at 200°C. After 20 minutes, put the pudding in the oven and bake it for about 40 minutes until risen and golden. Serve as a starter or, with a green salad, for lunch or supper.

Cheesy Eggs.

Serves 4

This has always been a great supper standby for us, eaten with a green veg or baked tomatoes.

6 EGGS
40G/1½ OZ BUTTER
40G/1½ OZ FLOUR
425ML/¾ PINT MILK
175G/6OZ GRATED CHEDDAR CHEESE
1 TEASPOON OF ENGLISH MUSTARD
SALT AND PEPPER

Set the oven at 200°C. Grease an ovenproof dish.

Boil the eggs for 9 minutes, then plunge them in cold water. Peel them, cut in halves long-ways and arrange the halves in the greased dish. To make the cheese sauce, melt the butter in a saucepan, stir in the flour and cook gently for two minutes, without letting it get brown.

Gradually add the milk, stirring all the time, until the sauce is smooth and creamy. You may not need all the milk. Off the heat, add the cheese and mustard and stir until the cheese has melted and the sauce is smooth again. Season with salt and pepper.

Bake in the oven for 15 to 20 minutes, until the sauce is brown and bubbly.

Gloucestershire Squab Pie.

Serves 4

Although I've lived in Gloucestershire for 36 years, I didn't eat this until I recently made it myself. I imagined the recipe was a local take on pigeon pie, but it is not. The filling very successfully combines lamb, onion and apple.

For the pastry:
225G/8OZ PLAIN FLOUR
55G/2OZ BUTTER
55G/2OZ LARD

For the filling:
FAT OR OIL
2 LARGE ONIONS, PEELED AND THINLY SLICED
FLOUR FOR DUSTING
$\frac{1}{2}$ TEASPOON ALLSPICE
$\frac{1}{2}$ TEASPOON NUTMEG
SALT AND PEPPER
675G/1$\frac{1}{2}$ LB LAMB FILLET, CUBED
1 LARGE COOKING APPLE, PEELED, CORED AND SLICED
150ML/$\frac{1}{4}$ PINT STOCK

Put the flour and roughly chopped lard and butter in a food processor and pulse until it's the texture of breadcrumbs. Add cold water a very little at a time and pulse until a firm dough is formed. Wrap the pastry in cling-film and put it in the fridge for half an hour at least.

Heat the fat or oil in a frying pan. Gently fry the onions for a few minutes, remove them from the pan and set them aside. Mix the flour, spices, salt and pepper, roll the lamb pieces in the seasoned flour and brown them quickly in the fat or oil.

Set the oven at 200°C.

Grease a 900ml/1$\frac{1}{2}$ pint pie dish and put in half the lamb. Put half the apple and onions on top. Repeat the layers. Deglaze the frying pan with the stock and pour it over the meat.

Roll out the pastry and cut a strip for the rim of the pie dish. Wet the rim of the dish, press the strip down. Wet the strip, then cover the dish with the rest of the pastry, trim and press the edges down well. Make a hole in the top for steam to escape.

Bake in the oven for 15 minutes. Reduce the temperature to 180°C and cook for 1 hour 15 minutes more.

Chipolata Casserole.

Carole Guise
Serves 4

Carole adds a tin of sweetcorn to the ingredients when she makes this for her grandchildren, but when I made it I left out the corn and my own grandchildren much enjoyed it for supper.

OIL FOR FRYING
450G/1LB PORK CHIPOLATA SAUSAGES
1 MEDIUM ONION, CHOPPED
3 RASHERS OF BACON, CHOPPED
1 DESSERTSPOON FLOUR
300ML/½ PINT MILK
3 TABLESPOONS OF PARSLEY, CHOPPED
2 TEASPOONS SOY SAUCE
50G/2OZ FRESH BREADCRUMBS
BUTTER

Set the oven at 175°C.

Fry the sausages until lightly browned, then remove them to an ovenproof dish. Fry the onions and bacon until they are cooked. Add the flour and stir for two minutes to cook the flour. Add the milk gradually, stirring until the mixture is thickened. Stir in the parsley and soy sauce. Pour the mixture over the chipolatas, sprinkle the breadcrumbs on top and dot the surface with butter. Bake the dish uncovered for about 30 minutes.

This can be prepared in advance and kept in the fridge until you bake it.

Mary's Proper Greek Moussaka.

Mary Spyromilio
Serves 4-6

Greece is the adopted country of my schoolfriend Mary. She is a wonderful granny and a brilliant cook, so I asked her for the best version of the Balkan equivalent of shepherd's pie. Mary says, "The secret of moussaka is that it should be dry – you use up tons of oil making it just to squeeze it all out! The tourist moussaka is nothing to do with the home-cooked one."

3 AUBERGINES
6 MEDIUM-SIZED POTATOES
OLIVE OIL
500G/1LB 2OZ MINCED LEAN LAMB
1 LARGE ONION, CHOPPED
2 CLOVES OF GARLIC, FINELY CHOPPED
200G/7OZ CAN OF CHOPPED TOMATOES
CHOPPED PARSLEY AND OREGANO
SALT AND PEPPER

Topping:
50G/1¾ OZ BUTTER
50G/1¾ OZ PLAIN FLOUR
400ML/14 FL OZ MILK
50G/1¾ OZ GRUYÈRE CHEESE, GRATED (OPTIONAL)
SALT AND FRESHLY GROUND BLACK PEPPER

Slice the aubergines thinly, sprinkle them with salt and leave for half an hour. Peel the potatoes and slice them thinly.

Set the oven at 180°C. Oil a large, shallow ovenproof dish.

Rinse the aubergine slices and squeeze them dry between two sheets of kitchen paper. In a large frying pan fry the slices in olive oil and lay them between two layers of kitchen paper to drain. Do the same with the potatoes.

Fry the onions and garlic lightly. Add the minced lamb and turn it to brown it. Add the chopped tomatoes and the herbs. Stir together and season.

Put a layer of potatoes into the dish, then a layer of aubergines. Put in the mince, then another layer of potatoes and aubergines.

For the topping: Melt the butter in a saucepan, add the flour and cook it for a few minutes but do not let it brown. Gradually add the milk, stirring until the sauce is smooth. Add the grated Gruyère if you are using it, and season with salt and pepper. Spread the sauce over the dish. It should be a thinnish layer.

Bake in the oven for about 45 minutes until the top is golden brown.

Macaroni Cheese.
Serves 4

Classic comfort food, highly rated by all age groups, macaroni cheese is quick and easy to make. In this recipe I have departed from British tradition and followed Heston Blumenthal's take on a traditional Lyonnaise dish. The use of Gruyère instead of Cheddar makes it a bit more grown-up, but it would still be good with Cheddar, or half Parmesan and half Gruyère. The use of cream instead of white sauce makes the dish lighter and richer at the same time.

200G/7OZ MACARONI
1 TABLESPOON OLIVE OIL
200ML/⅓ PINT DOUBLE CREAM
60G/2¼ OZ GRATED GRUYÈRE CHEESE
SALT AND PEPPER
1 CLOVE OF GARLIC
20G/½OZ BUTTER

Set the oven at 190°C.

Cook the macaroni according to the instructions on the packet. Drain it and, in a large bowl, turn it in the olive oil. Add the cream and cheese, season with salt and pepper and mix everything together. Rub the surface of a shallow ovenproof dish with the garlic, cut in half. Put the mixture in the dish, dot the surface with butter and bake for 15 minutes until golden brown.

Cornish Pasties.

Makes 4

Lunch in an edible envelope occurs all over the world, in the form of stuffed pitta bread, for example, or Chinese spring rolls or those crisp little Indian triangles filled with curried vegetables called samosas. In Scotland, steak, onions and suet baked in a pasty are known as bridies. A Cornish pasty without potato in the filling is called a hoggan.

On holiday in north Cornwall we used to queue early every day outside the local bakery, where the best pasties were to be had, to pick up our lunchtime picnic. Florence White's 1932 recipe from St Ives includes calf's liver as well as beef steak, which sounds rather good, but I have stuck to a more modern but authentic version from Rock.

SHORTCRUST PASTRY (SEE PAGE 80; USE BUTTER INSTEAD OF LARD)
350G/12OZ CHUCK STEAK, CUT INTO SMALL PIECES
1 ONION, CHOPPED
2 POTATOES, DICED
200G/7OZ TURNIP, DICED
1 LARGE CARROT, DICED
SALT AND PEPPER
1 BEATEN EGG

Set the oven to 200°C. Cover a baking sheet with parchment.

Roll out the pastry and cut it into 4 circles the size of tea plates. You may need to do this in two stages. Mix all the other ingredients together in a bowl, and season them well.

Pile the meat and vegetables in the centre of each pastry circle. Paint the edge of the pastry with beaten egg and pull the edges together on top (not at the side), crimping the edges so that no steam can escape. Put the pasties on the baking sheet and cook them in the oven for 20 minutes, then lower the heat to 150°C and cook for another 45 minutes.

If the pasties are for a picnic, as soon as they come out of the oven wrap each one in two layers of foil, wrap the four foil parcels in two tea towels, and put the whole parcel in an insulated box.

Picnics.

Tea carried out on a tray, to a rug spread under a shady tree at the bottom of the garden, seemed a treat when we were children. There were sandwiches cut into triangles, filled with Marmite and lettuce, tomato (the soggier the better), egg and cress, mashed sardines, or jam. And a whole cake. And wasps.

In August, picnic teas were sometimes carried in wicker baskets to the harvest field, and we earned our lemon squash and sandwiches by helping to stook the sheaves of oats, barley or wheat.

Trips to the beach were incomplete without sand in the sandwiches or tears from a toddler whose lunch had been snatched from his hands with delicate precision by Rex, our Labrador. There were always a few squares of dark chocolate "to warm you up" when you came out of the sea, teeth chattering.

Sometimes we wrapped sandwiches and ginger cake in greaseproof paper parcels, stuffed them in our pockets with an apple and bottle of ginger beer and took off on our bicycles for the day. Without watches, we had to guess when it was lunchtime, and had usually eaten our picnic by 11.

School sports days meant posh picnics with plates, knives and forks from a hamper in the boot of the car. Out came tupperware boxes of smoked salmon cornets, coronation chicken, strawberries and cream, and cherries (we surreptitiously used the stones as missiles). Picnics for point-to-points meant flasks of hot soup and Cornish pasties or sausage rolls. No picnic was complete without hard-boiled eggs (don't forget the salt, in a twist of greaseproof paper), and they were often provided, with sandwiches, for our lunch on the train going back to London. The upholstery of train seats still seems to give off that hard-boiled egg smell.

The picnic of all picnics was the annual river outing organized by our friends the Tullochs. Boats were hired and several families with children of assorted ages piled in. Each family contributed to the feast and everyone shared. The day always ended in total immersion for several teenagers, and on one occasion, a three-month-old baby had to be hauled, dripping, back into the boat. Every year there were tears, but far, far more laughter.

See Cornish Pasties opposite, Granny B's Sausage Rolls page 215, All-in One Fruit Cake page 177, Loney's Sticky Ginger Cake page 172.

Risotto with Chicken Livers.

Serves 3-4

Whenever we had chicken, my mother made stock from the carcass. To intensify the flavour, she boiled the stock, reducing it until it was almost syrupy. With it she made soup or risotto. This was one of her best, but had somehow been forgotten for several decades. I cooked it again recently. "Very good. It's a cracker," was the verdict.

225G/8OZ CHICKEN LIVERS
UP TO 600ML/1 PINT GOOD CHICKEN STOCK
2 TABLESPOONS OLIVE OIL, PLUS A LITTLE FOR THE LIVERS
1 ONION, CHOPPED
2 RASHERS OF STREAKY BACON, DICED
250G/9OZ ARBORIO RICE
½ GLASS OF WHITE WINE
SALT AND PEPPER
2 TABLESPOONS CHOPPED PARSLEY AND BASIL
115G/2OZ PARMESAN CHEESE

Cut the chicken livers into bite-sized pieces, removing any discoloured parts. Heat the stock in a saucepan.

In another large, heavy saucepan, cook the onion and bacon gently in the olive oil, until the onion is translucent. Add the rice and stir until it has absorbed the oil. Add the wine and let it bubble for a minute or two. (Don't leave out the wine, it really makes a difference.) Add enough hot stock to cover the rice and stir well. When the stock has been absorbed, add more, stirring from time to time to stop the rice sticking to the pan. After 20 minutes, taste the rice. If it is soft all through, it is cooked. If it is still a little gritty in the middle, continue adding stock and stirring.

In a small frying pan, fry the chicken livers gently in oil for just a couple of minutes. They should be pink in the middle. When the rice is ready, stir in the livers and chopped herbs. Add seasoning. Put the Parmesan on the table with a grater, for people to help themselves. Cheese bought in a piece has far more flavour than cheese sold ready-grated.

Variations: With a basis of good stock the risotto possibilities are almost infinite, including different combinations of meat, fish or shell-fish with various vegetables. Risotto can look rather grey and porridge-y, and a touch of green makes it more inviting. Try stirring in frozen peas near the end of cooking, or garnishing with chopped herbs, chives or finely sliced spring onion tops.

Tip: Some cooks put the risotto in the oven to cook after adding the stock, but if you want risotto with a really creamy texture, the stirring method on top of the cooker works best.

Pork Chops Auberge Saint Pierre.

Lyla Harling

Abracadabra! A speedy, trouble-free way of transforming ordinary grilled chops into a treat.

Per person:
ONE THICK PORK CHOP
1 OR 2 TEASPOONS DOUBLE CREAM
1 TABLESPOON GRATED STRONG CHEDDAR
MUSTARD TO TASTE

Make a thick paste with the cream, cheese and mustard. Grill the chops on both sides until cooked all through. Pile the cheese mixture on to the chops and put them under the grill until brown and bubbling.

Hungarian Goulash.

Serves 6

This recipe only works if you use good-quality paprika from a newly opened tin or packet. So throw away the one that has been lurking behind the other spices in your cupboard for three years, and buy some more.

2 TABLESPOONS SUNFLOWER OIL
3 ONIONS, PEELED AND CHOPPED
900G/2LB CHUCK STEAK, CUT INTO 3CM/1¼IN CUBES
3 TABLESPOONS SWEET HUNGARIAN PAPRIKA
SALT
2 TABLESPOONS TOMATO PURÉE
A GARLIC CLOVE, CRUSHED
A GLASS OF RED WINE
A BOUQUET GARNI
4 MEDIUM POTATOES PEELED AND CUT INTO 2.5CM/1IN CUBES
2 TEASPOONS CARAWAY SEEDS (OPTIONAL)
1 RED PEPPER DESEEDED AND CUT INTO THIN STRIPS
200ML/⅓ PINT SOUR CREAM.

Heat the oil in a frying pan, brown the onions and remove them to a casserole. Roll the beef in the paprika and brown it on all sides. Add any remaining paprika, the garlic, bouquet garni, a little salt, the tomato purée, the wine and enough hot water barely to cover the meat. Stir well, bring to the boil and simmer gently with the lid on for 2 hours. Boil the potatoes for 5 minutes, drain them and add to the stew with the caraway seeds, if used. Simmer for another 20 or 30 minutes until the potatoes are quite soft. Meanwhile, cook the red pepper gently in a little oil for a few minutes so that it still has a bit of bite. Stir it into the goulash. Serve with dollops of sour cream and, if liked, noodles or rice.

Andrew's Spinach Supper.

Serves 4

Eggs lying on a bed of spinach are covered with a blanket of brown and yellow speckled cheese sauce. Of the many dishes made with eggs and cheese, this is one of the best.

450G/1LB FRESH SPINACH OR A PACKET OF FROZEN SPINACH

¼ TEASPOON OF GROUND NUTMEG

4 LARGE EGGS

40G/1½ OZ BUTTER

2 TABLESPOONS FLOUR

425ML/¾ PINT MILK

115G/4OZ GRATED STRONG CHEDDAR CHEESE

1 TEASPOON OF ENGLISH MUSTARD

SALT AND PEPPER

Set the oven at 220°C. Grease a gratin dish.

Wash the spinach, removing any coarse ribs from the leaves. Put it in a large saucepan, add half a teaspoon of salt, cover and cook over a gentle heat for 7 minutes, stirring occasionally to stop the leaves sticking to the pan. Or defrost and heat the frozen spinach.

Meanwhile, make the cheese sauce. Melt the butter in a saucepan, stir in the flour and cook gently for 2 minutes, without letting it get brown. Add the milk gradually, stirring all the time, until the sauce is smooth and the consistency of cream. Off the heat, add the cheese and mustard and stir until the cheese has melted and the sauce is smooth again. Season with salt and pepper.

Drain the spinach, squeezing out as much water as possible. Chop roughly and return to the saucepan and stir, uncovered, to steam out any remaining moisture. Add the nutmeg and spread the spinach over the gratin dish. Make four indentations for the eggs. Break each egg into a cup and slide it carefully into an indentation.

Bake in the oven for 5 minutes or until the egg white is beginning to set. Carefully pour the sauce over and bake for a further 5 to 10 minutes until brown on top, or brown the dish under the grill.

Somerset Chicken.

Serves 4

Somerset, like Normandy, has a long history of growing apples, and orchards still flourish in both regions, although there are, alas, many fewer than in the past. In French cooking, *à la normande* implies the use of apples and/or cider in a dish. As you might expect, Somerset chicken also makes good use of these ingredients.

A LITTLE OIL AND 30G/1OZ BUTTER

1 ORGANIC OR FREE-RANGE CHICKEN WEIGHING BETWEEN 1.25 AND 1.5 KG/
4$\frac{1}{2}$ TO 5$\frac{1}{2}$ LB, JOINTED, OR 8 ORGANIC CHICKEN THIGHS

FLOUR FOR DUSTING

SALT AND PEPPER

1 ONION, CHOPPED

3 RASHERS OF STREAKY BACON, CUT INTO 1CM/$\frac{1}{2}$ IN PIECES

2 CELERY STICKS, CHOPPED

2 EATING APPLES, PEELED AND SLICED

300ML/$\frac{1}{2}$ PINT DRY CIDER

300ML/$\frac{1}{2}$ PINT CHICKEN STOCK

150ML/$\frac{1}{4}$ PINT CREAM

A BUNCH OF SAGE

Set the oven to 175°C.

Heat the oil in a frying pan and add the butter. Dust the chicken pieces in seasoned flour and quickly brown them in the butter. Remove them and put them on a plate while you cook the onion, bacon and celery for a few minutes, adding a little more butter if necessary.

Put the onion, bacon and celery mixture in the bottom of a casserole dish, spread the apple slices over, then lay the chicken pieces on top. Add 1 tablespoon of the seasoned flour to the juices in the frying pan, scrape and cook for a minute, then add the cider and stir until thickened. Add enough stock to make the sauce the consistency of thin cream. Pour it around the chicken, put the lid on the casserole and bake for 20-30 minutes, until the chicken is cooked so that, when you stick a skewer into it, the juice comes out clear, not pink.

Remove the chicken to a serving dish. Strain the sauce, boil to reduce it if necessary, then whisk in the cream and pour it over the chicken. Strip the sage leaves off their stalks and fry them in hot oil until they are crisp; it only takes a moment. Scatter them over each helping.

Braised Red Cabbage with Spicy Sausages.

Serves 6

The warm, spicy sweetness of slow-cooked red cabbage has a special affinity with pork sausages, ham or bacon.

1 SMALL RED CABBAGE
1 ONION, CHOPPED
30G/1OZ BUTTER
1 GARLIC CLOVE, FINELY CHOPPED
150ML/$\frac{1}{4}$ PINT RED WINE
2 TABLESPOONS BALSAMIC VINEGAR
3 TABLESPOONS SOFT BROWN SUGAR
4 EATING APPLES, PEELED, CORED AND SLICED
A BAY LEAF AND A STRIP OF ORANGE PEEL
1 TEASPOON CINNAMON
$\frac{1}{4}$ TEASPOON GROUND CLOVES
SALT AND FRESHLY GROUND BLACK PEPPER
450G/1LB POLISH KIELBASA OR OTHER SPICY SAUSAGE

Set the oven at 160ºC. Cut the cabbage into quarters, discarding the white stalk, and shred the rest. In a fire-proof casserole, soften the onion in the butter. Add the garlic and cook for a minute. Add the cabbage and all the other ingredients except the sausages, and stir to mix. Cut the sausages into chunks and lay them on top of the cabbage. Cover tightly and bake for 2 hours or longer. After an hour, check and, if all the liquid has been absorbed, add a little more wine or water. Adjust the seasoning before serving.

Variation: Instead of sausages, use chunks of smoky bacon.

Souvlaki.

Serves 4

The warm, herby scent of lamb kebabs cooked on wooden skewers brings back happy memories of holidays in Greece in the 1960s, enjoying the generous hospitality of our friends Mary and Spyro. It seemed that every time we got off a bus or a boat there was a stall selling souvlaki, and they tasted as good as they smelt.

Souvlaki also remind me of my 13th birthday, when my parents took me to dinner at Beoty's, a Greek restaurant in London. My schoolfriend Philippa came too. After carefully studying the menu she ordered a kebab, which came with bay leaves skewered between the chunks of meat, mushroom, onion and tomato. Seeing Philippa chomping valiantly at a bay leaf, my mother said gently and kindly, "You don't have to eat the bay leaves, you know." "Oh, I do know," Philippa replied, breezily, determined not to seem unsophisticated, "but I really like them," and washed the bay leaf down with a gulp of water.

4 WOODEN SKEWERS (SOAK THEM IN WATER FOR 30 MINUTES
BEFORE THEY ARE NEEDED)
700G/1LB 9OZ LEAN MEAT FROM A SHOULDER OR LEG OF LAMB
GRATED PEEL AND JUICE OF ONE LEMON
3 TABLESPOONS OF OLIVE OIL
3 GARLIC CLOVES, CRUSHED
2 BAY LEAVES, CRUMBLED
1½ TABLESPOONS OF DRIED OREGANO
SALT AND FRESHLY GROUND BLACK PEPPER
FRESH OREGANO, CHOPPED

Cut the meat into cubes of about 4cm/1½ in. Mix together all the other ingredients except the salt and the fresh oregano. Add the lamb and stir to coat the cubes with the marinade. Cover and leave in the fridge for at least 6 hours and preferably overnight.

Thread the cubes on to the skewers, sprinkle with salt and, when the grill (or barbecue) is hot, cook them for about 8 minutes, turning from time to time, and basting with the marinade. When cooked, sprinkle with fresh chopped oregano and serve in pitta bread envelopes, with Greek style tomato salad.

Variation: Pork can be used instead of lamb.

Very Good Tomato Sauce for Pasta.
Serves 6 or more

This is very easy to make, and tastes much better than anything ready-made out of a tin or a jar.

600G/1LB 5OZ TINNED ITALIAN PLUM TOMATOES
115G/4OZ SUN-DRIED TOMATOES
3 TABLESPOONS OLIVE OIL
1 LARGE ONION, CHOPPED
3 GARLIC CLOVES, PEELED AND THINLY SLICED
SALT AND FRESHLY GROUND BLACK PEPPER
A SMALL HANDFUL OF FRESH BASIL

Chop the tinned and sun-dried tomatoes. In a saucepan soften the onion in the olive oil, add the garlic and cook until the garlic just begins to colour. Add the tomatoes, lower the heat and simmer very gently, uncovered, for 25 minutes. Add salt and plenty of freshly ground pepper. At this stage it can be removed from the heat and put aside to be reheated later, or it can be frozen.

To serve, reheat and just before serving, add the basil leaves, roughly torn.

Toad in the Hole.

Serves 4

One veggie grandchild, one carnivore. Both love Toad-in-the-Hole –
I simply cook the sausages separately.
GRANNY FREARSON

This comforting and perennially popular variation on Yorkshire pudding needs no introduction. It used to be cooked using left-over meat, but nowadays it is always made with sausages. Toad in the hole can be nasty if the sausages are gristly and pallid, and the batter soggy instead of crisp, as some may remember from school dinners. So buy the best sausages you can get, and make sure the fat is really hot before the batter goes in. It is important to brown the sausages before the batter is added, and to serve the dish as soon as it is cooked, before it deflates.

8 BEST PORK SAUSAGES
2 TABLESPOONS OIL
125G / 4½ OZ FLOUR
3 MEDIUM EGGS AND 1 EXTRA EGG WHITE
300ML / ½ PINT WHOLE MILK
SALT AND PEPPER

Set the oven to 220ºC.

Put the flour, eggs, milk and seasoning in a blender and pulse in 10-second bursts, with the plunger left off to help aeration, till the batter is smooth. Let it rest for half an hour. Put the oil in a baking tin and heat it in the oven for 5 minutes. Add the sausages and cook for a few minutes or more until the fat runs and they are lightly browned.

Pour the batter around the sausages in the tin and bake for about 20 minutes until the batter is risen and golden brown. Check after 15 minutes. Put a bottle of tomato ketchup on the table.

Variation: Make individual toads in muffin tins, using chipolatas cut in three.

Leek and Bacon Tart.

Serves 4

Although quiche lorraine was, for some reason, considered unmanly, it became extremely popular in British home cooking in the 1960s. Since then, we have become accustomed to all sorts of imaginative variations on the theme, some more palatable than others. If any recipe could persuade a real man to eat quiche, this is it. The sweetness of young, fresh leeks, and the rich cream and egg yolk filling, make it one of the best.

SHORT-CRUST PASTRY (SEE PAGE 80)
30G/1OZ BUTTER
650G/1½ LB LEEKS, WASHED AND THE OUTSIDE LEAVES REMOVED
85G/3OZ SMOKED BACON
90G/3¼ OZ GRUYÈRE CHEESE, GRATED
4 EGG YOLKS
284ML/10 FL OZ SINGLE CREAM
SALT AND FRESHLY GROUND BLACK PEPPER

Set the oven at 190°C.

Roll out the pastry and use it to line a 20-22.5cm (8-9in) tart tin. Prick all over the bottom with a fork.

Trim and wash the leeks and thinly slice them across. Melt the butter in a frying pan and cook the leeks gently in the butter for 5 minutes until they start to get soft, but do not let them get brown. Spread them over the pastry case. Cut the bacon into 1cm/³⁄₈ in strips and cook for five minutes. Spread the bacon over the leeks and sprinkle the Gruyère evenly over them.

Beat the egg yolks and cream together, season with salt and freshly ground pepper, and pour carefully over the leek mixture. Bake for 25 to 30 minutes, until golden and set.

Head Mistress Chicken.
Serves 4

At my day school, parents ambitious for their daughters' success would invite our head mistress to dinner. Comparing notes, the girls discovered to their great glee that their parents' menus invariably featured chicken with mushrooms in a cream and white wine sauce. Miss Bowden must have got heartily sick of it, but her response was always the same, "Chicken, my dear, how lovely."

Now that chicken is no longer a luxury, it has become a quick and easy weekday dish, especially in this up-dated version. The more generous you are with the herbs, the better. It can be made with a whole chicken, jointed, or with chicken breasts which look more elegant. But thighs have more flavour.

8 FREE-RANGE CHICKEN THIGHS
1 TABLESPOON OLIVE OIL
1 ONION, CHOPPED
2 GARLIC CLOVES, CRUSHED
115G/4OZ MUSHROOMS, SLICED
1 LARGE GLASS OF WHITE WINE
200ML/$\frac{1}{3}$ PINT CRÈME FRAICHE
4 TABLESPOONS OF FRESH, CHOPPED PARSLEY, TARRAGON AND CHIVES.

Fry the chicken thighs in a large frying pan in the olive oil for about 10 minutes until they are golden. Add the onion, garlic and mushrooms and cook for five minutes.

Pour in the white wine and let it bubble until it is reduced by half. Stir in the crème fraiche, bring to the boil and simmer for a further 10 minutes or until, when the chicken pieces are prodded with a skewer, the juices run out clear, not pink. Stir in the herbs and eat with mashed potato, pasta or rice.

Variation: Instead of the herbs, stir in a tablespoon of Worcestershire sauce at the end.

Herby Lamb Chop Gratin.

Serves 4

This is a good bung-in-the-oven dish, needing very little advance preparation. The herbs can be varied; a mixture of rosemary and parsley is good.

4 LARGE LAMB CHOPS
4 TABLESPOONS BREADCRUMBS
2 TABLESPOONS LEMON THYME LEAVES, STRIPPED FROM THE STALKS
GRATED RIND OF $\frac{1}{2}$ LEMON
1 GARLIC CLOVE, CHOPPED FINE
SALT AND FRESHLY GROUND BLACK PEPPER
BUTTER

Set the oven at 190°C. Grease a shallow ovenproof dish.

Lay the chops in the dish. Mix together all the other ingredients except the butter and spread them over the chops. Dot small pieces of butter over the crumb mixture. Bake in the oven for about 30 minutes.

Tip: Whenever you have the tail end of a loaf of bread you know you can't use, make breadcrumbs and store them in the freezer until you need them for a gratin or stuffing.

Chapter 5.

LOVELY
FRESH
JOHN DORY
7.90 lb 17.42 kg

MACKE
2.99 lb

Fish on
Friday.

11 Recipes

We usually had fish on Fridays always with parsley sauce, a sauce rather neglected now in favour of the sharper but less subtle Tartare.
GUY HUNGERFORD

A huge baked cod with hard boiled egg sauce was always served for dinner on Good Friday, my mother presciently remarking that cod should be revered as a king of fishes, for feasts not fasting.
MADELINE WILKS
(Note: for parsley sauce and egg sauce, see page 45.)

Out of respect for the Christian tradition of fasting, fish invariably appeared at lunch or dinner not only on Good Friday but on Fridays all the year round. Nobody jumped for joy since it all too often seemed to be boiled cod; cod boiled, indeed, until the poor fish's flesh lost its firm and flakey texture and became like hard-to-chew and harder-to-swallow cotton wool. Lumpy white sauce did not help it to go down, either. The alternative to cod seemed to be a mouthful of equally hard-to-swallow herring bones. Of all the food that ever appeared on our plates, fish was the thing we would most gladly have parcelled up to send to those poor, starving children in China.

That was a long time ago. Now we know better than to insult fish by overcooking it, and can happily enjoy it on any day of the week.

Fish Baked on a Bed of Leeks.
Serves 4

The sweetness of young, fresh leeks enhances the flavour of any fish, which should also, of course, be very fresh.

3 MEDIUM OR 5 SMALL LEEKS
50G / 1¾ OZ BUTTER
4 FILLETS OF WHITE FISH OR 4 WHOLE FISH SUCH AS TROUT,
RED MULLET, OR MACKEREL
HALF A LEMON
SALT AND PEPPER

Set the oven at 220°C. Grease a large, shallow ovenproof dish large enough to hold all the fish in one layer.

Wash the leeks and slice them diagonally, very thinly. Melt the butter and sweat the leeks in it gently until they begin to soften. Remove the leeks with a slotted spoon and spread them on the bottom of the dish. Lay the fish on top of the leeks, squeeze the half lemon over them, season with salt and pepper, and dribble the buttery juice from the leeks over them. Bake until the fish are just cooked through. Test after 10 minutes by parting the flesh with a knife. If the flesh is opaque, it is cooked; if transparent, test again in a few minutes.

Variation: Try salmon steaks on a bed of shredded sorrel mixed with cream and chopped chives, dill and parsley. By the time the salmon is cooked, the sorrel will have wilted to the texture and colour of a cowpat, but it will have imparted its unique lemony flavour to the fish.

Fish Cakes.

Tessa Hayward
Makes 10-12 fish cakes

450G/1LB FLOURY POTATOES
225G/8OZ FRESH HADDOCK FILLET
MILK TO COOK THE FISH
225G/8OZ SMOKED HADDOCK FILLET
30G/1OZ BUTTER
2 TABLESPOONS OF FINELY CHOPPED PARSLEY
2 TABLESPOONS SNIPPED CHIVES
SALT AND PEPPER
FLOUR FOR DUSTING
2 EGGS, BEATEN
ABOUT 115G/4OZ HOME-MADE BREADCRUMBS
OIL AND BUTTER FOR FRYING

Peel the potatoes and boil them in a pan of salted water. While they cook put the fresh fish into a sauté pan, cover it with milk and bring to the boil. Simmer for 1 minute then remove the fish, using a slotted spoon. Put the smoked fish in the milk and simmer for 2 or 3 minutes until it is just cooked. Flake both pieces of fish, removing any stray bones or skin.

When the potatoes are cooked, drain them and mash until they are completely smooth, adding the butter and herbs. Carefully fold the flaked fish into the potato mixture and season well. Cool and chill in the fridge for half an hour to make the mixture easier to handle.

Put the flour, eggs and breadcrumbs into three separate small bowls. Flour your hands, take a heaped tablespoonful of the fish and potato mixture and shape it into a disc about 2cm/¾ in thick. Dip it first in the flour, then the egg, then the breadcrumbs, patting them to make them stick. Repeat until you have used up all the mixture.

Heat a little oil and butter in a frying pan and fry the fish cakes until they are hot all through and golden brown. Drain on kitchen paper. Eat them with tartare sauce.

Italian Baked Fish.

Carole Cox
Serves 6

This is an excellent dish of strong flavours, almost a meal in itself, to be eaten with crusty bread and a green salad.

25G/1OZ BUTTER

1 LARGE ONION, SLICED THINLY

2 GARLIC CLOVES, CHOPPED FINE

600G/1LB 5OZ POTATOES, NOT PEELED, CUT INTO 2CM CUBES

6 PLUM TOMATOES, ROUGHLY CHOPPED

200ML/$^1/_3$ PINT DRY WHITE WINE

200ML/$^1/_3$ PINT FISH STOCK MADE FROM THE SKINS OF THE FILLETS

200G/7OZ STONED GREEN OLIVES

1 SMALL RED CHILI, DESEEDED AND CHOPPED FINE

1KG/2LB 4OZ WHITE FISH FILLETS (COD, HADDOCK, POLLOCK)

SALT AND PEPPER

2 TABLESPOONS OF FLAT LEAVED PARSLEY, ROUGHLY CHOPPED

Preheat the oven to 200°C.

Melt the butter in a large flameproof shallow casserole and cook the onion until it begins to soften. Add the garlic and potatoes, and stir in the tomatoes. Add the wine and let it bubble over a high heat until reduced by half. Pour in the fish stock, add the olives and stir everything together. Cook in the oven for 20-25 minutes until the potatoes are tender. The dish can be prepared in advance up to this stage, allowed to cool and kept in the fridge until needed.

When you are ready to eat, reheat the vegetables (if necessary) in the oven for 10 minutes. Lay the fish among the potato and tomato mixture and baste it with the juices in the dish. Season with salt and pepper. Bake at 200°C for 7-10 minutes until the fish is just cooked. Scatter the chopped parsley over and serve.

Mum's Fish Pie.

Serves 6

My children still call it Granny's Fish Pie, and my grandchildren, Great-Granny's Fish Pie. For me it is Mum's, and the best there is.

150G/5½ OZ FROZEN PRAWNS
500G/1LB 2OZ SMOKED FILLET OF WHITE FISH (HADDOCK, POLLACK OR COLEY)
300G/10OZ FRESH WHITE FISH FILLET
200G/7OZ ORGANIC SALMON FILLET
700ML/1¼ PINTS WHOLE MILK
1 ONION, PEELED AND COARSELY GRATED
1 CARROT, COARSELY GRATED
1 STICK OF CELERY, CHOPPED
1 BAY LEAF
1 BUNCH OF FLAT-LEAVED PARSLEY
3 LARGE EGGS
50G/1¾ OZ BUTTER
70G/2½ OZ FLOUR
2 TABLESPOONS SNIPPED CHIVES
SALT AND PEPPER

For the mash:
900G/2LB FLOURY POTATOES
50G/1¾ OZ BUTTER
100ML/3½ FL OZ WHOLE MILK

Set the oven to 200°C.

Defrost the prawns in a sieve over a bowl, to save the water that comes out of them. Skin the fish fillets and put the skins into a saucepan with the water from the prawns, the milk, onion, carrot, celery, bay leaf and parsley stalks (save the leaves for later). Bring to the boil, remove from the heat and leave to infuse for half an hour.

Put the potatoes on to boil. Boil the eggs for 9 minutes, then plunge into cold running water. Peel them and chop roughly. When the potatoes are cooked, drain them and mash them with the butter and milk. Cut the fish into 2cm/³⁄₄ in cubes and mix in a bowl with the prawns and eggs.

Make the sauce: Strain the milk into a jug, melt the butter in a saucepan, add the flour and cook for a few minutes, stirring till smooth. Do not let it brown. Add the milk gradually, stirring all the time to keep it smooth. If it ends up lumpy, beat it with a balloon whisk. Season, and stir in the chopped parsley and chives. Then add the sauce to the fish and stir gently till the fish is all coated in the sauce. Put the mixture into a pie dish, spread the mashed potato over and draw furrows in the potato with a fork. Bake for about 20 minutes, until the top is getting brown.

Very Speedy Fish Pie.

Serves 6

This is based on Alice Thomas Ellis's fish pie, described in *Fish, Flesh and Good Red Herring* (Virago Press). The sauce, rather like an Italian salsa verde, makes it an unusual version of a classic dish, and easy as pie.

1KG/2.2LB HADDOCK FILLETS OR OTHER WHITE FISH, SKINNED AND BONED
3 SPRIGS OF THYME
BUNCH OF PARSLEY
4 TABLESPOONS OLIVE OIL
4 CLOVES OF GARLIC
SALT AND PEPPER
6 MEDIUM-SIZED POTATOES, BOILED AND PEELED
100G/3½ OZ BUTTER

Set the oven at 200°C. Butter an ovenproof dish.

Lay the fillets in the dish. Strip the leaves off the thyme sprig and whiz them in the small bowl of a food processor with the parsley, oil, garlic, salt and pepper. Pour the herb mixture over the fish. Slice the cooked potatoes and lay them over the fish, overlapping the discs. Dot with butter and bake for 25 to 30 minutes, until the fish is cooked and the top brown.

Moules Marinière.

Serves 4

Perhaps my opinion is coloured by nostalgia, but I am convinced that the best beaches in the world are round the coast of Britain. Our seaside combines golden sand washed clean by twice-daily tides, bracing surf, and comfortably warm rock pools full of sea anemones to poke and prawns to net. If you clamber from rock to rock, you can usually find, at low tide, encrustations of mussels. It is one of our family traditions at the seaside to eat at least one meal of mussels freshly picked from the rocks. Everyone, provided they are old enough to toddle and to hold a small bucket, joins in. As far as the mussels are concerned, though, size does matter; the bigger the better.

2 ¼ LITRES / 1 QUART MUSSELS
50G / 1¾ OZ BUTTER
1 SHALLOT, 2 CLOVES OF GARLIC AND A BUNCH OF PARSLEY,
ALL ROUGHLY CHOPPED
A LARGE GLASS OF WHITE WINE OR DRY CIDER
ANOTHER TABLESPOON OF CHOPPED PARSLEY
200ML / ⅓ PINT DOUBLE CREAM

Put the mussels in a large bowl of cold water, discarding any broken ones and any that are open and do not close when the shell is tapped sharply with a knife. Scrub any dirt off the shells, scraping off barnacles and yanking out the beards. Rinse them in two lots of clean water.

In a saucepan large enough to hold all the mussels, melt the butter and gently cook the shallot, garlic and parsley for a few moments. Add the wine or cider and the same quantity of water and bring to the boil. Add the mussels, cover the pan and boil fiercely for 3 minutes. When the mussels open they are ready. Remove them with a slotted spoon, and divide them among four heated serving bowls. Boil any unopened mussels for a minute or two more. If they don't open, discard them.

Strain the mussel broth through muslin to remove any sand and grit. Put it in a saucepan, add the cream, stir well and pour the sauce over the mussels. Scatter on the chopped parsley.

Rob's Seduction Sole.
Serves 2

In his bachelor days my husband sometimes used to invite young ladies to dine a deux at his flat. He always cooked the same dish: fillets of Dover sole with condensed mushroom soup poured over them, baked in the oven. It was usually a success; at any rate there were no complaints. By the time I met him his signature dish had become sautéed lambs' kidneys with sherry. I had no complaints either.

Fresh ingredients taste incomparably better than tinned soup, so here is a non-soupy version of seduction sole, almost as quick and easy.

2 FILLETED DOVER SOLES (OR OTHER WHITE FISH)
30G/1OZ BUTTER
1 ONION, FINELY CHOPPED
115G/4OZ SMALL MUSHROOMS, FINELY SLICED
½ A GLASS OF WHITE WINE
2 TABLESPOONS CHOPPED PARSLEY
150ML/¼ PINT DOUBLE CREAM
SALT AND PEPPER

Butter an ovenproof dish and lay the fish fillets in it. In a small saucepan, melt the rest of the butter, add the chopped onion and cook until transparent. Do not let it brown. Add the mushrooms and wine and boil until the wine has almost all evaporated. Add the parsley and cream. Season to taste. All this can be done in advance.

Thirty minutes before you want to eat, turn on the oven to 220°C. Fifteen minutes before, heat the sauce and pour it over the fish. Put the dish in the oven and bake for 10 minutes, or until the fish is just cooked.

Plaice Rolls.

Amanda Hornby
Serves 4

These ordinary, easy ingredients are made special by the way they are presented.

12 SMALL FILLETS OF PLAICE (3 FOR EACH PERSON)
BUTTER
PARSLEY SAUCE (SEE PAGE 45)
SALT AND PEPPER

Butter a shallow ovenproof dish big enough to hold the rolled fillets in one layer. Roll up each fillet and lay, join downwards, in the dish. Pour the parsley sauce over, cover the dish with foil and bake for 15 to 20 minutes.

Tuna and Bean Salad.

Lunch in a tin. Well, two tins, actually.

A TIN OF BUTTER BEANS
A TIN OF TUNA
$^1/_2$ A SPANISH ONION, THINLY SLICED
$^1/_2$ A LEMON
OLIVE OIL
SALT AND PEPPER

Drain the tuna and beans and roughly mix them together. Scatter the onions on top, squeeze lemon juice over and drizzle with olive oil. Season with a little salt and freshly ground black pepper.

Stuffed Haddock Baked in Foil.

Serves 4

Served with home-made Hollandaise sauce, this makes a good dinner-party dish.

1 MEDIUM ONION, FINELY CHOPPED
75G/2¾ OZ BREADCRUMBS FROM A LOAF A DAY OR TWO OLD
55G/2OZ GRATED PARMESAN CHEESE
2 TABLESPOONS CHOPPED PARSLEY
GRATED RIND AND JUICE OF ½ A LEMON
SALT AND PEPPER
1 EGG, BEATEN
2 LARGE FILLETS OF FRESH HADDOCK
BUTTER

Heat the oven to 200°C.
Make the stuffing: soften the onion in butter and mix with the breadcrumbs, cheese, parsley, salt and pepper in a bowl. Add the lemon juice and enough egg just to bind the ingredients together.

Grease a large piece of foil with butter. Lay one fillet on the foil. Spread the crumb mixture over the fillet and cover with the second fillet. Dot with butter. Wrap the foil round to make a leak-proof package and place in a baking tin to save the juices when it is opened. Bake in the oven for 20 minutes.

Smoked Haddock with Poached Eggs.

Arbroath Smokies are the gourmet's choice, but "ordinary" smoked haddock is delicious too (buy un-dyed fish). This is one of the quickest, easiest, most satisfying dishes to cook for lunch or supper.

Gently simmer in milk or milk and water a piece of fish per person. Keep the fish warm while you poach the required number of eggs. Eat with brown bread.

Chapter 6.

Saturday
Stews.

14 Recipes

My mother's stews were greatly appreciated on shooting lunch days.
I think the secret was always using shin and cooking it for a very long time.
The dumplings that went with them were also very good.
TEEN COOKE

Many of these dishes owe their melting tenderness to long, slow cooking, and can be left, barely simmering, on the back burner or in a low oven while you all go out. They provide warming, satisfying fuel for anyone who has been outdoors, whether walking, playing football in the park, or battling down the high street, loaded with carrier bags. They need something to sop up the delicious gravy, and in many people's food memories, dumplings (see page 47) fulfil this role. If you don't make dumplings, serve these stews with baked, mashed or plain boiled potatoes, or with rice or pasta.

Another advantage of stews and casseroles is that they can be prepared a day or two in advance and reheated. Often the flavours are actually improved and intensified by this process.

Billabong Stew.

Val Marriott

Serves 4-6

Just the sort of food the Jolly Swagman in "Waltzing Matilda" dreamed about: a hearty, satisfying, strongly flavoured stew.

900G/2LB STEWING STEAK

4 MEDIUM ONIONS

6 CARROTS

SEASONED FLOUR

2 TABLESPOONS WORCESTERSHIRE SAUCE

2 TABLESPOONS TOMATO KETCHUP

2 TABLESPOONS WINE VINEGAR

2 TABLESPOONS SOFT BROWN SUGAR

300 ML/½ PINT WATER

DRIED HERBS

SALT AND PEPPER

Set the oven at 190°C.

Cut the steak into bite-sized pieces. Slice the onions and carrots. Roll the steak pieces in seasoned flour and put alternate layers of steak and vegetables in a deep casserole dish, finishing with a layer of veg. Mix together all the liquids with the herbs, sugar and seasoning and pour over. Cover tightly and put in the oven. Turn the oven down to 150°C and cook the stew for 3 hours, stirring halfway through. Good with a baked potato.

Bobotie.
Serves 6

This is the most amazing South African dish. Everyone I cook it for adores it.
I usually double or treble the amount and do it in a huge dish for a party.
It is quite delicious... also a very economical way of feeding a lot of people.
CAROLE COX

Don't be put off by the long list of ingredients. Except for Mrs Ball's chutney, which most South Africans consider an essential ingredient (it is obtainable from Sainsbury's), you probably have most of them in the store cupboard, and putting them together is easy.

Rice and lentils:
15ML/$\frac{1}{2}$OZ SUNFLOWER OIL
150G/5$\frac{1}{2}$ OZ BROWN RICE
150GM/5$\frac{1}{2}$ OZ BROWN OR GREEN LENTILS, PICKED OVER AND RINSED
500ML/18 FL OZ WATER
$\frac{1}{2}$ TEASPOON EACH OF SALT, CUMIN, GROUND CORIANDER, TURMERIC
1 TEASPOON SUGAR
1 x 400G/14 FL OZ TIN OF CHOPPED TOMATOES WITH THEIR JUICE
1 STICK OF CINNAMON
2 STAR ANISE

Meat mixture:
1 SLICE OF BREAD, CRUSTS CUT OFF
300ML/$\frac{1}{2}$ PINT MILK
25ML/1 FL OZ SUNFLOWER OIL
1 ONION, CHOPPED
2 GARLIC CLOVES, CHOPPED
2 TEASPOONS CURRY POWDER
$\frac{1}{2}$ TEASPOON TURMERIC
$\frac{1}{4}$ TEASPOON GRATED NUTMEG
2 TEASPOONS BROWN VINEGAR
2 TABLESPOONS MRS BALL'S CHUTNEY

500G / 1LB 2OZ MINCED BEEF
125G / 4½ OZ SEEDLESS RAISINS
1 TEASPOON SALT
1 BEATEN EGG

Topping:
1 EGG
RESERVED MILK
A PINCH OF SALT
A PINCH OF TURMERIC
100G / 3½ OZ DESSICATED COCONUT
2 BAY LEAVES
GARAM MASALA FOR DUSTING

Set the oven at 180°C.

Rice and lentils: Put the oil in a large saucepan, add all the other ingredients and bring to the boil, stirring just once to mix. Cover and simmer very gently for one hour or until the liquid is absorbed and the rice and lentils are cooked. Remove the cinnamon stick and anise.

Meat mixture: Put the bread to soak in the milk. Heat the oil and fry the onions and garlic. Mix in the spices, vinegar and chutney. Squeeze the milk out of the bread, and reserve the milk. Add the bread, the mince, raisins and salt to the pan and keep turning over a low heat until the mince is no longer pink. Remove from the stove and add the beaten egg, mixing well.

To assemble: Oil a deep 23cm/9in pie dish and spread half the rice mixture over the base. Spoon the mince mixture over in an even layer. Top with the remaining rice mixture.

Topping: Beat the egg into the reserved milk, add the salt, turmeric and coconut and pour evenly over the bobotie. Stick the bay leaves in here and there and dust with garam masala.

Stand the pie dish in a large roasting tin and pour in hot water to come halfway up the pie dish. Bake in the oven for 1 to 1½ hours.

Anne's Beef Stew.

Anne Lascelles
Serves up to 6

During the holidays, at Gemeaux, in the month of August, when we arrived
in my grandmother's dark kitchen on Sunday after Vespers, it was lit by a ray
of sunshine in which the dust and the flies were dancing, and there was a sound
like a little bubbling spring. It was a daube, which since midday had been
murmuring gently on the stove, giving out sweet smells which brought tears
to your eyes. Thyme, rosemary, bay leaves, spices, the wine of the marinade,
and the fumet of the meat were becoming transformed… into a delicious
whole, which was served about seven o'clock in the evening, so well cooked
and so tender that it was carved with a spoon.
PIERRE HUGUENIN, 1936

And she peered into the dish, with its shiny walls and its confusion of savoury
brown and yellow meats, and its bay leaves and its wine, and thought:
This will celebrate the occasion.
TO THE LIGHTHOUSE BY VIRGINIA WOOLF

My sister-in-law's simply named "beef stew" has all the qualities ascribed to
a *daube de boeuf*. Her magic ingredient is sun-dried tomatoes.

4 LARGE ONIONS

OLIVE OIL

1KG/2LB 3OZ BRAISING BEEF CUT IN 2.5CM/1IN SLICES

2 TINS CHOPPED TOMATOES

1/2 BOTTLE RED WINE

A SPRIG EACH OF ROSEMARY AND THYME, AND 2 BAY LEAVES

140G/5OZ SUN-DRIED TOMATOES IN OIL

BEEF STOCK (OPTIONAL)

600G/1LB 5OZ MUSHROOMS

2 GARLIC CLOVES, CHOPPED FINE

CHOPPED PARSLEY

SALT AND PEPPER

Peel the onions, halve them and slice as thinly as possible. In a large saucepan, fry them in olive oil until golden. Remove from the heat. Cut the beef into bite-sized pieces. Heat some olive oil in a large, heavy frying pan and brown the meat in small batches. Add it to the onions in the saucepan.

Add the tinned tomatoes, the wine and the herbs (except the parsley). Reserve the oil from the sun-dried tomatoes, chop them and add to the mixture. If more liquid is needed, add stock or water. Bring to the boil and simmer very gently top of the stove or in a slow oven, until the meat is tender, about 2 hours.

Meanwhile, chop the mushrooms into chunks, halves or quarters, depending on their size. Heat some olive oil in a frying pan, add the chopped garlic and stir. Add the mushrooms and the reserved oil from the sun-dried tomatoes. When the mushrooms are nearly cooked, add them and the chopped parsley to the stew and season with salt and plenty of freshly ground black pepper.

Like most stews, it is, if anything, improved by being kept in the fridge for a day or two and reheated. It also freezes well.

Variation: Add stoned black olives half an hour before the end of cooking.

Coq au Vin.
Serves 4

We kept our own chickens and preserved their eggs in enamel buckets. My brother and I took it in turns to feed them before we went to school. When their laying days were over my father would bravely "pull their necks". We watched from a safe distance as they flapped for a few seconds on the path. Then we would have boiled chicken with egg sauce. Heavenly!
ALISON McMAHON

The Scottish way with an old boiler is Cock-a-leekie, somewhere between a soup and a stew. In France, *coq au vin*, a rich, winey stew, is traditionally made from a cockerel in his young prime, full of flavour but less tender than a bird bred for roasting. Next best was a hen whose egg production had dwindled. For those of us who have to buy our meat, a free-range organic bird is the nearest equivalent.

1 CHICKEN, WITH GIBLETS IF AVAILABLE
500ML/18 FL OZ CHICKEN STOCK
250G/9OZ STREAKY BACON, ROUGHLY CHOPPED
50G/1¾ OZ BUTTER
1 TABLESPOON OLIVE OIL
250G/9OZ PICKLING ONIONS, PEELED
50G/1¾OZ FLOUR
SALT AND PEPPER
A SHERRY GLASS OF BRANDY
500ML/18 FL OZ RED WINE
PARSLEY, THYME, BAY LEAF
3 CELERY STICKS, CUT INTO 4CM/1½ IN LENGTHS
4 GARLIC CLOVES, CRUSHED
4 TOMATOES, SKINNED, DESEEDED AND CHOPPED
250G/9OZ BUTTON MUSHROOMS
SALT AND PEPPER

If you have the bird's giblets, add them to the chicken stock and simmer until needed. Joint the chicken into 4 or 6 pieces or get the butcher to do this for you. In a frying pan, brown the chopped bacon in the oil and butter, and with a slotted spoon transfer it to a flameproof casserole. Brown the onions and transfer them to the casserole.

Dust the chicken pieces with the seasoned flour and brown them all over. Pour over the brandy and light it. When the flames have died down, put the chicken pieces in the casserole. Pour the red wine into the frying pan and deglaze the pan. Pour the wine over the chicken, then do the same with the stock, having strained off the giblets.

Add the herbs, celery, garlic and tomatoes, stir, bring to the boil and simmer very gently on a hotplate or in the oven at 150°C, for about 1½ hours, until the chicken is tender. Cook the mushrooms in a little butter for a few minutes.

Strain off the stock and boil vigorously in a wide shallow saucepan until it is reduced by half or more to make a rich sauce. If it needs thickening, whisk in, a little at a time, some *beurre manié* (equal quantities of butter and flour mashed together until smooth).

Add the sauce and mushrooms to the casserole, and heat again. Serve with potatoes, boiled or mashed.

Lancashire Hot Pot.

Serves 4

The ingredients are similar to those of that other traditional, comforting one-pot dish, Irish Stew, but with the addition of a couple of lambs' kidneys and, according to some Lancastrians, black pudding. Unlike Irish stew, the lamb is browned before putting it in the pot.

600G/1LB 5OZ BEST END OR MIDDLE NECK LAMB CHOPS
2 LAMBS' KIDNEYS, QUARTERED AND THE CORE REMOVED
25G/1OZ BUTTER
OIL FOR FRYING
1 LARGE ONION, SLICED
750G/1LB 10OZ POTATOES
1 BAY LEAF
SEASONED FLOUR FOR DUSTING
2 LARGE CARROTS, PEELED AND CUT IN LARGE CHUNKS
1 MEDIUM TURNIP, PEELED AND CUT IN CUBES
1½ TEASPOONS WORCESTERSHIRE SAUCE
500ML/18 FL OZ STOCK OR WATER
SALT AND PEPPER

Set the oven at 200°C. In a pan, fry the onion gently in oil until it is soft. Peel the potatoes and slice them about the thickness of a 50p coin. Put the bay leaf, then half the potatoes, with the onion, in a large, deep casserole. Dust the chops with seasoned flour and brown them in the frying pan, in batches. Arrange them over the potatoes in the casserole. Flour and brown the kidneys and tuck them in around the chops. Add the carrots and turnip, filling in any gaps. Add the Worcestershire sauce to the stock or water, and bring to the boil.

Meanwhile, arrange the rest of the potatoes on top of the meat and vegetables, in overlapping circles. Pour the hot stock over, until the potatoes are barely covered. Cover the pot and put it in the oven. After 20 minutes, turn the oven down to 140°C and cook for 90 minutes. For the last 30 minutes take the lid off the pot so that the top layer of potatoes gets brown and crisp. If necessary, finish the browning under the grill.

Navarin of Lamb.

This is a summer dish, to be made with new season's lamb and fresh young vegetables.

$^1\!/_2$ LEG OF LAMB, BONED (ABOUT 1.25KG/2LB 12OZ)
75G/2$^1\!/_2$ OZ BUTTER
1 TABLESPOON OLIVE OIL
300ML/$^1\!/_2$ PINT DRY WHITE WINE
300ML/$^1\!/_2$ PINT CHICKEN STOCK
300ML/$^1\!/_2$ PINT TOMATO JUICE
250G/9OZ SMALL NEW POTATOES
250G/9OZ VERY SMALL ONIONS, PEELED
250G/9OZ BABY CARROTS
250G/9OZ BABY TURNIPS
250G/9OZ BABY COURGETTES, CUT IN CHUNKS
185G/6$^1\!/_2$ OZ BROAD BEANS
3 TABLESPOONS FLOUR
4 TABLESPOONS CHOPPED CHERVIL

Cut the lamb in cubes about 4cm/1$^1\!/_2$ in square. In a casserole melt 30g/1oz of the butter with 1 tablespoon of olive oil and brown the lamb all over. Heat the wine, stock and tomato juice together and pour the mixture over the meat. Cover and simmer gently. After 1 hour add the potatoes, onions, carrots and turnips. Simmer for another 30 minutes, then add the courgettes. After 15 minutes add the broad beans, season with salt and pepper, and cook for 10 minutes more. Mix the flour and 45g/1$^1\!/_2$ oz butter to a paste and add in small pieces to thicken the stew, stirring all the time. Sprinkle the chervil over before serving.

Rabbit with Lentil Purée.

Run, rabbit, run, rabbit, run, run, run,
Here comes the farmer with his gun, gun, gun.
He'll get by without his rabbit pie,
So run, rabbit, run, rabbit, run, run, run.

In the immediately postwar years, rabbit did duty as the poor man's chicken, chicken being a delicacy and a treat. It was my mother's proud boast that she could cook rabbit in such a way as to convince my father he was eating chicken. My cousin remembers eating rabbit and bacon pie, and rabbit stew: "I loved it," she says, "such tender meat."

This recipe is adapted from one of eight rabbit recipes given by Constance Spry. She recommends soaking the rabbit pieces overnight in water and vinegar, to whiten the flesh. This would certainly add to the chicken illusion, but is not otherwise necessary.

1 RABBIT, JOINTED BY THE BUTCHER
2 TABLESPOONS FLOUR, SALT AND PEPPER
50G/1¾ OZ BUTTER
150G PUY LENTILS, PICKED OVER AND RINSED
1 MEDIUM ONION, CHOPPED
2 CLOVES OF GARLIC, CRUSHED
1 STICK OF CELERY, SLICED
A BOUQUET GARNI OF PARSLEY, THYME AND BAY
2 TABLESPOONS DOUBLE CREAM
MORE SALT AND PEPPER

Dust the rabbit joints with the seasoned flour. In a frying pan, melt the butter and turn the rabbit joints in batches, until they begin to colour, but do not let them brown. Put them in a fireproof casserole with the lentils, onion, garlic, celery and bouquet garni. Season with salt and pepper and add enough water barely to cover them. Put on the lid and simmer very gently on top of the stove or in the oven at 150°C, for 2 hours, until the rabbit is very tender.

Put the rabbit joints in a covered dish in a low oven to keep warm. Strain off most of the stock and whiz the vegetables in a blender or food processor, adding enough stock to make a fairly lax purée. Reheat the lentil purée, stir in the cream and adjust the seasoning. Put the lentil purée in the centre of a serving dish and arrange the rabbit joints around it.

Oxtail Stew.
Serves 4

Long, slow cooking yields meltingly tender meat and rich, vinous sauce.

2 OXTAILS CUT IN SHORT LENGTHS
1 MARROW BONE OR PIG'S TROTTER (OPTIONAL, TO ENRICH THE DISH)
2 CARROTS, 2 ONIONS, 2 CELERY STICKS, 1 SMALL TURNIP,
ALL ROUGHLY CHOPPED
THINLY PARED ZEST OF $\frac{1}{2}$ AN ORANGE
A BUNCH OF PARSLEY, THYME AND BAY LEAVES, TIED WITH COTTON
$\frac{1}{2}$ A BOTTLE OF GOOD RED WINE

Soak the oxtail pieces in cold water for two hours to remove some of the blood. Drain and put them in a large saucepan with all the ingredients except the wine. Cover with cold water and bring slowly to the boil, skimming off any scum that forms. Cover and simmer very gently on a hotplate or in a very low (120°C) oven for 3 hours or more, until the meat is tender and coming away from the bone.

With a slotted spoon, take out the oxtail pieces and put to one side. Remove the trotter or marrow bone and the vegetables and strain the liquid through muslin into a clean pan. Add the wine and boil over a high heat to reduce. Keep boiling until it reaches a rich and slightly syrupy consistency.

Meanwhile, remove the meat from the oxtail bones. Heat it in the sauce and serve with mashed potatoes or parsnip-and-potato mash, and Savoy cabbage, shredded fine and steamed for a few minutes.

Slow Roasted Pork Belly with Cider.

Serves 6

There is a long tradition of cooking rich meats, such as pork or goose, with apples and cider, specially in the West Country. The sharpness of the apples balances the unctuous, herby meat, and the crackling is irresistible.

3 GARLIC CLOVES, CRUSHED

2 LARGE BRAMLEY APPLES, PEELED, CORED AND THICKLY SLICED

A BIG SPRIG OF ROSEMARY

6 SPRIGS OF THYME

A BUNCH OF PARSLEY

12 SAGE LEAVES

SALT AND PEPPER

2.25KG/5LB BELLY OF PORK, THE SKIN WELL SCORED

500ML/18 FL OZ DRY CIDER

Set the oven to 175°C.

Put the garlic, apple slices and herbs on the bottom of a roasting tin. Season. Lay the pork, skin side up, on top and pour the cider over it. Rub salt into the skin. Cover in foil and cook in a moderate oven for 2½ hours or until the meat is tender.

Place under a hot grill to crisp up the crackling, watching all the time, in case it burns.

Poulet Grand-Mère.

Serves 6

This recipe appeared in *Ma Cuisine*, by the great French chef Escoffier. In the language of classical French cooking, the epithet "grand-mère" signifies good, simple home-cooking. If you can't get the chicken's liver (or that of another chicken), leave it out.

1 ORGANIC CHICKEN, ABOUT 2KG/4½ LB, AND ITS LIVER
4 TABLESPOONS BUTTER
90G/3¼ OZ LEAN BACON, DICED
15 BABY ONIONS, BLANCHED AND PEELED
SALT AND PEPPER
3 MEDIUM POTATOES, CUBED
STUFFING:
1 MEDIUM ONION, FINELY CHOPPED
1½ TABLESPOONS BUTTER
90G/3¼ OZ GOOD SAUSAGE MEAT
3 TSP CHOPPED PARSLEY
40G/1½ OZ FRESH WHITE BREADCRUMBS
SALT AND PEPPER

For the stuffing: Cook the onion in the butter until golden. Add the sausage meat and stir to break it up and mix it with the onion. Chop and add the chicken liver. Cook it for 1 minute then, off the heat, add the parsley and breadcrumbs. Season to taste. When the stuffing has cooled, put it inside the chicken.

For the chicken: In a casserole big enough to take the chicken and vegetables, melt the butter and add the chicken, bacon and onions, and salt and pepper to taste. Cover and cook over a very low heat for 20 minutes, stirring and turning the chicken occasionally. When the chicken and onions are golden brown, add the potatoes. Cover and cook very gently, stirring occasionally, on top of the stove or in the oven at 120°C for about 20-25 minutes, when the chicken should be very tender and the potatoes browned.

Pheasant and Chestnut Casserole.

Serves 4

Twenty years ago we planted a sweet chestnut tree in the garden. After the hot summer of 2006 we had a really good crop of plump chestnuts for the first time, and I was so proud of them that I went through the tedious process of peeling them several times without complaining. However, chestnuts can be bought ready peeled, vacuum packed or in tins. The recipe for Somerset Chicken on page 90 is good made with pheasant too.

2 PHEASANTS
30G/1OZ BUTTER
1 LARGE ONION, CHOPPED
225G/8OZ PEELED CHESTNUTS
1 TABLESPOON FLOUR
1 GLASS RED WINE
450ML/16 FL OZ STOCK
2 TEASPOONS BALSAMIC VINEGAR
2 TEASPOONS REDCURRANT JELLY
GRATED RIND AND JUICE OF $\frac{1}{2}$ AN ORANGE
A BOUQUET GARNI
SALT AND PEPPER

Set the oven at 180°C.

Cut each pheasant in half along the breastbone. Brown the halves in the butter and put them in a casserole. Slowly brown the onion and chestnuts, adding more butter if necessary. Add to the pheasant.

Cook the flour in the remaining butter for a minute or two, then add the wine, then the stock. Stir until thickened and smooth. Add the vinegar, orange rind and juice and redcurrant jelly. Season to taste.

Put the bouquet garni in the casserole and pour the sauce over the pheasants. Cover and cook for 1 hour. Before serving, taste the sauce and adjust the seasoning. If the sauce is too thin, strain it off and boil to reduce it.

Variation: Instead of chestnuts, add prunes.

Spag. Bol.

Sandra Smith-Gordon
4 helpings

Apart from macaroni cheese, spaghetti bolognese was the only pasta dish we knew when I was a child. It has been popular with children of each new generation – something to do with slurping up the worms one by one. It may come as a surprise to find Spag. Bol. in the "Slow Stews" chapter, but long, slow cooking is the secret of a good Bolognese sauce.

Sandra's recipe described as optional the second clove of garlic, the wine and the mushrooms but I think they are all essential, so I have included them.

500G/1LB 2OZ MINCED BEEF
1 TIN CHOPPED TOMATOES
1 LARGE ONION, FINELY CHOPPED
2 CLOVES OF GARLIC, FINELY CHOPPED
140G/5OZ TOMATO PURÉE
1 OXO CUBE
1 BAY LEAF
1 GLASS OF RED WINE
100G/3½ OZ MUSHROOMS, CHOPPED SMALL
SALT AND PEPPER

Put the beef, tomatoes, onion, garlic and tomato purée in a large saucepan or casserole and stir well till everything is thoroughly mixed and there are no lumps of meat.

Crumble in the Oxo cube and add the bay leaf. Add the wine and enough water to make a sloppy mix. Bring to the boil, stirring regularly. Turn down the heat, cover and simmer very gently on top of the stove for at least two hours, stirring occasionally. Or cook it, covered, in the oven for 2 or 3 hours at 150°C. Half an hour before the end of cooking, season and add the mushrooms. If the mixture becomes too dry, add a little more water. If it is too thin, leave the lid off towards the end of the cooking.

This recipe freezes very well so it is worth while doubling it up and freezing half. You can also make it a day or two in advance and keep it in the fridge.

Lamb with Aubergines and Cinnamon.

Serves 6

The exchange of recipes in families is a two-way affair. This gently spiced Middle Eastern lamb dish came from my daughter Sophy, and is adapted from one by Josceline Dimbleby.

1.3KG/3LB LAMB NECK FILLETS
2 TABLESPOONS GROUNDNUT OIL
40G/1½OZ BUTTER
3 LARGE GARLIC CLOVES, THINLY SLICED
4CM/1½ IN FRESH GINGER ROOT, PEELED AND FINELY CHOPPED
800G/1LB 12OZ TINNED CHOPPED TOMATOES
JUICE OF 1½ LEMONS
3 MEDIUM-SIZED AUBERGINES
2 TABLESPOONS TOMATO PURÉE
1½ TABLESPOONS HONEY
2 STICKS OF CINNAMON
SALT AND FRESHLY GROUND BLACK PEPPER
55G/2OZ PINE NUTS

Set the oven at 170°C.

Slice the lamb into pieces about 2.5cm/1in thick. Heat the oil and butter in a large fireproof casserole over a fairly high heat. Add the lamb and cook, stirring constantly, for 8 to 10 minutes until well browned. Remove from the heat.

Add the garlic, ginger and tomatoes to the lamb. Put the lemon juice in a large bowl. Cut the unpeeled aubergines into cubes of about 4cm/1½ in, stirring them into the lemon juice as you go. Add them to the casserole.

Stir the tomato purée and honey into 600ml/1¼ pints of hot water and add to the casserole with the cinnamon. Season with salt and freshly ground black pepper and stir the mixture well.

Bring to the boil on top of the stove, cover and cook in the oven for 2 hours until the lamb is tender. In a deep frying pan, over a fairly high heat, toss the pine nuts until they are lightly browned. Just before serving the casserole, fish out the cinnamon sticks and scatter the pine nuts over the dish.

Very Slow Shoulder of Lamb.
Serves 6-8

I use two bits of shoulder – v. good value – All the fat disappears and the meat all falls off the bone. You can put more beans in – I think I do.
CAROLE COX

This is one of the most meltingly delicious of all meat dishes, specially if made a day or two in advance and reheated for an hour. A shoulder is quite a fatty joint, and although Carole says the fat all disappears in the cooking, the lamb is even better cooked in advance, allowed to get cold, and surplus fat removed before reheating it.

1 LARGE-ISH OR 2 SMALLER PIECES OF LAMB SHOULDER
2 LARGE TINS OF HARICOT BEANS
2 LARGE ONIONS
10 SHALLOTS
6 TOMATOES, QUARTERED
10 WHOLE CLOVES OF GARLIC, PEELED
1 TIN OF ANCHOVIES
2 BAY LEAVES
3 BRANCHES OF ROSEMARY
SALT AND FRESHLY GROUND BLACK PEPPER
3 TABLESPOONS TOMATO PURÉE
300-400ML/$\frac{1}{2}$-$\frac{3}{4}$ PINT OF DRY WHITE WINE

Heat the oven to 220°C.

Put all the ingredients into a large casserole, cover and cook for an hour at 220°C, followed by 6-8 hours at 100°C.

Chapter 7.

Vegetable
Dishes and
Salads.

29 Recipes

Vegetables used merely to play a humble supporting role in the drama of Meat and Two Veg. As a result, not much trouble was taken over preparing them. Reminiscences are mostly negative: "Vegetables were always overcooked – houses reeked disgustingly of cooked cabbage… cauliflower, broad beans, carrots, beetroot were all covered with thick floury blankets of white sauce…" Another person remembers that her mother grew wonderful vegetables in the garden, but always ruined them by overcooking, "and they were far too big: she thought it was a 'waste' to pick veg when they were still tiny, so all the broad beans were the size of conkers and the beetroots like tennis balls."

Homegrown fruit and vegetables were just as likely to put children off eating up their greens as those bought from the greengrocer. Slugs did not discriminate between the two, and more than one usually lurked in a complex network of tunnels that led to the heart of a cabbage or lettuce. If you made a fuss, "extra meat ration!" was the bracing reply.

So eating vegetables was for many children a penance undertaken before they were allowed to leave the table. In the days of wartime blackout, carrots were the only popular vegetable, as being able to see in the dark seemed a worthwhile reward for eating them. In some families, every time carrots appeared on the table, the children asked ritual question, "Are they really good for your eyesight?" just for the pleasure of being answered with another question: "How often do you see a rabbit wearing spectacles?"

Most people of my generation remember our first banana, but it was not only bananas that we were deprived of when we were growing up. Mediterranean vegetables such as aubergines, peppers and globe artichokes were unknown to us before the 1960s, and the only herbs we had ever seen were parsley, thyme and bay leaves. No basil, no tarragon, no coriander, and only a cautious smidgin of garlic.

One of the great culinary improvements during my lifetime is the huge variety of fruit and vegetables available at all seasons, together with excellent advice on how to cook them so they retain all their goodness and taste delicious. Even the old familiar standbys like carrots and cabbage are transformed, so that at last we can appreciate and celebrate them. One grandmother remembers rather enjoying school meals, "but not the cabbage which of course was over-cooked. I now love it – I usually shred it and stir fry with garlic – or cook it lightly then stir fry with previously fried onions and caraway seeds."

In this chapter, I have included several vegetable dishes, such as dear old cauliflower cheese, that are substantial enough to stand alone at lunch or supper. Others are not traditional but will, perhaps, become classics of the future.

There are also plenty of ways to gussie up everyday vegetables, without having to refer to a recipe. Garnish them with crispy bacon bits, fried breadcrumbs, snipped chives, chopped parsley, crumbled walnuts, toasted almonds, or chopped anchovies. Or dribble a little olive oil over them and add a splash of balsamic vinegar.

Beans with Garlic and Pine Nuts.
Tessa Hayward

It is now considered such a crime to overcook any vegetable, that nobody dares to speak out when vegetables are served underdone. There is a fashion in restaurants for serving French beans so undercooked that they squeak against your teeth. That is not what *al dente* means. To test vegetables for doneness, the most reliable way is not to poke them with a knife, but to fish a piece out of the pan and bite it.

375G/12OZ GREEN BEANS, WASHED AND TOPPED AND TAILED
50G/1¾OZ BUTTER
50G/1¾OZ PINE NUTS
2 GARLIC CLOVES, CRUSHED
SALT AND PEPPER

Put the beans into boiling, salted water. Melt the butter in a small saucepan and, while the beans are cooking, turn the pine nuts in the butter until they start to brown. Add the garlic and seasoning, stir well and set aside until the beans are ready. Drain the beans, mix with the butter, nuts and garlic, and serve immediately.

Variation: You can use split almonds instead of pine nuts.

Greens with Bacon and Onion.
Serves 4

This is a good way to spruce up any green vegetable.

ABOUT 450G/1LB OF GREEN VEG
1 MEDIUM ONION
3 RASHERS OF STREAKY BACON
50G/2OZ BUTTER

Wash the vegetables and if using cabbage or another leafy vegetable, shred the leaves. Break cauliflower or broccoli into florets.

Chop the onion finely and snip the bacon into strips with kitchen scissors. Melt the butter in a large saucepan and fry the onion and bacon until they begin to colour. Add the greens, turn them in the butter, then put the lid on and cook over a gentle heat for from 5 to 10 minutes, shaking the pan to stop the contents sticking.

Cauliflower Cheese.
Serves 2 as a main dish

This trusty old friend is best made with strongly flavoured cheese: mature Cheddar, Lancashire, Parmesan or a combination of any two of these.

ONE MEDIUM-SIZED CAULIFLOWER
50G / 1¾ OZ BUTTER
2 TABLESPOONS FLOUR
200ML / ½ PINT MILK
100G / 3½ OZ GRATED CHEESE
½ TEASPOON MUSTARD
A PINCH OF NUTMEG

Set the oven at 220°C. Grease an ovenproof dish.

Cut the cauliflower into florets, and slice any remaining stalk. Steam for 5 minutes until barely tender. Meanwhile, melt the butter in a saucepan, add the flour and cook, stirring constantly for 1 or 2 minutes. Add the milk gradually, stirring until thickened and smooth. Add the grated cheese, mustard and nutmeg, and stir until the cheese has melted.

Put the cauliflower into the dish, pour the sauce over and bake in the oven until the top is brown and bubbly.

Creamed Spinach.

Serves 2

I loathed spinach as a child, perhaps because we were given plain boiled whole leaves with tough stalks and traces of gritty soil lurking in them. This is a much more child-friendly method.

500G/1LB 2OZ SPINACH LEAVES, THE YOUNGER THE BETTER
1 SMALL ONION, GRATED
½ CARROT, GRATED
1 BAY LEAF
FRESHLY GROUND BLACK PEPPER
A PINCH OF NUTMEG
250ML/9 FL OZ WHOLE MILK
50G/1¾ OZ BUTTER
25G/1OZ/1 HEAPED TABLESPOON FLOUR

Wash the spinach in lots of water and if there are coarse stalks, strip the leaves off and discard the stalks. Lightly steam or blanch the leaves, squeeze out excess liquid and chop them roughly. Add the onion, carrot, bay leaf, a twist of black pepper and pinch of nutmeg to the milk, bring to the boil and leave to infuse for 10 minutes, then strain the milk. Melt the butter, stir in the flour and cook for 2 minutes. Add the milk a little at a time, stirring until thick and smooth. You may not need to use all the milk; the sauce should be thick. Simmer it for 1 minute, mix in the spinach, adjust seasoning and serve.

Carrots Vichy.

Serves 2

The large, dirty carrots delivered in winter organic veg boxes are a lot better than they look, and are usually sweeter and fuller flavoured than the clean young supermarket kind.

500G/1LB 2OZ CARROTS
TEASPOON CASTER SUGAR
25G/1OZ BUTTER
400ML/14 FL OZ WATER
CHOPPED PARSLEY OR TARRAGON

Slice the carrots into rounds about the thickness of a £1 coin. Put them into a saucepan with the sugar, butter and water, bring to the boil and simmer until the water has evaporated and the carrots are tender. Add a little more butter and serve with the parsley or tarragon sprinkled over.

Courgette Frittatas.

Serves 2 as main course, 4 as a side dish

This recipe is adapted from one contributed to the *Daily Telegraph* by a reader. It makes a delicious summer lunch dish, or starter.

350G/12OZ COURGETTES, COARSELY GRATED
1 MEDIUM ONION, GRATED
2 GARLIC CLOVES, CRUSHED
50G/2OZ SELF-RAISING FLOUR
75G/3OZ GRATED CHEDDAR CHEESE
2 EGGS, BEATEN
A LITTLE MILK
SALT AND PEPPER
OIL FOR FRYING

Place all the ingredients except the oil in a bowl and mix well, adding enough milk to bring the mixture to a dropping consistency. Heat a little oil in a large frying pan. Put heaped tablespoons of the mixture into the pan and cook for 5 minutes, turning once, until brown. Serve at once, with tomato sauce (see page 93) or tomato salad on the side.

Creamed Sprouts with Chestnuts and Bacon.

Supper for 2, or as a side dish

I used to think the one thing that spoils Christmas dinner is the tradition that you must have Brussels sprouts with the turkey, but this recipe, adapted from *The River Cottage Year*, has completely converted me.

250G/9OZ CHESTNUTS
500G/1LB 2OZ BRUSSELS SPROUTS
25G/1OZ BUTTER
2 TABLESPOONS DOUBLE CREAM
SALT AND PEPPER
6 RASHERS OF STREAKY BACON

Roast the chestnuts in a dry, heavy frying pan, turning frequently, until they are cooked through. It doesn't matter if the skins turn black. When they are cool enough to handle, peel them, removing the inner skin as well as the outer shell. Or use tinned or vacuum packed cooked chestnuts.

Remove any tired outer leaves from the sprouts. There is no need to cut a cross on the base. Put them into boiling, salted water and simmer till just tender, 8-10 minutes. Drain them and whiz in a food processor with the butter and cream. Season to taste, remembering the bacon will add salt. Roughly crumble the chestnuts into the sprout puree, and turn on to warm plates.

Cut the bacon into strips and fry until crisp. Scatter the bacon over the purée.

Gardener's Pie.

6 generous helpings

This all-vegetable version of shepherd's or cottage pie is an improved version of an austere war-time dish, named "Woolton Pie" after the Minister for Food from 1940 to 1943. Lord Woolton's Pie attracted much mockery, but Alice Thomas Ellis's recipe, described in her book *Fish, Flesh and Good Red Herring* (Virago Press), is, in spite of its humble ingredients, not at all austere and makes a delicious lunch or supper dish, or an accompaniment to roast lamb.

For the base:

1 KG/2.2LB OF MIXED WINTER VEGETABLES, WHATEVER IS AVAILABLE,
FOR EXAMPLE AN ONION, A CELERY STICK, A LARGE CARROT, 2 JERUSALEM
ARTICHOKES, ½ A CAULIFLOWER, SOME SWEDE
2 TABLESPOONS OLIVE OIL
STOCK OR WATER
SALT AND PEPPER

For the topping:

900G/2LB FLOURY POTATOES, PEELED
50G/2OZ BUTTER
ABOUT 400ML/14 FL OZ MILK
115G/4OZ GRATED CHEDDAR CHEESE

Set the oven at 220°C.

Chop the onion and dice all the other vegetables into equal-sized pieces. Heat the olive oil in a wide, shallow saucepan and add the vegetables. Over the heat, turn them in the oil until they start to colour. Add enough stock or water to stop them sticking to the pan, and stir occasionally, until the liquid has evaporated. At this stage the vegetables should still be crunchy. Season them to taste and put them in a pie dish. Don't worry if the mixture seems rather dry; the vegetables will release their juices during cooking.

Meanwhile, boil the potatoes and mash them with the butter, milk, cheese and plenty of freshly ground black pepper. Cover the pie with the mash and cook in the oven until the top is brown.

Cheesy Baked Aubergines.

Serves 4-6

The addition of plenty of cheese makes this another substantial veg dish to lunch or sup off.

4 LARGE AUBERGINES, SLICED LONGWAYS
OLIVE OIL
350G/12OZ TOMATO SAUCE (SEE PAGE 93)
350G/12OZ FRESH MOZZARELLA CHEESE, SLICED
5 TABLESPOONS OF FRESHLY GRATED PARMESAN

Set the oven at 200ºC. Grease a large, shallow, ovenproof dish. Lay baking parchment on two baking trays.

Brush the aubergine slices lightly on both sides with olive oil, put them on the baking trays and bake in the oven until just cooked. Don't worry if they seem dry; the tomato sauce and cheese will all melt together to make a lovely moist mixture.

Prepare the tomato sauce and spread a thin layer of sauce over the bottom of the dish. Cover it with the aubergine slices, overlapping. Lay the mozzarella slices over the aubergines. Pour the rest of the tomato sauce over and sprinkle the Parmesan on the surface. Bake for 20 minutes and eat warm, but not hot, with good bread and green salad.

Jerusalem Artichoke Soufflé.

Serves 2 for supper or lunch, 3-4 as a starter

This unusual and delicious soufflé, from *Steam Cuisine* by Tessa Hayward, is light and subtly flavoured. It can be steamed but I usually cook it in the oven. If you have never attempted a soufflé before, don't be daunted. Success comes more often than failure, and even if your soufflé fails to rise, it will still taste good.

700G/1½ LB JERUSALEM ARTICHOKES
50G/2OZ BUTTER PLUS EXTRA FOR GREASING THE DISH
40G/1½OZ FLOUR
200ML/⅓ PINT MILK
4 EGGS, SEPARATED
SALT AND PEPPER

Set the oven at 200°C. Grease a 1.5 litre/2¾ pint soufflé dish.

Peel the artichokes. They are so knobbly and misshapen that, after peeling, this quantity will yield the required 350g/12oz. Steam or boil them for 15-20 minutes until they are tender. Purée them in a food processor or blender.

In a saucepan, melt the butter, stir in the flour and cook for a minute or two. Add the milk slowly, stirring constantly until the sauce is thick and smooth. Off the heat, stir in the artichoke purée, then the egg yolks. Season with salt and pepper. Whisk the egg whites until stiff and fold them into the mixture. Pour into the soufflé dish and bake in the oven for about 30 minutes or until it has risen and the top is lightly browned. A sharp knife inserted should come out clean.

Variation: For courgette soufflé, make a purée of 450g/1lb of cooked courgettes instead of artichokes, and add 5 tablespoons of grated Gruyère cheese.

Parsnip Fritters.

Serves 4

We loved it when my mother cooked fritters, whether sweet or savoury, and regarded them as a special treat.

200G/7OZ PLAIN FLOUR
SALT AND PEPPER
2 TABLESPOONS OLIVE OR SUNFLOWER OIL
250ML/9 FL OZ BEER PLUS 2 TABLESPOONS
2 EGG WHITES
3 OR 4 LARGE PARSNIPS, DEPENDING ON SIZE
OIL FOR FRYING

First make the batter. Whiz the flour, seasoning, oil and beer in the blender till smooth. Put the batter in a bowl, cover and leave it to rest for 15 minutes. Stir in 2 more tablespoons of beer then beat the 2 egg whites and fold them in. Set the batter on one side for half an hour.

While the batter is resting, cut the parsnips into slices or wedges of fairly uniform size, and boil until barely tender. Let them cool.

Put the parsnip pieces in the batter and stir gently till they are thoroughly coated. Heat the oil in a thick frying pan. When it is smoking hot, using tongs, fish out the parsnip pieces from the batter and fry a few at a time on both sides, draining each batch on kitchen paper.

Serve them on a bed of spinach, and/or with tomato sauce.

Variations: Make fritters with courgettes sliced longways, celeriac cut into discs, large carrots sliced longways, aubergines, sliced into discs. Mix them up for a veggie *fritto misto*.

Pea and Lettuce Risotto.

Serves 4

If you grow lettuces, sooner or later there'll be a glut; your family will rebel at green salad twice a day, and you'll have bolting lettuces on your hands. This pretty, summery risotto will save at least one from relegation to the compost heap.

600ML/1 PINT LIGHT CHICKEN STOCK
2 TABLESPOONS OLIVE OIL
1 ONION, CHOPPED
2 GARLIC CLOVES, FINELY CHOPPED
1 CELERY STICK, CHOPPED
400G/15oz ARBORIO RICE
½ GLASS OF WHITE WINE
350G/1 oz FROZEN PEAS, DEFROSTED
1 LETTUCE, WASHED, DRIED AND SHREDDED INTO NARROW RIBBONS
CHOPPED HAM (OPTIONAL)
SALT AND PEPPER
50G/2oz FRESHLY GRATED PARMESAN CHEESE
2 TABLESPOONS CHOPPED CHIVES

Heat the stock in a saucepan. In another large, heavy saucepan, cook the onion, garlic and celery gently in the olive oil, until the onion is translucent. Add the rice and stir until it has absorbed the oil. Add the wine and let it bubble for a minute or two. Add enough hot stock to cover the rice and stir well. When the stock has been absorbed, add more, stirring from time to time to stop the rice sticking to the pan. You may not need all the stock. When the rice is nearly cooked, stir in the peas, lettuce, ham and Parmesan, and season.

Sprinkle the chives over the top and serve it immediately. Put more Parmesan on the table with a grater, for people to help themselves.

Pease Pudding.

Serves 4

This split pea and peppercorn purée comes from Ruth Watson via River Cottage, and is a delicious take on old-fashioned pease pudding, or the cold pease porridge the man-in-the-moon burnt his mouth on. It is excellent with ham, gammon, bacon or roast game.

250G/9OZ SPLIT PEAS
1 SMALL ONION, PEELED AND HALVED
1 LARGE CARROT CUT INTO CHUNKS
1 CELERY STICK, ROUGHLY CHOPPED
1 BAY LEAF
25G/1OZ BUTTER
SALT AND A PINCH OF SUGAR
1 TABLESPOON GREEN OR PINK PEPPERCORNS PICKLED IN BRINE

Put the peas, vegetables and bay leaf in a saucepan and add enough water to cover them by 1cm/½ in. Bring to the boil and cook until the peas are soft. Remove the vegetables and bay leaf and mash or process the peas to a rough purée. Add the butter and season with salt and a pinch of sugar. Mix in the peppercorns and reheat, thinning with a little hot water or stock if necessary. Eat hot.

Stuffed Peppers.

Serves 4

In the last 50 years, peppers have graduated from exotic to everyday ingredients. Being already completely hollow, they just cry out to be stuffed. You can use green, yellow or red peppers, or combine all the colours, but the red ones are the sweetest. This dish can be made in advance and reheated.

5 LARGE RED PEPPERS, HALVED LENGTHWISE AND DESEEDED
150G/5½ OZ FRESH WHITE BREADCRUMBS
12 ANCHOVY FILLETS
12 BLACK OLIVES, STONED
3 GARLIC CLOVES
2 TABLESPOONS CHOPPED PARSLEY
1 TABLESPOON CAPERS
2 TEASPOONS CHOPPED MARJORAM
FRESHLY GROUND BLACK PEPPER
3 TABLESPOONS OLIVE OIL

Set the oven at 160°C. Grease a shallow ovenproof dish.

Put four of the peppers aside and chop the remaining one with all the other ingredients except the olive oil. Or put the pepper, roughly chopped, in a food processor, add the other ingredients except the breadcrumbs, and pulse until everything is chopped and mixed, but not mushy. Add the crumbs.

Fill the 8 half peppers with this mixture and put them in the dish. Dribble the olive oil over them, cover loosely with foil and bake for 40-45 minutes or until the peppers are soft. Cook uncovered for a further 10 minutes to brown the tops, or flash under the grill.

Three Root Mash.

Easily the nastiest thing about school dinners was mashed swede, lumpy and watery. My research tells me I am not alone in remembering how hard it was to swallow. And yet, swedes don't have to be unpalatable. They simply need to be cooked with care and well seasoned. Anyone who doubts they'll ever be converted should try this root vegetable mélange.

450G/1LB FLOURY POTATOES, PEELED AND CUT UP
280G/10OZ SWEDES
280G/10OZ CARROTS
280G/10OZ PARSNIPS
70G/2½ OZ BUTTER
ABOUT 150ML/¼ PINT MILK
SALT AND PEPPER

Boil the potatoes in a saucepan. Clean and peel the root vegetables, and cut them into fairly uniform pieces. Boil them in another saucepan, until tender. When all are cooked, mash the potatoes with the butter and as much milk as is needed. Purée the roots in a food processor or mash them by hand and mix them with the mashed potatoes. Season with salt and lots of freshly ground black pepper. Eat the mash with roast meat, or with a few rashers of bacon for supper.

Tip: Potatoes will turn to rubber if processed by machine; it is always better to mash them by hand.

Upside-Down Shallot Tart.

Serves 4

This recipe comes from *It's Raining Plums*, a collection of *Daily Telegraph* readers' recipes edited by Xanthe Clay, who described it as "supremely good, dark and savoury as roast meat."

900G/2LB SHALLOTS
50G/1¾ OZ BUTTER
3 TABLESPOONS DARK BROWN SUGAR
2 TABLESPOONS BALSAMIC VINEGAR
1 TABLESPOON WORCESTERSHIRE SAUCE
4 TABLESPOONS WATER
1 TABLESPOON FRESH SAGE, CHOPPED
340G/12OZ SHORTCRUST PASTRY (SEE PAGE 80)

Peel enough shallots to cover the base of a 20-25cm/8-9in ovenproof frying pan. Cook them in boiling water for 5 minutes. Drain them well. Heat the butter in the pan and fry the shallots until golden. When the shallots are coloured all over, add the rest of the ingredients, except the pastry, and simmer until the shallots are bathed in dark syrup. (You can make the tart in advance up to this point.)

Roll out the pastry into a circle a little larger than the pan and lay it over the shallots. Tuck in the edges. Bake at 200°C for 20-25 minutes until the pastry is golden and cooked all through. Invert on to a plate so that the shallots are on top. Eat warm.

Salads.

A generation ago salad was predictable and depressing: a few limp lettuce leaves, with or without a young slug or caterpillar; a hard, watery tomato, sliced or quartered; some cucumber slices; spring onions; a slice or two of hard-boiled egg; and perhaps a few radishes. (Fresh radishes from the garden are wasted in mixed salads. Far better to pull them, give them a quick wash and serve them in a separate little bowl to eat with butter.)

Salads were seldom dressed, olive oil being available only from the chemist in a small square bottle, for treating earache. Instead, a bottle of gloopy, vinegary salad cream would be passed around.

Tomato Salad.

Peeling a few tomatoes takes no time at all, and it makes all the difference.

2 RIPE MEDIUM SIZED TOMATOES PER PERSON

OLIVE OIL

SALT AND PEPPER

1 SWEET ONION, FINELY CHOPPED

FRESH BASIL

Put the tomatoes in a bowl and pour boiling water over them. After 30 seconds, take them out and put them in cold water. The skins should then slip off easily.

Slice the tomatoes and put them in a glass or earthenware dish. Trickle olive oil over them, season with salt and pepper and scatter the chopped onion and some torn basil leaves over.

Variations: Various ingredients can be added, such as black olives or feta cheese, but the general rule is to keep it simple, and only use one or two ingredients at a time.

Barley Salad.

Lyla Harling
Serves 4 as a main dish, 6 as a side dish

This is a welcome new take on a traditional ingredient, pearl barley, once a familiar component of Scotch broth and homely stews. With a leafy salad it makes a good lunch.

225G/8OZ PEARL BARLEY
470M/17 FL OZ CHICKEN STOCK OR WATER
1 BUNCH SPRING ONIONS, SLICED
1 BUNCH RADISHES, SLICED
1 CUCUMBER, PEELED, DESEEDED AND DICED
1 RED PEPPER, DESEEDED AND DICED
3 TABLESPOONS CHOPPED PARSLEY
1 TABLESPOON CHOPPED LEMON THYME
2 TABLESPOONS SNIPPED CHIVE
4 OR 5 CORNICHONS, CHOPPED
1 TABLESPOON CAPERS, CHOPPED

Dressing:
3 TABLESPOONS OLIVE OIL
2 TABLESPOONS LEMON JUICE
3 GARLIC CLOVES, CRUSHED
SALT AND FRESHLY GROUND BLACK PEPPER

Put the barley and stock or water and a pinch of salt in a saucepan, bring to the boil and simmer until the barley is tender, 30-40 minutes. Drain and allow the moisture to steam off. Mix all the dressing ingredients together and pour the dressing over the barley. Stir, then spread the barley in a shallow dish to cool. Stir in all the chopped vegetables and herbs.

Variation: The ingredients can be varied according to what is available. A rice or bean salad can be made in the same way.

Salade Nicoise.

Serves 4

This standby for summer lunches went out of favour in our household for a while, but has made a comeback, specially when climbing French beans are glutting in the garden, and tiny toms (favourite variety: Sungold) in the greenhouse. The composition of a salade Nicoise varies according to what ingredients are available, but, as Elizabeth David wrote, it "should be a country salad, rather than a fussy chef's concoction." It was originally conceived as an hors d'oeuvre, but can be robust enough to make a complete meal, eaten with warm, crusty bread. Making this salad look appealing is part of the fun.

2 HEARTY LETTUCES
4 HARD-BOILED EGGS, SHELLED AND CUT IN HALF
8 ANCHOVY FILLETS
1 TIN OF TUNA
ABOUT A DOZEN LITTLE TOMATOES
ABOUT 225G/8OZ COOKED FRENCH BEANS
ABOUT 12 BLACK OLIVES
A TABLESPOON OF CAPERS, RINSED AND DRIED

Dressing:
6 TABLESPOONS OF VERY GOOD OLIVE OIL
1 TABLESPOON TARRAGON VINEGAR
1 GARLIC CLOVE, CRUSHED
1 TEASPOON DIJON MUSTARD
SALT AND PEPPER

Shake the dressing ingredients together in a screw-top jar. Taste and adjust seasoning.

Arrange the salad components prettily in a shallow salad bowl. At the table, pour the dressing over, mix and eat.

Celeriac Remoulade with Walnuts.

Serves 4

Celeriac, with its refreshing crunch and slightly aniseed flavour makes a great winter salad, and the addition of walnuts works a treat.

JUICE OF $\frac{1}{2}$ LEMON
1 MEDIUM CELERIAC ROOT
4 TABLESPOONS MAYONNAISE, PREFERABLY HOME-MADE
1 TEASPOON DIJON MUSTARD
1 TABLESPOON SOUR CREAM
PEPPER
50G / 1¾ OZ WALNUTS, CHOPPED

Squeeze the lemon juice into a bowl of cold water. Peel the celeriac and coarsely grate it by hand or in a food processor, putting it into the lemony water as you go, to stop it turning brown. Mix the mayonnaise, mustard, and sour cream and season with freshly ground black pepper. The mayo is probably salty enough. In a saucepan, blanch the celeriac for 1 minute. Drain it and pat it dry on kitchen paper. Mix the celeriac with the mayo. In a dry frying pan, lightly toast the walnuts. When cool, sprinkle them over the celeriac.

Chicory and Orange Salad.
Serves 4

My mother used to make this salad to eat with roast wild duck. The orange and ginger combination makes the dressing special (it is delicious with any leafy salad).

4 CHICORY HEADS
2 ORANGES
A BUNCH OF WATERCRESS

Dressing:
1 GARLIC CLOVE, CRUSHED
1 TEASPOON GRATED ROOT GINGER
1 TEASPOON FRENCH MUSTARD
1 TEASPOON CASTER SUGAR
100ML/3½ FL OZ SUNFLOWER OIL
1 TABLESPOON WHITE WINE VINEGAR
SALT AND PEPPER

Put into a screw-top jar the grated zest and juice of half an orange. Add the rest of the dressing ingredients except the vinegar and salt and shake the jar thoroughly. Add the vinegar a little at a time, tasting until it is right. Adjust the seasoning.

Using a sharp, serrated knife, peel the remaining 1½ oranges, removing all the white pith. Cut out the segments, leaving the membranes behind. Slice the chicory heads across and divide them, the orange segments and watercress between 4 plates. Give the dressing a final shake and pour some over each salad.

Rob's Lunchtime Salad.

The ingredients depend on what happens to be in the garden: two or more kinds of lettuce, rocket and chives usually feature; much the same leaves and herbs that are found in a supermarket bag of mixed green salad, but with more flavour because they are freshly picked. The dressing is an on-going combination of oil and vinegar, seasoned and shaken vigorously in a screw-top jar, and topped up from time to time. If the oil and vinegar are of the best quality, nothing more elaborate is needed.

3 OR 4 RASHERS OF STREAKY BACON
2 SLICES OF BREAD, CRUSTS REMOVED, CUT INTO CUBES
SUNFLOWER OIL FOR FRYING
SALAD LEAVES

Dressing:
GREEK VIRGIN OLIVE OIL
BALSAMIC VINEGAR
SALT AND FRESHLY GROUND PEPPER

Fry the bacon rashers until crisp; fry the bread croutons in the bacon fat until golden brown, adding oil if needed. Snip or crumble the bacon.

Wash and dry the leaves and put them in a salad bowl. Pour the dressing over and add the bacon and croutons. Toss everything together.

Potatoes.

I's not surprising that potatoes play an important part in people's food memories when they have always been such an important part of our diet. It seems miraculous that a food with such nourishing qualities should be easy to grow, available at all seasons, and cheap. So it's not surprising that culinary creativity has come up with so many ways of making spuds delicious.

Some people remember "Grandma's mash," or "Gran's potato cakes," while others remember potatoes as part of an ensemble: "stewed chops with mash to soak up all that lovely gravy;" and "mince and tatties with greens, served in Nan's deep blue and white bowls."

Best Ever Roast Potatoes.

I remember a postwar pantomime song which started, "I do want my Sunday potato, with whale-meat tomatoes won't go." Rationing meant that, for some families, whale was the only meat available for the Sunday roast.

At least the Sunday roast potato was not rationed. Brown and crunchy on the outside, soft and fluffy inside, is how we liked them, and still do. To achieve it, you need the right kind of potato to start with, like Maris Piper or King Edward: floury, not waxy. Peel the potatoes and cut them into fairly uniform sizes, then boil them in salted water for 7 or 8 minutes, no less, or the outsides will not be fluffy enough to crisp up. Drain them in a colander and leave for a few minutes so that the moisture steams off them. Then swirl them around in the colander to rough up the surface of each potato. Sprinkle them lightly with salt.

Make sure the fat (goose fat for the best results, lard for next best) is hot and at least 5mm/¼ in deep when you put them in, around the Sunday joint if there is room, otherwise in a separate roasting tin, on a shelf above the joint. Spoon fat over them before putting them in the oven, and roast them for 45 minutes, turning them over once or twice to brown evenly. Season with salt and pepper before serving.

Best Ever Mash.

There was a world of difference between school mash which was lumpy and home mash which was somewhere between fluffy and creamy. I'm ashamed to admit that, later, I fell for the best ever TV advertising campaign and bought Smash (deconstructed mashed potato, you just added water) to make the topping for my shepherd's pie, but I knew in my heart of hearts that the best mash is always home-made.

As with roast potatoes, you can only get good results if you use a floury variety of potato. Some experts cook potatoes in their skins, then peel them before mashing; others put the cooked potatoes through a sieve or a ricer to make sure they are free of lumps. Neither method is particularly practical in the average domestic kitchen, but, by observing four rules, you can get really good results.

1. Make sure the potatoes are thoroughly cooked so they are soft all through.

2. When you drain the potatoes after boiling them, leave time for steam to escape: the drier they get, the better the mash will be.

3. Heat the milk and butter together until they are almost at boiling point and put the potatoes into the milk and butter, not vice versa.

4. When the potatoes are thoroughly mashed and smooth, beat the mash with a wooden spoon. The more air you can get into them, the better they will taste. And season them well with salt and freshly ground pepper.

There are almost limitless variations on the mash theme: as well as other root vegetables (see page 146) mash can be flavoured with horseradish, curry powder, nutmeg, chopped herbs, onions, chutney or grated cheese.

It would be easy to fill a book with potato recipes, and it is difficult to reduce the choice to just a few, but those offered here are held in great affection.

Potato Salad.

Whenever you make mayonnaise, increase the quantity and put some aside for a potato salad next day. A really good potato salad doesn't always have to be made with so-called salad potatoes. Indeed, in my experience, La Ratte, Pink Fir Apple and the more widely available Charlotte taste better hot than cold, while Arran Pilot is excellent for potato salads. If you have a garden, these varieties are worth growing. The shortest time between plot and pot ensures that satisfying but fleeting earthy taste.

When you are in a hurry, make potato salad the quick way: mix a few tablespoons of Hellmann's with a teaspoon of mustard, a squeeze of lemon juice and lots of freshly ground black pepper.

Stir in the potatoes, sliced or cubed and snip chives or dill over.

For a change, a specially good potato salad can be made with small, whole new potatoes served warm with a vinaigrette dressing (see page 207). Cook them until they are just tender, drain them and while still warm, stir them into the dressing with some chopped spring onions and mint.

Milly-Molly-Mandy Potatoes.
Ruth Biddiss

This potato dish was described in one of Joyce Lankester Brisley's *Milly-Molly-Mandy* books (girls of my generation will remember M-M-M and Little Friend Susan).

1 BAKED POTATO PER PERSON
BUTTER
SALT AND FRESHLY GROUND BLACK PEPPER
GRATED CHEESE (OPTIONAL)

Take the tops off the baked potatoes, as if they were boiled eggs. Scoop out the middle, mash it with lots of butter, salt and pepper, and cheese if you like. Put the cap back on and return the potato to the oven to crisp up.

Potato Gratins.

With the aid of the slicing gadget on a food processor, gratins are a joy to make. A shallow dish of sliced potatoes with milk, cream or stock, and sometimes with onions, garlic and/or cheese added, is baked in the oven until the potatoes are soft underneath and browned and crisp on top. The gratin dish should be buttered or oiled, which makes it easier to wash up later, and the potatoes well mixed with the cream or other wet ingredient before they are put in the dish.

The richest version is gratin dauphinois, made with half a pint of cream to 1 lb potatoes. Addressing my mother's generation, Elizabeth David wrote, "If it seems to the thrifty-minded outrageously extravagant…, I can only say that to me it seems a more satisfactory way of enjoying cream than pouring it over tinned peaches or chocolate mousse."

In a gratin savoyard, the sliced potatoes are cooked in meat stock and topped with grated Gruyère. Ruth Biddiss remembers a gratin from her childhood: "Peel potatoes, cut into matchsticks, put in a dish with lots of butter and some milk, garlic and ground pepper, parsley. Lots of blobs of butter on top. Put in the oven to cook slowly."

Pan Haggerty.
Serves 4-6

This robust, comforting supper dish from the North Country is traditionally cooked on top of the stove and served straight from the frying pan, but it can also be cooked in the oven in a gratin dish if that is more convenient.

900G/2LBS POTATOES
4 MEDIUM ONIONS
50G /2OZ BUTTER
2 TABLESPOONS SUNFLOWER OIL
225G/8OZ LANCASHIRE OR STRONG CHEDDAR CHEESE, GRATED
SALT AND PEPPER

Finely slice the potatoes and onions (easily done in a food processor). Heat the butter and oil in a large, fairly deep frying pan; remove from the heat and put in the potatoes, onions and cheese in layers, adding salt and pepper to each layer and ending with a layer of cheese. Cover and cook slowly for about 30 minutes, until the potatoes and onions are soft. Remove the lid and brown under the grill for a few minutes.

Mustard Potatoes.

Shona Anderson
Serves 6-8

A good and unusual variation on the potato gratin theme.

6 LARGE FLOURY POTATOES SUCH AS MARIS PIPER
284ML / ½ PINT DOUBLE CREAM OR CRÈME FRAICHE
200ML / ⅓ PINT MILK
2 GARLIC CLOVES, CRUSHED
5 GENEROUS TABLESPOONS WHOLEGRAIN MUSTARD
SALT AND FRESHLY GROUND BLACK PEPPER
60G / 2¼ OZ BUTTER

Set the oven at 190°C. Grease an ovenproof dish with a little of the butter.

Peel the potatoes and slice them finely. Put them in a bowl of cold water to soak out the starch. Put the cream or crème fraiche, milk, garlic and mustard into a saucepan and bring to the boil. Season.

Drain the potatoes and layer them in the dish, seasoning each layer. Pour the mustard mixture over and dot with butter. Cover the dish with foil and bake for 1 hour or until the potatoes are soft. Remove the foil and cook for a further 10 to 15 minutes until brown and bubbling.

Champz.

Serves 6

Good on its own or to accompany cold meat. So simple, so soothing, so wicked.
LYLA HARLING

In Ireland, at Halloween, they leave a bowl of champ under a hawthorn bush for the fairies.

900G/2LB FLOURY POTATOES
300ML/½ PINT MILK
4 TABLESPOONS CREAM
1 BUNCH OF SPRING ONIONS, FINELY CHOPPED
SALT AND PEPPER
85G/3OZ BUTTER

Boil the potatoes till they are soft and mash them with the milk and cream. Season with salt and lots of freshly ground pepper. Stir in the chopped spring onions. Serve very hot with a big lump of butter melting in the middle of each helping.

Chapter 8.

Teatime.

21 Recipes

*There are few hours in life more agreeable than the hour dedicated to the
ceremony known as afternoon tea.*
THE PORTRAIT OF A LADY BY HENRY JAMES

*Sail me on a silver sun
Where I know that I'm free,
Show me that I'm everywhere
And get me home for tea.*
ALL TOO MUCH BY THE BEATLES

The institution of afternoon tea has acquired mythical status. Once upon a time
there was a tea shop in every high street, serving crumpets, cucumber and
fish paste sandwiches, scones with jam and cream, and "fancies". The latter
were a selection of small cakes and pastries: lemon curd tarts, custard tarts, cup
cakes with pastel icing and crystallized violets, fairy cakes, cream slices,
meringues, arranged on tiered plates. As well as ye olde village tea shoppe
there were tea rooms in hotels and department stores, safe places for women
to meet in the days when they wouldn't have dared enter a pub without a man
to escort them, places where they could indulge in a good gossip and treat
themselves to something naughty but nice.

When we were children the ultimate food treat was tea at Gunter's in
Mayfair in London, where you could have iced coffee instead of tea to drink,
and where the sandwiches were tinier and the cakes more delicious than any-
where else. We were taken there for birthday treats, or as a reward for undergoing the ordeal of buying school uniform at Daniel Neal's. Almost as good
was Fuller's, with a tea room above and a cake shop downstairs where you
could buy a famous Fuller's walnut cake to take home. Both were eventually

eclipsed by the 1950s and 60s craze for coffee bars. But now tea is in fashion again, and if you want to have tea with all the trimmings at the Ritz or Claridges, you have to book a table months in advance.

Teatime meant different things to different families, but in most households it induced a calm, leisurely atmosphere. At my country grandparents' house we had tea at a small round table in the library, spread with an embroidered white cloth. The pretty cups and plates had an elaborate cream and gilt pattern, and the paraphernalia of teapot, hot water jug, strainer, slop basin and sugar tongs were set out on a large black papier maché tray decorated with painted flowers. The butter came in little balls with a criss-cross pattern on their surface, and the jam was decanted into a cut-glass jar. There was always a plate of sandwiches and one of bread and butter – my grandfather was fond of saying, "When I was your age we had butter or jam on our bread, never both." My grandmother would give him a look, and pile a spoonful of strawberry jam on to my bread and butter. However, the rule of bread and butter before cake was always strictly applied.

When I asked friends what they remembered about teatime it unleashed a wave of nostalgia for sandwiches. They were very different from the robust triangles in rigid wrappers on offer at lunchtime in supermarkets and cafés. One friend remembered her grandmother's maid, Kate, making "the best cucumber and tomato sandwiches I have ever had, slightly soggy. The tomatoes must be skinned and very finely sliced. The cucumbers sliced and drained with salt. Crusts cut off the bread, white pepper." Others spoke of egg and cress sandwiches, the cress grown on a flannel on the bathroom windowsill; of Shipham's meat paste or salmon paste in little glass jars; of Marmite and lettuce, and sandwich spread out of a Heinz bottle. The bread was always white, always wafer thin, and the crusts had always been removed.

Tea at London Granny's was always the same. Hot buttered toast, sandwiches filled with an anchovy paste of her own concoction, known as "Silver Wedding", and a yellow sponge cake with a crusty top, for which I give the recipe below.

At home, it is the winter weekend teas eaten in front of the fire that I remember: crumpets soaking up melting butter like sponges, or hot toast spread with dripping, and, if you were lucky, some of the meaty jelly at the bottom of the dripping bowl. One friend recalls a pregnancy craving for toast and dripping.

These teatime reminiscences pre-date electric toasters. Crumpets and bread were toasted either under the grill of an electric or gas cooker, or at an open fire, speared on a three-pronged toasting fork. One of my correspondents remembers making toast on an upturned electric fire; it is something of a miracle that she survived to tell the tale.

Other teatime treats remembered include brown bread and butter spread with banana or treacle or chocolate spread and, at school, peanut butter scooped out of the pot with a pencil. Someone else remembers staying at her granny's house and going for a Sunday afternoon walk, to find, on their return, little mountains of mashed potato which had been baking slowly in the oven, deliciously crunchy outside and potato-ey inside.

Only one thing spoilt our childhood teatimes: milk to drink was compulsory. It usually appeared in a silver christening mug, making it somehow taste of silver, and it was never really cold. As far as unwelcome phrases go, "Drink up your milk" was the next most dreaded phrase after "eat up your greens". School offered no escape; at break tepid milk was handed out in glass bottles with a straw stuck through the silver foil top.

There are some people for whom the whole point of teatime is not the crumpets, the sandwiches, the cake or the biscuits, but the cuppa. Brewing a perfect cup of tea is not difficult, but you have to take some trouble. For a start, you must brew a pot of tea, not just a mugful. Fill the kettle with cold water straight from the tap, to oxygenate the tea. Then warm the teapot by swilling it out with hot water. Put the tea in the warm pot. Then observe the rule, "always take the pot to the kettle, not the kettle to the pot." This is because the water must be boiling when poured on to the tea.

The argument about whether you should put the milk in first or last can get quite heated. I prefer last, so that you can see, by the colour, how much you are putting in. I also think that, if the milk goes in first, the hot tea cooks it a little, and I don't like the taste of cooked milk. The only reason milk used to be put in first was as a precaution to protect fragile china cups from cracking.

This seems a good place to mention elevenses which don't quite merit a chapter on their own, but were at one time an important element in our eating pattern. In our house everyone stopped what they were doing sharpish at 11 and sat round the kitchen table. We drank tea, always from a cup, or cocoa or Ovaltine from a mug. Instant coffee had not been invented, except Camp coffee essence in a bottle with a picture on the label of a man wearing a turban. The cake tin with the remains of a weekend cake or gingerbread would be brought out, or a biscuit tin of chocolate digestives, bourbons and custard creams all jumbled up together.

It was at elevenses rather than at teatime that we went through the ritual of fortune-telling in the tea-leaves. To indulge in this, when you have drunk the tea in your cup, you swirl the dregs around and tip them out, leaving the tea-leaves in the cup. If you look at the tea-leaves long enough, a picture will emerge, in the same way as, to an imaginative person, a cloud might look like a rabbit. We each hoped for a long piece of stalk among the tea-leaves, signi-fying a tall dark stranger.

Cakes, Large and Small.

I read somewhere that cake contained almost everything that was
required to sustain the human frame: eggs, flour, fat, sugar.
It was comforting to know, when the children would eat little else.
FRANCINE YORKE

Before the advent of modern kitchen gadgets, cake making was something of a labour of love, involving a lot of elbow grease. The words "beat the butter and sugar until white" caused the heart to sink. But now that most kitchens are equipped with an electric whisk and a food processor, cake making is a breeze.

Paradoxically, although it has become so easy to make cakes, they seldom make an appearance in most households. This is a shame; teatime may not be the ceremonial affair it used to be, but it is still a great pleasure to bring out the cake tin and cut a slice to eat with a mug of tea or coffee.

Angel Cake USA.
Ray Phillimore

Ray was my aunt and also my godmother. She was a wonderful cook in general, and a wonderful cake maker in particular. I used to go and stay with her often when I was a child, and we always made cakes together.

Ray's husband was in the Royal Navy and they were stationed for a time in Washington, DC. She brought back an American cookbook with mouth-watering colour photographs of cakes covered in thick, rich frosting, at a time when few English books of any kind had coloured illustrations. I used to drool over them. Angel cake and devil's food cake are the two I remember best, perhaps because of their names.

Angel cake is supposed to be made in a special tin with a fairly narrow hole in the middle, but if that is hard to come by, a ring mould can be used instead.

Give angel cake a try instead of making meringues when you have egg whites to use up. It is lovely with fresh summer fruits, stewed fruit or fruit ice cream or sorbet.

For the cake:
50G/1¾ OZ PLAIN FLOUR
10G/¼ OZ CORNFLOUR
140G/5OZ CASTER SUGAR
5 EGG WHITES
A PINCH OF SALT
½ TEASPOON CREAM OF TARTAR
1 TABLESPOON WATER
1 TEASPOON VANILLA ESSENCE

For the icing:
350G/12OZ ICING SUGAR
HOT WATER

Set the oven at 135°C.

Sift the flour with the cornflour and 1 tablespoon of the sugar on to a shallow dish to dry. In a large bowl, using a hand-held electric whisk, beat the egg whites with the salt, cream of tartar and cold water until they are stiff enough to stand in peaks, but not dry. Fold in the sugar a tablespoonful at a time, add the vanilla and fold in the flour, sifting it over the mixture, a tablespoon at a time. Lightness is what you are after.

Pour the mixture into an ungreased tin and bake in the oven for 35 minutes, then increase the temperature to 165°C for another 10 minutes. Allow to cool before turning out and covering with icing.

Make the icing: Sift the icing sugar into a bowl. Add some hot water a very little at a time, beating it smooth until it is the consistency of thick cream. Pour it over the cake and smooth with a palette knife dipped in hot water.

Chocolate Cake.

I was planning to follow angel cake with its antithesis, devil's food cake, a rich and sticky chocolate cake that I also used to make with my godmother Ray. They say the devil has all the best tunes, and I thought he had the best chocolate cake until I made it again the other day. It was overpoweringly sweet, and when I checked the recipe it did indeed include 350g/12oz sugar.

So I have gone back to a cake I know and love, based on an Elizabeth David recipe. It is equally chocolate-y, equally gooey, but with quarter the amount of sugar. As with devil's food cake, you may need a spoon to eat it.

175G/6OZ BITTER CHOCOLATE
1 TABLESPOON RUM
1 TABLESPOON STRONG BLACK COFFEE
85G/3OZ BUTTER
85G/3OZ CASTER SUGAR
85G/3OZ GROUND ALMONDS
3 EGGS, SEPARATED

Set the oven at 145°C. Butter a shallow 18-20cm/7-8in cake tin.

Break up the chocolate and put it in a bowl with the rum and coffee. Put the bowl over a pan of hot water to melt the chocolate. Put the butter, sugar and ground almonds in a saucepan. Stir the chocolate mixture well and add it to the saucepan. Stir everything over a low heat until it is well mixed. Remove it from the heat and stir in well-beaten egg yolks. Whisk the whites until stiff and fold them in. Turn the mixture into the tin and cook in the oven for about 45 minutes. Allow the cake to cool and turn it out of the tin carefully, as it is very fragile. Eat it as it is, or with slightly sweetened, lightly whipped cream.

Custard Tarts.

We sometimes used to buy custard tarts to eat on the way home from school. "No eating in the street" was a strict rule so it was a guilty pleasure. I use this orange-y pastry to make mince pies, but it is good for any sweet tart.

For the pastry:
225G/8OZ PLAIN FLOUR
55G/2OZ BUTTER
55G/2OZ LARD
A PINCH OF SALT
1 TABLESPOON ICING SUGAR
GRATED RIND AND JUICE OF 1 ORANGE

For the filling:
1 EGG AND 2 EXTRA YOLKS
25G/1OZ SUGAR
15G/½ OZ FLOUR
300ML/½ PINT SINGLE CREAM
15G/½OZ MELTED BUTTER
NUTMEG

Make the pastry: Put everything except the orange into a food processor. Whizz until the mixture looks like fine crumbs. Add the grated rind of the orange and whiz for 2 seconds. Add the juice of the orange a spoonful at a time until the dough forms a single lump.

Wrap in cling-film and refrigerate for one day or up to a week.

Set the oven at 200°C.

Roll out the pastry and use it to line some patty tins.

Make the filling: In a bowl, mix the egg, the yolks, the sugar and the flour together. Add the milk and butter and stir until well mixed.

Put a spoonful of the mixture in each of the patty tins. Sprinkle a little nutmeg on each tart. Bake for 15 to 20 minutes until the custard is just set. It will get firmer as it cools.

Chocolate Eclairs.

Makes about 12

When, as children, we were occasionally taken out to a tea shop, I always had my eye on the chocolate éclair on the plate of mixed small cakes, hoping nobody would get to it before me. Later I learned to make choux pastry at home, and cream-filled profiteroles coated in thick, dark chocolate sauce became one of my dinner party puddings.

For the choux pastry:
300ML/½ PINT WATER
115G/4OZ BUTTER
140G/5OZ FLOUR
4 EGGS, LIGHTLY BEATEN
300ML/½ PINT DOUBLE CREAM

For the icing:
85G/3OZ UNSWEETENED CHOCOLATE
350G/12OZ ICING SUGAR
1 TEASPOON VANILLA EXTRACT
WATER

Set the oven to 220°C. Lay a sheet of baking parchment over a baking tray.

Sift the flour on to a sheet of paper. Put the butter and water into a saucepan and bring the mixture to the boil. Remove from the heat and quickly shoot all the flour in from the sheet of paper, and immediately beat just until the mixture is smooth and comes away from the sides of the saucepan. Do not over-beat at this stage.

Add the egg gradually, beating vigorously at each stage. You may not need to use all the egg; add just enough to make the mixture smooth, glossy and stiff enough to hold its shape, not wet. Pipe or spoon the mixture on to the prepared baking tray, in strips about the thickness and length of your forefinger. Leave plenty of space between them as they will more than double in size.

Bake in the oven for 20 minutes or until golden brown, firm and dry. If they are soft to the touch, or have little beads of sweat, cook them for a little longer. When they are cold, split the éclairs and fill with the cream, stiffly whipped.

Make the icing: melt the chocolate in a little water, over a very low heat. Stir it until it is smooth and add the icing sugar, vanilla and enough water to make it a creamy consistency. Dribble the icing over the éclairs and leave until the icing is set.

Variation: Flavour the cream and the icing with strong black coffee and a little sugar.

Chocolate Biscuit Cake.

Tessa White

Much loved by at least three generations, and very easy to make.

1 PACKET OF MARIE OR RICH TEA BISCUITS
115G/4OZ BUTTER
115G/4OZ BROWN SUGAR
115G/4OZ COCOA
115G SULTANAS/4OZ
1 EGG
A GOOD DOLLOP OF GOLDEN SYRUP

Break the biscuits into small pieces (get the children to do that). Melt the butter and stir in all the other ingredients. Add the biscuits last. Put in a greased tin and keep in the fridge until needed.

Loney's Sticky Ginger Cake.

Loney, my country grandmother's cook, used to make this loaf-shaped cake. Dark, sticky and dense, it improves with keeping, and should not be eaten until at least 24 hours after baking. If my grandfather was not there at teatime, we were allowed to spread butter on it. We used to take a few slices, wrapped in greaseproof paper, in our pockets when we went on long bike rides.

Loney was always vague about her recipes, but my cousin Tessa Hayward, who also ate Loney's food in her youth, reconstructed it for her *Magimix Cake Book*, now out of print, alas. This is her recipe.

Tip: When weighing treacle or golden syrup, use a hot spoon and cover the pan or bowl of the scales with flour to stop the syrup sticking.

225G/8OZ PLAIN FLOUR
100G/3½ OZ SOFT DARK BROWN SUGAR
1½ TEASPOONS GROUND GINGER
3 TABLESPOONS MILK
½ TEASPOON BICARBONATE OF SODA
100G/3½OZ BUTTER, SOFTENED
2 EGGS
225G/8OZ BLACK TREACLE
50G/1¾OZ GOLDEN SYRUP
5 KNOBS STEM GINGER, DRAINED OF ITS SYRUP
75G/2½ SULTANAS
1 TABLESPOON CHUNKY MARMALADE

Set the oven at 160°C. Grease a 20cm/8in cake tin or a small loaf tin and line the bottom.

Put the flour, sugar and ground ginger into a food processor and whiz for 5 seconds to mix and aerate them. In a small saucepan bring the milk to blood heat and stir in the bicarbonate of soda. Add the milk mixture, butter, eggs, treacle and golden syrup to the bowl and process for 5 seconds.

Scrape down the sides of the bowl and add the ginger, each knob cut into about 5 pieces, the sultanas and the marmalade. Pulse about half a dozen times to mix everything in, then pour it all into the prepared tin. Bake for 1 hour, then turn the oven down to 150°C, cover the cake with a piece of greaseproof paper and bake for a further 45 minutes or until a skewer plunged into the centre comes out clean. Leave the cake for 5 minutes before turning it out on to a rack to cool.

London Granny's Crusty Sponge Cake.

This cake appeared regularly for Sunday tea, after a long walk in the park and Gentleman's Relish sandwiches. I think it was the only cake our London Granny knew how to make, and very good it was: yellow and sponge-y inside, with a sweet, crusty top. Granny always made it in a rectangular loaf tin, but a round cake tin is fine.

5 EGGS, SEPARATED
300G/10OZ CASTER SUGAR
1 TEASPOON VANILLA EXTRACT (OR USE VANILLA SUGAR)
190G/6½OZ FLOUR

Preheat the oven to 165°C. Grease a loaf or cake tin and line the base with baking parchment.

Put the egg yolks and 200g/7oz of the sugar into a bowl and whisk over a gentle heat until the mixture is pale and mousse-like. Add the vanilla. Sift the flour. Whisk the egg whites until stiff and whisk in the rest of the sugar. Fold the flour and egg whites into the yolk mixture and pour it all into the prepared tin. Bake for between 40 minutes to 1 hour.

If you like, split the cake and fill it with jam, fresh fruit with whipped cream, or butter icing.

Nusskuchen.

My mother made exceedingly good cakes, but she was also famous in the family for her vagueness. The occasion when she absentmindedly baked a cake using soap powder instead of flour is often described with glee and a certain amount of exaggeration, some versions insisting that a mass of soapsuds floated out when the oven door was opened.

Nusskuchen, a light but moist cake, made from a Constance Spry recipe, was one of her specialities, and we often had it for pudding rather than tea. The hazelnuts give it a rich, crunchy texture. It can be filled with jam and/or whipped cream, but the slightly tart apple filling is perfect.

For the cake:
60G/2¼ OZ HAZELNUTS, SHELLED AND PEELED
115G/4OZ BUTTER
115G/4OZ CASTER SUGAR
2 EGGS AND 1 EXTRA EGG WHITE
115G/4OZ FLOUR
2 LEVEL TEASPOONS BAKING POWDER
2 TABLESPOONS VERY STRONG COFFEE
2 TABLESPOONS MILK

For the filling:
450G/1LB APPLES
RIND AND JUICE OF 1 LEMON
2 TABLESPOONS APRICOT JAM

For the icing:
115G/4OZ GOOD UNSWEETENED CHOCOLATE
2 TABLESPOONS STRONG COFFEE
15G/½ OZ UNSALTED BUTTER
VANILLA OR RUM TO FLAVOUR

Make the cake: Set the oven to 175°C. Grease and line a shallow cake tin.
Grind the hazelnuts in a food processor. With an electric whisk, beat the

butter until cream, add the sugar and go on beating until the mixture is very pale. Beat in the eggs but not the extra white, and the nuts, flour and coffee. Stir in the milk, the baking powder and last of all, the egg white, whipped stiff. Pour the mixture into the tin and bake for 20 to 30 minutes. When the cake is cool, split it and fill it with the apple. Pour the icing over the top.

Make the filling: Peel, core and slice the apples. Put them in a saucepan with the grated rind and juice of the lemon and the apricot jam. Cook until soft and cool before using.

Make the icing: Break up the chocolate, add the coffee and heat gently until the chocolate is just melted. Remove from the heat, stir until smooth, then add the butter and flavouring and stir again. Pour it over the cake.

Madeleines.

I include this recipe in case you wonder about the taste experience that unlocked Proust's memory. To *rechercher* his *temps perdu* properly you need shell-shaped moulds to bake the little cakes in, and a lime *tisane* to dip them in. But they are good with any brew of tea, or with fruit fool or mousse.

55G/2OZ CASTER SUGAR
2 EGGS
½ TEASPOON VANILLA
50G/1¾OZ FLOUR, SIFTED
50G/1¾OZ UNSALTED BUTTER, MELTED
ICING SUGAR FOR DUSTING

Set the oven to 190°C. Grease the madeleine moulds and dust them with flour.

Whisk the sugar, eggs and vanilla (or use vanilla sugar) until thick and mousse-like.

Lightly fold in the flour, then the melted butter. Fill each mould three-quarters full and bake for 7-10 minutes. When cool, dust lightly with icing sugar.

Lemon Drizzle Cake.

Helen Thomas

I used to make this cake the hard way, creaming the butter and sugar by hand. My niece Helen's version is better than mine. This is her quick and easy recipe.

140G/5OZ SELF-RAISING FLOUR
115G/4OZ BUTTER
115G/4OZ CASTER SUGAR
2 DESSERTSPOONS LEMON CURD
2 EGGS
GRATED RIND OF 1 LEMON
JUICE OF $1/2$ A LEMON
2 TABLESPOONS SUGAR FOR TOPPING

Set the oven at 175°C. Grease and line a loaf tin.

Put all the ingredients in a food processor and blend for 2 minutes. Put the mixture into the tin and bake for 30 minutes or until firm.

While the cake is still warm, and before turning it out of the tin, pour over the lemon juice and sprinkle sugar on top.

Swiss Roll.

75G/$2^1/2$ OZ SELF-RAISING FLOUR
3 EGGS
75G/$2^1/2$ OZ CASTER SUGAR
ABOUT 3 TABLESPOONS RASPBERRY JAM
EXTRA CASTER SUGAR

Preheat the oven to 200°C. Grease a Swiss roll tin and line it with baking parchment.

Sift the flour. In a large bowl, whisk the eggs and sugar together until the mixture is thick and mousse-like. Fold the flour into the egg mixture, a little at a time. Pour the mixture into the prepared tin and bake it in the oven for 8 to 10 minutes. It is important not to overcook it.

Meanwhile, warm the jam to make it easier to spread. Cut a sheet of grease-proof paper larger than the tin. Sprinkle caster sugar on it. Turn the cake out on to the sugared paper, peel the paper off the base of the cake and spread the jam over it. Before rolling the cake up, with a sharp knife score a line 2.5cm/1in in from the edge, right across the short end, but only cutting through half the thickness. This makes it easier to start rolling it. Leave the roll to get completely cold before serving.

All in One Fruit Cake.

This recipe is adapted from one by Mary Berry. The cake will keep well,
stored in an airtight tin. I just wrap mine in clean foil when cold;
it's nice just as it is or spread with butter.
MARLENE NOBLE

175G/6OZ SOFT MARGARINE OR BUTTER
175G/6OZ SUGAR
GRATED RIND OF 1 ORANGE
4 EGGS, BEATEN
225G/8OZ SELF-RAISING FLOUR
350G/12OZ MIXED DRIED FRUIT
75G/2½OZ GLACÉ CHERRIES, HALVED
1 TABLESPOON RUNNY HONEY OR GOLDEN SYRUP
50G/2OZ CHOPPED WALNUTS

Set the oven at 160°C. Grease and line a 23cm/9in cake tin.

In a food processor or by hand, beat all the ingredients together well for 2 or 3 minutes, put the mixture into the tin and smooth the top. Bake for about 2½ hours, until a skewer or knitting needle stuck in the centre comes out clean. If necessary, lay a piece of foil over the cake halfway through baking so the top doesn't get too brown. Allow the cake to cool before turning it out.

Biscuits.

Belgium Shortbread.

This recipe was given to me by my mother-in-law and has been a firm favourite with both my children and grandchildren. It is very easy to make and keeps well in an airtight tin. I always make a couple for our village fete.
KAY HOLME

250G/9OZ SELF-RAISING FLOUR
140G/5OZ CASTER SUGAR
1 EGG, BEATEN
175G/6OZ BUTTER
PINCH OF SALT
100G/4OZ STONED DATES, SLICED THINLY
5-6 TABLESPOONS SEEDLESS RASPBERRY JAM
A LITTLE MILK FOR GLAZING
WALNUTS FOR DECORATION

Set the oven to 180°C. Grease and flour an 18-20cm/7-8in shallow cake tin.

Whiz the butter, sugar and flour in a food processor until it is the texture of breadcrumbs. Add the beaten egg, and pulse until it forms a pastry-like dough. Divide the dough in half, shape each half into a ball and roll out to about 1.5cm/½ in thick so that it fits the tin. Use one half to line the cake tin. Spread a layer of jam over the dough, then a layer of dates. Place the second half of the dough over and press it to fit inside the tin. Brush the top with a little milk to glaze and decorate with walnut halves.

Bake for about three-quarters of an hour. When cold, store in an airtight tin.

Brandy Snaps.

*My mother made meringues and brandy snaps for our birthday parties
— still enjoyed by the grandchildren.*
KAY HOLME

The brandy is in the cream filling, not in the snaps. They are excellent without the filling, served with rhubarb fool or gooseberry fool.

115G/4OZ BUTTER
115G/4OZ CASTER SUGAR
115G/4OZ GOLDEN SYRUP
115G/4OZ PLAIN FLOUR
$^{1}/_{2}$ TEASPOON GROUND GINGER
JUICE OF $^{1}/_{2}$ A LEMON
$^{1}/_{2}$ PINT DOUBLE CREAM
2 TABLESPOONS BRANDY

Set the oven at 175°C. Line two baking sheets with baking parchment.

Melt the butter, sugar and syrup together. Add the flour, ginger and lemon and mix everything together thoroughly. Drop teaspoonfuls of the mixture on to the baking sheets 15cm/6in apart (they will spread when cooked). Bake until golden brown. While they are still warm and pliant, roll each one round the handle of a wooden spoon and slip it off.

Whip the cream with the brandy until stiff. Fill the snaps with the cream just before you eat them.

Choc Chip Cookies.

This recipe from the *River Cottage Family Cookbook* has been a hugh success in our family. Both grownups and children love making them and eating them. The cookies can be eaten warm, more or less straight from the oven, or cold, and they keep well, stored in an airtight tin.

100G/3½OZ GOOD DARK CHOCOLATE
125G/4½OZ UNSALTED BUTTER
100G/3½OZ GRANULATED SUGAR
75G/2½OZ SOFT BROWN SUGAR
1 FREE-RANGE EGG
2 TEASPOONS VANILLA EXTRACT
150G/5½OZ PLAIN FLOUR
½ TEASPOON BAKING POWDER
A PINCH OF SALT

Set the oven at 175ºC. Line two baking sheets with baking parchment.

Chop the chocolate into little chunks and set aside. Heat the butter in a small saucepan very gently until it has just melted.

Meanwhile, put the two types of sugar into a mixing bowl. Pour in the melted butter and beat well with a wooden spoon. Add the egg and vanilla and beat until well blended. Sift the flour, baking powder and salt into the bowl and stir them into the mixture, then stir in the chopped chocolate. Drop heaped dessertspoonfuls on to the lined baking sheets, leaving plenty of space between them.

Bake for 8 to 10 minutes until the cookies are just turning golden brown. Leave to harden for a couple of minutes before transferring them to a wire cooling rack.

Gipsy Creams.

Christian Buchan

*We regarded these as very exotic! They were the speciality of
a neighbour, Chrissie Buchan.*
ANN HARTHILL

For the biscuits:
85G/3OZ BUTTER
3 LEVEL TABLESPOONS GOLDEN SYRUP
175G/6OZ FLOUR, SELF-RAISING OR PLAIN
15G/½OZ COCOA
55G/2OZ SUGAR
55G/2OZ ROLLED OATS
2 TABLESPOONS MILK

For the filling:
150G/5½OZ ICING SUGAR
55G/2OZ CHOCOLATE, MELTED
75G/2¾OZ BUTTER

Set the oven at 165°C. Line one or more baking trays with baking parchment.

In a saucepan, melt the butter and syrup. Stir in the sifted flour and cocoa, the sugar and rolled oats. Add the milk and mix. Form the mixture into walnut sized balls and place them on a baking tray. Flatten the biscuits with a fork dipped in hot water. Bake for 20 minutes.

Make the filling: Beat together all the ingredients and when the biscuits are cold, sandwich them in pairs.

Crow's Nicky-Nacky Men.

The feast of St Nicolas on the 6th December is celebrated in most Northern
European countries, and special cookies are baked for the occasion. In Basel,
in Switzerland, these brioche-type buns, shaped like gingerbread men, are tradi-
tional. St Nick, or Nicky-Nacky, is the rather sinister equivalent of Santa Claus.
He is dressed in black, and carries a birch switch, and a sack full of nuts
and oranges with which good little girls and boys are rewarded, while BAD
kiddies are carted off in the sack never to be seen again. Needless to say the
children were terrified, and even I got goose-bumps when this bearded figure
emerged with his lantern from the foggy gloom of a December evening.
However, the making of the little bread men made up for these horrors, and
having got most of the dough on the floor, we would eat them hot from the
oven with butter and a bowl of pumpkin soup, every 6th December.
CAROLINE FUGLISTALLER (CROW)

Grattima dough:
500G / 1LB 2OZ PLAIN FLOUR
1 TEASPOON SALT
1 PACKET OR 7G DRIED YEAST
50G / 1¾OZ SUGAR
GRATED PEEL OF ½A LEMON
80G / 2¾OZ BUTTER
250ML / 9 FL OZ MILK
1 EGG YOLK

Set the oven at 200°C. Line a baking sheet with baking parchment.

Sieve the flour and salt into a bowl, add the yeast, sugar and lemon peel.
Mix together and make a well in the middle. Melt the butter over gentle heat,
add the cold milk and pour into the flour mixture. Mix, knead and slap to make
an elastic dough. Place in a clean bowl and cover with cling-film and allow to
rise in a warm place till doubled in volume.

Turn out on to a floured board and cut into 16 equal pieces and form into
little men. Allow to rise for 20 minutes. Paint with beaten egg-yolk. Chill for
10 minutes. Bake for 20 minutes

Orange Jumbles.

To say that they are indescribably charming really describes them.
AMBROSE HEATH

My mother made these from Ambrose Heath's recipe. We ate them at tea, at elevenses and to accompany mousses, fools or ice cream.

115G/4OZ ALMONDS, SHREDDED
115G/4OZ CASTER SUGAR
85G/3OZ BUTTER, SOFTENED
55G/2OZ FLOUR
GRATED RIND AND JUICE OF 2 ORANGES

Set the oven at 165°C. Line a baking tray with baking parchment.

In a bowl, mix the almonds, sugar, butter, flour and grated orange rind. Gradually beat in the orange juice (you may not need it all) until the mixture is a stiff dropping consistency.

Drop teaspoonfuls of the mixture, set well apart, on to the baking tray. Bake for 7-10 minutes until golden.

Mary's Biscuits.

Amanda Hornby

The Mary with whom these biscuits originated cooked for three generations of the Hornby family, and her recipe has now been passed on to a fourth.

SUGAR, PLAIN FLOUR AND BUTTER, EACH TO THE WEIGHT OF 1 LARGE EGG

Set the oven to 175°C. Line a baking tray with baking parchment.

Beat the butter and sugar together until fluffy. Add the egg and half the flour and beat again. Add the rest of the flour and a little milk if the mixture is too stiff. Pipe or spoon the mixture on to the baking tray, well spaced apart. Cook until light brown and curling at the edges. Before they cool, wrap each one round the handle of a wooden spoon, to curve it.

Fork Biscuits.

My mother used to make these when I was very little, and I "helped" by pressing the fork on each biscuit.

140G/5OZ SELF-RAISING FLOUR
115G/4OZ MARGARINE (OR BUTTER), SOFTENED
50G/1¾OZ CASTER SUGAR
GRATED RIND OF ½ A LEMON OR ORANGE

Set the oven to 175°C. Line a baking sheet with baking parchment.

Beat the sugar into the margarine or butter. Add the citrus rind, then gradually work the flour into the mixture. Make the mixture into balls the size of a walnut and put them on the baking sheet. Flatten each ball using a fork dipped in water. Bake for 15-20 minutes.

Variation: To make chocolate fork biscuits, replace 30g of flour with 30g of powdered chocolate.

Flapjacks.

This is the basic recipe, very easy to make. You can vary it almost infinitely by adding chopped nuts and/or one or more kinds of dried fruit, such as raisins and sultanas, snipped dried apricots, dates, dried cranberries, or candied citrus peel. You can also add chocolate to the fruit or nuts, or use chocolate on its own.

100G/3½OZ BUTTER
75G/2¾OZ SOFT BROWN SUGAR
4 TABLESPOONS GOLDEN SYRUP
275G/9¾OZ ROLLED OATS

Set the oven to 180°C. Grease a shallow baking tin.

Melt the butter, sugar and syrup together in a saucepan. Add the oats and stir until they are coated with the syrup mixture. Stir in any additions such as fruit, nuts or chocolate. Put the mixture into the tin, to about 1cm/⅜ in deep. Bake for 20-25 minutes until golden. Leave the flapjack mixture in the tin to cool, then cut it into wedges or rectangles.

Chapter 9.

Soups and
Savouries.

32 Recipes

The way our meals are structured has changed enormously in the last 50 years. My mother and some of her friends were stuck in a time warp, trying to produce single-handed the sort of meals that their own mothers had achieved simply by having a word with the cook each morning. Yet many women like my mother became not merely competent, but excellent, cooks, and were entirely self-taught. It helped that, with a few exceptions, they did not go out to work: cleaning their houses and feeding their families was their full-time job and they did it as well as they were able.

Today it seems extraordinary that they prepared (and ate) a three-course dinner every night: soup or another starter; meat or fish with two veg; and finally, a pudding or savoury. Nowadays soup has been promoted to a main dish for lunch or supper, and we like it to be robust. Clear consommé, or a delicate cream of asparagus, do not make a satisfying meal, so the recipes given here are mostly for more substantial soups. Other starters, served in large helpings, accompanied by good bread and perhaps a salad, can also be promoted to main-course status to satisfy hearty appetites for lunch or supper.

Savouries have tended to disappear from the culinary repertoire, or shrunk into mere cocktail snacks. They deserve a revival. In the old days, they were served instead of and occasionally as well as, puddings, and were often more popular, especially with men. My mother thought it worthwhile to keep in her kitchen library, a whole volume (albeit a slim one) on the subject of savouries. It was simply called *Good Savouries* by Ambrose Heath, and is the source of some of the recipes given here.

Soups and Accompaniments.

*In my grandparents' house dinners and lunches started with soup which
was said to prepare your stomach for what was coming: consommé,
broth with pearl barley, vegetable soup thick and thin, or whatever I
suppose suggested itself to Kate whose stockpot was always
on the bubble.*

GUY HUNGERFORD

When I got home from school my mother was often making soup. I would
take over from her the task of rubbing cooked vegetables through a hair
sieve with a wooden spoon, while Mum stirred something on the stove. Then
I'd disappear upstairs to do my homework before laying the table in the dining room, ready for supper when Dad got back from the office.

While we ate, I filled them both in about my day; whom the maths mistress
had vented her sarcasm on, how my best friend had got an order mark for being
cheeky, and how unfair it was that I had only got C-minus for my History
essay, based, as usual, on my mother's knowledge and wisdom. My brother was
at boarding school, so in term time he missed out on the pleasurable daily
routine of cooking and eating together.

My mother knew that most soups benefit from being dressed up. She
garnished smooth, creamy soups with crunchy croutons made from yesterday's bread cut into cubes and fried in dripping or oil or butter. A swirl of
cream in each bowl, with parsley, chives or coriander snipped over the top also
makes soup more appealing, and grated cheese can be sprinkled over minestrone and other vegetable soups.

Bramley Apple and Celeriac Soup.

Serves 4

This comes from a collection of recipes from farmers and their families, published by the Wessex Foundation to promote local fresh produce.

2 ONIONS, CHOPPED
2 GARLIC CLOVES, CHOPPED
OIL FOR FRYING
2 MEDIUM CELERIAC ROOTS
2 BRAMLEY APPLES
1 LITRE/1¾ PINTS OF WATER
A FEW SAGE LEAVES, CHOPPED
SALT AND PEPPER
2 TABLESPOONS CREAM

In a saucepan, cook the onions and garlic in a little oil, until soft but not brown. Add the celeriac, peeled and cut into cubes, the apples, peeled, cored and sliced, and the sage. Add the water, bring to the boil and simmer gently, uncovered, for 30 minutes or until the celeriac is tender.

Allow the soup to cool slightly, then liquidize it, reheat and season to taste. If it is too thick, add a little water; if too thin, boil to reduce and thicken it. Finally, stir in a little cream.

Cullen Skink.

Serves 4

Other recipes have appeared with flour added which makes us scream with horror. Flour to thicken is just not traditional. The steeped oatmeal gives a lovely silky texture.

Mrs Ann Smith Harthill of Cullen, Morayshire

There are various versions of this Scottish half-soup, half-stew, but this one, coming as it does direct from Cullen, can claim to be authentic.

1.3kg/3lb floury potatoes
1 onion, quartered
1 tablespoon of oatmeal soaked in 300ml/½ pint of warm milk
2-3 fillets of good, un-dyed, smoked haddock
salt and pepper
a nut of butter

Peel and cut up the potatoes. Put them in a pan with the onion, cover with water, bring to the boil and simmer until the potatoes are soft. Add the milk and oatmeal to the pan and stir gently.

Lay the haddock on top and simmer gently for 10 minutes or so until the fish is cooked. Lift the fish out and either reserve it to serve whole or flake it to put back in the pan. Crush the potatoes but leave a bit of texture. Check the seasoning, adding salt (if needed, the fish will already be quite salty), freshly ground pepper and the nut of butter.

Gazpacho.

Tessa Hayward
Serves 4

This refreshing cold Spanish soup was a trendy, exotic starter for summer dinner parties in the 1960s, but it was not originally a party piece. Alice B Toklas (bosom friend of Gertrude Stein), travelling in Spain in the 1950s, was told, "Gazpachos are only eaten by peasants and Americans." In *The Alice B Toklas Cookbook* she gave recipes for different versions of the dish from Malaga, Seville and Cordoba. The gazpacho of Segovia, she wrote, has a more vulgar appeal, being "outrageously coarse." The coarseness depends on whether the soup is sieved or not, and on the size of the diced vegetables. Half the fun of gazpacho is helping yourself from the pretty, fresh-looking dishes of finely diced cucumbers, tomatoes, peppers, etc. Served with robust bread and some cheese, it is all you need for lunch in the garden.

For the soup:
2 SLICES OF BREAD, CUT FROM A WHITE LOAF AT LEAST A DAY OLD
1 MEDIUM SIZED GREEN PEPPER, DESEEDED AND ROUGHLY CHOPPED
8 MEDIUM RIPE TOMATOES
½ CUCUMBER, PEELED
3 GARLIC CLOVES, CRUSHED
1 TABLESPOON OF WINE VINEGAR
6 TABLESPOONS OF OLIVE OIL
SALT AND PEPPER

For the garnish:
2 HARD-BOILED EGGS, CHOPPED
1 SPANISH ONION, FINELY CHOPPED
½ CUCUMBER, PEELED AND DESEEDED
2 TOMATOES, PEELED AND DESEEDED
1 GREEN PEPPER, DESEEDED
2 SLICES OF BREAD FOR CROUTONS
ICE CUBES

Make the soup: Cut the crusts off the bread and soak it in water. Squeeze it out and put it in a food processor or blender with the green pepper, the tomatoes, the cucumber roughly chopped, the garlic, vinegar and olive oil. Whiz until everything is well blended. If you want a smooth soup, sieve it to get rid of any bits of tomato and pepper skin. For a more peasanty dish, leave it as it is. Chill the mixture.

Make the garnish: Dice the ingredients very small and put into separate small bowls or ramekins. Dice the bread for the croutons and fry them in olive oil. To serve, put a few ice cubes in each person's bowl and pour the soup over. Put the bowls of garnish on the table for everyone to help themselves.

Potage Crécy.

Serves 6

If you drink up your soup you will be able to see in the dark.

450G / 1LB CARROTS
4 MEDIUM POTATOES
40G / 1½ OZ BUTTER
½ A MEDIUM ONION, CHOPPED
1 TEASPOON SUGAR
SALT
1 LITRE / 1¾ PINTS CHICKEN OR VEGETABLE STOCK OR WATER
A BUNCH OF PARSLEY, CHOPPED VERY FINE

Peel and chop the carrots and potatoes. Melt the butter in a saucepan and add the onion, carrots and potatoes, the sugar and a pinch of salt. Cook the mixture gently until the butter is absorbed. Add the stock, bring to the boil and simmer until the carrots and potatoes are soft. Liquidize: the mixture should not be too smooth. Adjust the seasoning, heat and add a little more butter and the parsley.

Parsnip with Orange and Ginger.

Serves 4, hot or cold

This soup has been highly praised by people who thought they hated parsnips. It is adapted from a recipe in *It's Raining Plums*, a book of *Daily Telegraph* readers' recipes edited by Xanthe Clay.

450G/1LB PARSNIPS, PEELED AND ROUGHLY DICED
1 MEDIUM ONION, CHOPPED
50G/1¾OZ BUTTER
1 TABLESPOON FLOUR
GRATED RIND AND JUICE OF 1 ORANGE
2½ CM/1IN FRESH GINGER, GRATED
850ML/1½ PINTS VEGETABLE STOCK
150ML/¼ PINT SINGLE CREAM (OPTIONAL)

In a large saucepan, soften the onion in the butter. Stir in the parsnips, flour, ginger and orange rind. Gradually add the stock, stirring until the mixture is smooth. Bring it to the boil and simmer for about 20 minutes, until the parsnips are soft. Liquidize the soup and stir in the orange juice. Season, pour into bowls and swirl some cream into each bowl. If the soup is to be eaten cold, allow it to cool before stirring in the cream.

Heinz Tomato Soup.

For most of us, this is comfort food of the highest order. Keep a few tins in the larder or store cupboard.
Open the tin, heat and eat.

Garlicky Spinach Soup.

Serves 4

This soup was an important stage in my conversion from loathing to loving spinach.

2 PACKETS OF FROZEN SPINACH
2 GARLIC CLOVES, CRUSHED
30G/1OZ BUTTER
1 TABLESPOON FLOUR
200ML/$\frac{1}{3}$ PINT MILK
PINCH OF NUTMEG
SALT AND PEPPER
100G/$3\frac{1}{2}$OZ GRATED CHEESE

Put the spinach and garlic in a saucepan and cook until the spinach has thawed and is heated through.

Meanwhile, melt the butter, stir in the flour and add the milk gradually, stirring all the time until the mixture is thick and smooth. Liquidize the spinach and the sauce until smooth, adding some stock or water to thin if necessary. Season with salt, pepper and nutmeg. Heat and eat, serving the grated cheese separately to sprinkle over the soup.

Minestrone.

Minestrone is a meal in a bowl. It is also a moveable feast, the ingredients varying according to what is in the market at one season or another, and according to which part of Italy you come from. In England the market rules also apply, so there is no "correct" recipe. The one given below is a suggestion only, and can be infinitely adapted. If you find it calming to sit down for half an hour with a chopping board and a sharp knife or mezzaluna, and the radio for company, you will enjoy making minestrone.

The time taken will be much less if you use tinned haricot beans.

115G/4OZ DRIED HARICOT BEANS
OLIVE OIL
2 ONIONS, CHOPPED
2 GARLIC CLOVES, CHOPPED FINE
115G/4OZ BACON LARDONS
4 TOMATOES, PEELED AND CHOPPED OR A TABLESPOON OF CONCENTRATED
TOMATO PURÉE
MARJORAM, THYME, BASIL AND PARSLEY, CHOPPED
2 CARROTS
2 SMALL POTATOES
2 STICKS OF CELERY
1 LEEK, FINELY SLICED
½ A SMALL SAVOY CABBAGE
55G/2OZ SMALL PASTA SHAPES
SALT AND PEPPER
75G/2¾OZ FRESHLY GRATED PARMESAN

Soak the haricot beans overnight. Next day, in a large saucepan, soften the onions in olive oil, add the garlic and bacon, and mix well. Add the tomatoes or tomato purée, the drained haricot beans and a good tablespoon of herbs. Pour in 1.5 litres/2¾ pints of hot water and boil gently for 2 hours.

Dice the carrots, potatoes and celery. Finely slice the leek and cabbage.

When the soup has been cooking for 2 hours, add the carrots and simmer for 10 minutes. Add the potatoes, celery and leek, and simmer for 10 minutes more or until the vegetables are cooked. Add the cabbage and pasta shapes. Adjust the seasoning and stir in 2 tablespoons of Parmesan. Put the rest of the Parmesan on the table for people to help themselves.

Variations: Instead of haricot beans, use red kidney beans, rice or lentils. In summer, use baby broad beans, added at the end of cooking.

Use any herbs or vegetables that are in season: spinach, courgettes, French beans, celeriac, turnips.

Green Pea Soup.

Serves 4, hot or cold

This pretty soup can be made almost instantly and is good hot or cold.

1 SMALL ONION, FINELY CHOPPED
25G/1OZ BUTTER
700G/1½LB FROZEN PEAS
600ML/1 PINT CHICKEN STOCK
A FEW SPRIGS OF MINT
2 TABLESPOONS CREAM
SALT AND PEPPER

Cook the onion gently in the butter until transparent, 5 to 10 minutes. Add the peas, the stock and a few mint leaves, bring to the boil and simmer for a few minutes until the peas are cooked. Liquidize, reheat and season. Pour into bowls, adding a swirl of cream to each, and a sprinkling of chopped mint. If you are eating the soup cold, stir in the cream after it has cooled, and add some finely diced cucumber.

Parsley Soup.

Serves 6, hot or cold

1 SMALL ONION, CHOPPED
30G/1OZ BUTTER
1 GOOD BUNCH OF PARSLEY, ABOUT 115G/4OZ
450G/1LB NEW POTATOES, ROUGHLY DICED
850ML/1½ PINTS CHICKEN STOCK (LIQUID NOT JELLIED)
300ML/½ PINT MILK
SALT AND PEPPER
150ML/¼ PINT CREAM

In a large saucepan, soften the onion in the butter. Put a few springs of parsley aside for garnishing the soup and roughly chop the rest. Add the potatoes and parsley to the saucepan and stir until the butter is absorbed. Add the stock and milk, season and bring to the boil. Cover and simmer for 30-40 minutes or until the potatoes and parsley are soft.

Liquidize the soup, return it to the pan and reheat. Adjust the seasoning, pour the soup into bowls and swirl a little cream into each. Scatter some chopped parsley on top. If you are going to eat the soup cold, allow it to cool, stir in the cream and refrigerate it until needed.

Variations: The formula of potatoes, chicken stock and onion as a basis for different soups is tried and tested. Experiment with mixed herbs, spinach and sorrel, and other combinations.

Rob's Veg Soup

Serves 4

Rob and I both remember our mothers making something very like this warming and satisfying soup, and in winter Rob makes it for lunch about once a fortnight. The ingredients vary according to what we happen to have, but the base is always a good chicken stock thickened with potato, and it always tastes good. The better the stock, the better the soup. The thick consistency combined with chunky bits of vegetable makes it different from and more of a meal than other veg soups. A batch will provide at least one lunch for four people or two lunches for two. If there are cooked vegetables left over from other meals, they can be chopped up and added near the end of cooking.

2 LARGE POTATOES
2 LARGE CARROTS
2 LEEKS
1 PARSNIP
1 LARGE ONION
BUTTER OR OIL
1 GARLIC CLOVE, CRUSHED
1.2 LITRES/2 PINTS CHICKEN STOCK OR HALF STOCK, HALF WATER
1 BAY LEAF, A BUNCH OF PARSLEY, A SPRIG OF THYME

Peel and dice or slice the vegetables. Soften the onion in oil or butter. Add the rest of the vegetables and the garlic, and stir until the butter is absorbed. Add the stock, the bay leaf, thyme and a few parsley stalks, bring to the boil and simmer until all the vegetables are cooked (25 to 30 minutes). Remove the bay leaf and thyme stalk and liquidize half the soup, making sure the balance has plenty of potato to thicken the soup. Stir everything together and heat.

Variations: Add other vegetables – beans, celeriac, chopped spinach or cabbage, chopped smoked bacon, chopped cooked chicken, ham or game. If you have pheasant stock to use up, add more parsnips to the soup – they have an affinity.

Leek and Potato Soup.

Serves 4, hot or cold

We have this soup so often in the winter that I could make it blindfold, yet we never tire of it. It is known as *potage bonne femme* in France, and, since the ingredients are nourishing and cheap, the epithet signifies a housewife who is frugal as well as a good cook. The recipe scrubbed up well for 1960s dinner parties as *crème vichyssoise*, served chilled with cream and chopped chives added.

450G/1LB POTATOES, PEELED AND DICED
2 LARGE LEEKS, CLEANED AND THINLY SLICED
40G/1½OZ BUTTER
1 LITRE/1¾ PINTS WATER
1 TEASPOON SUGAR
SALT AND PEPPER
CREAM
CHOPPED PARSLEY, CHERVIL OR CHIVES

Melt the butter and stir in the leeks. When they are beginning to soften but not brown, add the potatoes, the water, sugar and a pinch of salt. Bring to the boil and cook for 25 minutes or until the potatoes and leeks are soft. Liquidize the soup and adjust the seasoning. When it is hot, pour the soup into bowls and add a swirl of cream and scattering of herbs to each. If it is to be eaten cold, allow it to cool then stir in the cream and refrigerate it.

Variation: For a more robust lunchtime soup, liquidize half the soup and return it to the pan with the remaining half full of bits.

Velouté Johnny (Onion Boys' Soup).

Serves 6

The onion man in his Breton beret crossed the channel once a year, and arrived on his bicycle, the handlebars festooned with his wares strung in golden brown garlands fastened with straw. Mum would rush to the door to practice her rusty French on him.

This recipe is adapted from one in *Cuisine Grandmère* by Jenny Baker. It is called after the onion "boys" (they were pretty ancient) from Roscoff and is very comforting, specially when you have a cold.

25G/1OZ BUTTER
450G/1LB ONIONS, CHOPPED
350G/12OZ POTATOES, PEELED AND CUT IN CHUNKS
1 LITRE/1¾ PINTS STOCK
SALT AND PEPPER
1 EGG YOLK
1 TABLESPOON CRÈME FRAICHE
CHIVES

Melt the butter in a saucepan and gently fry the onions for 5 to 10 minutes until soft but not brown. Add the potatoes and stock, bring to the boil and simmer for 20 minutes or until the vegetables are tender, then liquidize. In a small bowl, beat the egg yolk and crème fraiche together and stir in a ladleful of the soup. Add this to the soup and heat again without boiling. Ladle the soup into bowls, snip chives over each helping and serve with croutons.

The Potter's Loaf.

Peter Lascelles

"Serve with fresh, crusty bread" hardly needs saying at the end of a soup recipe. Good bread turns a bowl of soup into a meal, and a home-baked loaf, warm and crusty from the oven, is a wonderful treat. My brother Peter makes the best bread, perhaps because he is a potter and has honed his kneading skills on recalcitrant clay. His loaves were much in demand at the Clargill Head Pottery at Alston, in the days when he and his family ran a café alongside the pottery, which is still there. We always look forward to the potter's loaves when we visit each other.

For creative satisfaction nothing beats making bread, except perhaps throwing a perfect pot on the wheel. What's more, it is good exercise.

Here are Peter's instructions verbatim (N.B. preparation and cooking time is about 20 hours):

The best results are obtained by using much less yeast than the yeast packet tells you, so that the dough takes all night for its first rising. For some reason the flavour of bread is improved by long rising and also by using as little water as you can get away with. Measure the quantities carefully and knead the dough in a bowl, stopping when the last of the flour has been absorbed. If this takes less than 15 minutes, you have used too much water and should reduce the amount next time.

750G/1LB 10OZ STRONG WHITE FLOUR
2 TABLESPOONS SALT
1 TEASPOON DRIED YEAST
455ML WATER

For glaze:
1 EGG
2 TABLESPOONS MILK

Mix flour, salt and yeast together in a large bowl. Clear a space in the middle and pour the water into the well. With a large fork mix most of the flour with the water. There should be a thick paste in the middle and dry flour around the outside. Keeping a layer of dry flour between your hands and the wet mix, gather dough from the outside and push it down into the middle. Rotate the bowl slightly and repeat the process. Go on doing this, rotating the bowl each time. Initially you will need to press the gathered dough into the middle very gently but as the dough stiffens you can be more forceful without getting your hands mired with dough. This process continues for 15-20 minutes when all the free flour should have been absorbed and the dough become uniform in texture.

Turn the ball of dough upside down in the bowl. Wet a tea-towel, wring it out and place it over the bowl. Put a sheet of plastic (a slit up shopping bag for instance) over the tea-towel to stop it drying out. Leave at room temperature overnight.

In the morning (before 7am if you want the bread ready by midday), knead again for half a minute. Cover and leave to rise for 2 hours. Grease a 40cm/ 16in rectangular baking tray.

Turn the dough out on to a floured surface. Gather dough from the far side of the lump and push it down into the middle. Rotate the lump through 180 degrees and repeat. Where the dough from back and front meet down the middle, press together with thumb and forefinger along the length of the join. Repeat this whole cycle twice, so that the loaf becomes long and thin.

Place the loaf diagonally across the baking tray with the pressed together line on top.

Replace the damp cloth and plastic sheet and leave to prove for 2 hours.

Whisk the egg and milk together thoroughly and brush on to the loaf. Glazing is essential to get a crisp, delicate crust. Place in a cold oven set to 150°C, switch the heat on and bake for 68 minutes (or 150°C for an hour in an AGA).

Garlic Bread.

2 SHORT LOAVES OF FRENCH BREAD OR 1 LONG LOAF CUT IN HALF
100G/3½ OZ BUTTER, SOFTENED
2 GARLIC CLOVES, CRUSHED
CHOPPED HERBS (OPTIONAL)

Set the oven at 220ºC. Slice the bread diagonally into slices about 5cm/2in wide, cutting almost but not quite through to the bottom of the loaf. Mash the butter, garlic and herbs (if used) together until well mixed and really soft. Spread it generously on both sides of each slice of bread, push the loaves back into shape and spread any surplus butter over the tops of the loaves. Wrap each loaf or half loaf in foil and bake for 15 to 20 minutes. Unwrap the foil just before eating.

Other Starters and Savouries.

Savouries, the passion of the average Englishman and the bete noire of the ordinary housewife… make an admirable ending to a meal, like some unexpected witticism or amusing epigram at the close of a pleasant conversation… A large number of the savouries here given could be used in the service of hot or cold hors d'oeuvre, or for such frivolous entertainments as fork luncheons, cocktail parties and so on.

GOOD SAVOURIES BY AMBROSE HEATH

As Ambrose Heath implies, many savouries are quick and easy to prepare and cook, and make instant, emergency lunches or suppers. Keep some tins of sardines, anchovies and soft roes in the larder. Some of the recipes are for starters which have gone out of fashion over the years, but deserve reviving as light main courses.

Lord Melville.

This recipe comes from my aunt Joyce Kaye's kitchen notebook. I have not been able to find out anything about the peer whom the crispy bacon savouries are named after, but they make delicious snacks to have with drinks.

10 OR MORE VERY THIN SLICES OF STREAKY BACON

2 EGGS, BEATEN

ABOUT 115G/4OZ BREADCRUMBS

OIL FOR FRYING

Cut the bacon rashers in half. Dip each piece in the beaten egg, shake off the surplus egg, and coat with breadcrumbs. In a large frying pan, heat enough oil to cover the pan to a depth of 5mm/$\frac{1}{4}$ in. Fry the bacon pieces until they are brown and very crisp.

Crudités.

Serves 6

This is one of those starters that can be converted into a satisfying main course for lunch. If you have 15 minutes to spare, it is worth making your own mayonnaise, for creative pleasure, as much as for the excellent results. Even the best bought mayonnaise doesn't compare. Part of the attraction of this dish is the eye appeal of crisp, colourful raw vegetables arranged on a large platter with a bowl of garlicky mayonnaise in the centre.

For the mayonnaise:
3 EGG YOLKS
300ML/½ PINT OLIVE OIL, AT ROOM TEMPERATURE
½ TEASPOON SALT
WHITE WINE VINEGAR OR LEMON JUICE
2 CRUSHED GARLIC CLOVES

The crudités:
6 SMALL EGGS, HARDBOILED
1 CUCUMBER
1 GREEN PEPPER
1 RED PEPPER
3 CELERY STICKS
RADISHES
6 MEDIUM OR 12 SMALL CARROTS
1 SMALL OR ½ A LARGE CAULIFLOWER

Make the mayonnaise: Put the oil in a measuring jug. In a bowl, beat the egg yolks with the salt. Add the oil, drop by drop, stirring all the time with a wooden spoon. When the sauce begins to thicken, pour it in a thin, steady stream, stirring constantly. From time to time add a little vinegar or lemon juice from a teaspoon. When all the olive oil is used up the mayonnaise should be thick and gloopy. Now is the time to add any extra flavouring, tasting as you go: in this case simply garlic, but on other occasions it might be chopped spinach and watercress for a *sauce verte*, mustard for potato salad, or herbs of your choice.

Prepare the crudités: Leave the hard-boiled eggs in their shells. Cut the cauliflower into individual florets. Leave a short stalk on the radishes; cut the rest of the vegetables lengthways into batons about 1cm x 7cm ($\frac{1}{3}$ in x $2\frac{3}{4}$ in), leaving the carrots whole if they are small.

Tip: To rescue curdled mayo, start again with a fresh egg yolk, and add the curdled mixture little by little. If you fail again, try tipping the whole thing into a blender and blitzing it.

Warm Chicken Liver Salad.
Serves 4

The last-minute cooking takes only a few minutes, so this is an easy first course as well as a good lunch or supper dish.

450G/1LB CHICKEN LIVERS CUT INTO BITE-SIZED PIECES
OLIVE OIL
MIXED GREEN SALAD LEAVES, SUCH AS LETTUCE, ROCKET, BABY SPINACH

Dressing:
2 TABLESPOONS WHITE WINE OR TARRAGON VINEGAR
2 TEASPOONS DIJON MUSTARD
SALT AND PEPPER
$\frac{1}{3}$-$\frac{1}{2}$ CUP OLIVE OIL

Toss the salad in the dressing and arrange it on four plates. Heat 2 tablespoons of olive oil in a frying pan, throw in the chicken livers and cook turning frequently, for 2 or 3 minutes; they should remain pink inside. Put the livers in the middle of the salad leaves on each plate and drizzle on any juices that are left in the pan.

Egg Mousse.

Serves 6

This rich and creamy dish featured as a starter for dinner parties in the 1970s and I still have a weakness for it. With a leafy salad and crusty bread it makes a meal on it's own for summer lunch.

5 EGGS, BOILED FOR 9 MINUTES THEN PLUNGED IN COLD WATER
300ML/½ PINT CHICKEN STOCK
15G/½ OZ POWDERED GELATINE
1 TEASPOON WORCESTERSHIRE SAUCE
150ML/¼ OZ DOUBLE CREAM
SALT AND PEPPER
WATERCRESS AND LUMPFISH ROE TO GARNISH

Shell the eggs, put the whites to one side and sieve the yolks into a basin. Warm a cupful of stock and sprinkle the gelatine over it. Stir it until the gelatine has dissolved, then stir the melted gelatine and the Worcestershire sauce into the rest of the stock. Season to taste. Chop the egg whites and partially whip the cream.

When the stock begins to jell, quickly stir it into the egg yolks. Fold in the cream and, last, fold in the egg whites. Pour the mixture into a soufflé dish or glass bowl, cover it with cling-film and put it in the fridge to set. Just before serving, spoon a pile of lumpfish caviar on to the centre of the dish and arrange dressed watercress around the rim.

Marinated Kipper Fillets.

Serves 6 as a starter, 4 for lunch

What better way to get your fix of oily fish than with this once-trendy, easy starter? Make it a day in advance, to give the marinade time to impart its flavours.

8 KIPPER FILLETS
2 SHALLOTS, CHOPPED
4 TABLESPOONS OLIVE OIL
3 TABLESPOONS WINE VINEGAR
1 BAY LEAF
2 TABLESPOONS CHOPPED FRESH DILL
2 TABLESPOONS CHOPPED PARSLEY
GRATED RIND OF 1 LEMON
1 TEASPOON CASTER SUGAR
SALT AND PEPPER
1 SWEET ONION, THINLY SLICED
LEMON WEDGES

Remove the skin from the kipper fillets and tweeze out any remaining bones. With scissors, cut the fillets into diagonal strips and put them in a china serving dish. Mix the shallots, oil, vinegar, herbs, lemon rind, sugar and seasoning all together and pour over the kippers. Cover the dish with cling-film and refrigerate for at least 24 hours.

Eat with thinly sliced sweet onion scattered over the kippers, and lemon wedges to squeeze over. Put a plate of buttered brown bread on the table.

Potted Shrimps.

Serves 12

My father, who loved puns and malapropisms, called them "slotted pimps." They came in blue cardboard tubs and were popular with us all. Potting your own shrimps may seem like stuffing a mushroom (life is too short to do it), but that's because you've never tried it. Delicious home-potted shrimps given to us a starter by our friend Diana Royden inspired me to have a go. The prawns come ready peeled, so it is quick and easy, and if you make a big batch, you can freeze some for future use.

200G/7OZ BUTTER
1KG BROWN SHRIMPS, PEELED
2 STICKS OF MACE OR 1/2 TEASPOON GROUND MACE
1/2 TEASPOON FRESHLY GRATED NUTMEG
1/4 TEASPOON CAYENNE PEPPER
3 LEMONS, QUARTERED
BROWN BREAD FOR TOAST

In a saucepan, melt the butter with the spices over gentle heat. Add the shrimps and stir to mix thoroughly and heat through, but do not let the mixture boil. Remove the mace sticks if used and divide the mixture among 12 small ramekins. Level the tops and leave in the fridge to set. When they are set, spoon a thin layer of clarified butter over each one. Serve with freshly made, hot brown bread toast and a lemon wedge.

Devils on Horseback.

A classic savoury, still encountered as a canapé at drinks parties.

Per person:
3 OR 4 SOFT PRUNES, STONED
3 OR 4 ALMONDS, PEELED
SALT, PAPRIKA AND CAYENNE
2 THIN SLICES OF STREAKY BACON
BREAD FOR TOAST

Set the oven at 200°C. Line a baking tray with parchment.

Season the almonds with a little salt, paprika and a small pinch of cayenne. Tuck each almond into a prune and wrap the prune in half a slice of bacon. Lay the devils on the baking tray with the join of the bacon underneath and cook in the oven for 7-10 minutes, until crisp. Serve them on hot buttered toast with the crusts cut off.

Variations: Instead of almonds, put anchovies, chopped chutney or olives in each prune. Instead of prunes, wrap up pieces of chicken liver sprinkled with finely chopped onion, parsley, salt, pepper and cayenne. These are all devils. Angels on horseback are oysters wrapped in bacon.

Sardines on Toast.
Serves 2

If you keep a few tins of sardines in the store cupboard, you are never without a meal.

8 TINNED SARDINES
1 TEASPOON GRATED ONION
1 TEASPOON FRENCH MUSTARD
1 TEASPOON WORCESTERSHIRE SAUCE
1 TEASPOON TOMATO KETCHUP
2 SLICES OF BREAD
OIL FROM THE SARDINE TIN

Mash up the sardines with all the other ingredients except the bread and oil. Toast the bread slices or fry them in the oil from the sardine tin; add a little butter if needed. Pile the sardine mixture on the toast and grill until it is hot and bubbling.

Variation: Simply lay sardines straight from the tin on to toast and grill them.

Jansson's Temptation.
Serves 4

A classic Swedish dish, although nobody seems to know who Mr Jansson was.

6 MEDIUM-SIZED POTATOES, PEELED
2 TINS OF ANCHOVIES IN OIL
1 LARGE ONION, SLICED
150ML/ ¼ PINT DOUBLE CREAM
FRESHLY GROUND BLACK PEPPER

Set the oven at 200°C.

Cut the potatoes into thick matchsticks. Pour the oil from the tins of anchovies into a large frying pan and cook the onion until it is soft. Add the potatoes and cook until the oil is absorbed. Take the pan off the heat and stir in the anchovies and cream. Season with pepper (the anchovies supply the salt), and turn the mixture into a gratin dish. Bake in the oven for about 30 minutes until crispy on top.

Mushrooms on Toast.

Serves 4

If they are available, it is worth using wild mushrooms for the extra flavour.

500g / 1lb 2oz mushrooms
1 garlic clove, chopped
bacon fat or butter
2 sprigs of thyme
salt and pepper
1 tablespoon cream
4 slices of bread
chopped parsley

Slice the mushrooms. In a small saucepan, soften the garlic in the bacon fat or butter. Add the mushrooms, thyme and seasoning and cook for 5 minutes, stirring occasionally. Meanwhile, make the toast. Stir the cream into the mushrooms, and pile the mixture, piping hot, on to the toast. Scatter the parsley over.

London Granny's Cheese Straws.

Part of the Sunday lunch routine at our London grandparents' flat was, for the grownups, the very dry martini that preceded lunch. Granny would bring out a gadget which looked like a mincing machine but was armed with spikes instead of blades. Ice cubes were fed in, the handle was turned, and crushed ice came out at the other end, ready for the cocktail shaker. Unlike 007's favourite tipple, Granny's dry martini was made with gin not vodka, and was shaken very vigorously, not stirred.

With the cocktails went potato crisps, home-made in a cauldron of smoking, spluttering oil, and kept fresh in a large glass sweet jar, and cheese straws, light and crumbly.

60G/2¼OZ STRONG CHEDDAR CHEESE
90G/3¼OZ PLAIN FLOUR
10G/¼OZ CORNFLOUR
50G/1¾ OZ SOFTENED BUTTER
1 LARGE EGG YOLK
SALT AND FRESHLY GROUND BLACK PEPPER
A LITTLE COLD WATER
CAYENNE PEPPER (OPTIONAL)

Chop the cheese roughly into cubes of about 1cm/½ in and put it in a food processor with the flour and cornflour. Whiz until the cheese has turned to fine crumbs. Add the soft butter and the egg yolk. Season and pulse. If the mixture does not quickly form a lump, add ½ a teaspoon of cold water and pulse again. If necessary add a little more water until a firm dough has formed. Wrap it in cling-film and leave in the fridge for 30 minutes. Set the oven to 200°C.

On a floured surface, roll the dough out to about 5mm/¼ in thick and cut it into strips about 10cm/4in long and 1.5cm/½ in wide. Put them on a baking sheet or tin covered in baking parchment and bake for 7-8 minutes. Remove from the oven and sprinkle cayenne pepper over the cheese straws very sparingly, if wanted. When they have cooled a little, transfer them to a wire rack. When completely cold, they will keep in an airtight tin for a day or two.

Tip: The less the dough is processed or handled, the lighter and crisper the finished product will be.

Granny B's Sausage Rolls.

The better the sausages, the better the results; it is worth buying the best. Children love making sausage rolls, to eat in the garden or take on picnics further afield. Granny B used to make her own puff pastry, but the ready-made variety is fine.

A PACKET OF FLAKY OR PUFF PASTRY
500G/1LB 2OZ SAUSAGES
1 EGG, BEATEN

Set the oven at 220°C.

Take the sausages out of their skins; divide the pastry into three and, on a floured surface, roll out one piece into a long rectangle, 13cm/5in wide. Arrange one-third of the skinned sausage meat in a continuous roll, making one long sausage, the length of the pastry. Brush one long edge of the pastry with the beaten egg, then fold the pastry over and seal the join. Cut into individual rolls about 6cm/2½ in long.

Repeat the process with the other two pieces of pastry. Put the rolls on a baking tray lined with parchment and bake at the top of the oven for 20 to 25 minutes. Check after 15 minutes to make sure they are not burning, and cover with foil if they are getting too brown.

Welsh Rabbit.

(This, rather than "rarebit", is said by some to be the correct spelling.)
Serves 4

Well, many's the long night I've dreamed of cheese — toasted mostly.
TREASURE ISLAND BY ROBERT LOUIS STEVENSON

200G/7OZ STRONG CHEDDAR OR CHESHIRE CHEESE, GRATED
1 TEASPOON MUSTARD
4 TABLESPOONS OF BEER
FRESHLY GROUND BLACK PEPPER
4 SLICES OF BREAD

In a bowl, mix all the ingredients except the bread. Toast the bread and spread the cheese mixture over it, right up to the edge so that the toast will not burn. Grill until the cheese is browned and bubbling. Eat immediately, with more mustard if wanted, and a good splash of Worcestershire sauce.

Variation: For added Welshness, soften a finely sliced leek in butter and spread a layer on the toast, under the cheese.

Tip: To get the Worcestershire sauce evenly spread over your Welsh Rabbit, make a lattice pattern on the top with a knife, before sloshing on the sauce.

Gougère.

Serves 6

This ring of cheese-flavoured choux pastry uses roughly the same basic ingredients as Yorkshire pudding batter, but is as French as Yorkshire pud is British. Gougère is delicious sliced and eaten as it is, hot or cold, but can also be filled with a leafy salad, chopped tomatoes with basil, hot chicken and mushrooms, ham and leeks in béchamel sauce – or any other filling your ingenuity suggests.

300ML/½ PINT MILK
115G/4OZ FLOUR; 55G/2OZ BUTTER
4 EGGS
85G/3OZ GRUYÈRE CHEESE, CUT INTO SMALL CUBES
SALT AND PEPPER

Set the oven at 190°C. Line a baking tray with parchment.

Sift the flour on to a sheet of paper. Put the milk into a saucepan, add the butter cut in small pieces and ⅓ teaspoon of salt. Boil until the butter and milk have amalgamated. Shoot the flour in, all in one go, and stir until the mixture comes away from the sides of the pan. Whisk the eggs lightly and beat them into the mixture a little at a time (this stage can be done in a food processor). You may not need to use the last bit of egg; the mixture should remain stiff enough to hold its shape. Continue beating until the mixture is smooth and shiny. Stir in the cheese.

Put tablespoons of the mixture on to the baking sheet in a circle, diameter 18-20cm/7-8in, leaving a space of about 7cm/2¾in diameter in the centre. Make another circle on top of the first one and roughly level the sides and top with a palette knife. Bake in the centre of the oven for about 45 minutes. It is done when it is golden brown and firm to the touch. Serve it hot or put it on a wire rack to cool.

Devilled Biscuits.

Good eaten hot with very cold cream cheese and radishes.

1 TABLESPOON BUTTER, SOFTENED
1 TEASPOON CHUTNEY
A DASH OF WORCESTERSHIRE SAUCE
THIN WATER BISCUITS

Mix the butter, chutney and Worcestershire sauce to a paste. Spread it thinly on the biscuits and put them in a hot oven for 5 minutes.

Soft Herring Roes on Toast.
Serves 4

This was one of my father's favourites, but I never tasted it myself until I tried it out for this book. Delicious.

500G/1LB 2OZ SOFT ROES, TINNED OR FROZEN AND DEFROSTED
100G/3½OZ BUTTER
FLOUR FOR DUSTING
SALT AND PEPPER
4 SLICES OF BREAD
2 TABLESPOONS CAPERS, ROUGHLY CHOPPED

Turn the roes in the seasoned flour and shake off the surplus. Heat a frying pan and add half the butter. When it is foaming, fry the roes gently for 5-7 minutes, turning once. Meanwhile, toast and butter the bread. Lay the roes on the toast and scatter capers on top.

Stuffed Eggs.

The preparation of cold eggs is not limited by classical rules;
it rests with the skill and artistic imagination of the operator.
ESCOFFIER

The humble hard-boiled egg gets a make-over; the principle is to cut the eggs in half, remove the yolks and mix them with other, well-seasoned ingredients, moistened with a little cream or mayonnaise. The mixture is then piled back into the cavities in the egg whites. Small eggs, done in this way make good snacks to eat with drinks. Larger eggs, with salad, make a summer lunch. Here are some fillings:

MIXED FRESH HERBS WITH FINELY CHOPPED ONION
CHOPPED OLIVES AND RED PEPPERS
MASHED SARDINES, TUNA, ANCHOVIES OR CRAB MEAT
GRATED CHEESE AND A DASH OF WORCESTERSHIRE SAUCE
CHOPPED MUSHROOMS COOKED IN A LITTLE CREAM WITH CHOPPED PARSLEY
PRAWNS AND MAYONNAISE
CURRY POWDER AND A LITTLE CHOPPED CHUTNEY

Chapter 10.

Puddings.

41 Recipes

When I asked other grandparents to recall the puddings of their childhood, treacle tart, queen of puddings and castle puddings came out top of the pops, and only a few puddings provoked strong negative reactions. The slimy suet casing of Spotted Dick was recalled with loathing, as were lumpy custard, junket and blancmange, also known as mold, or shape. But the hatred had usually developed because these puddings were dished up at school, not home. Every Sunday evening, at one girls' boarding school, round castles of blancmange were served in a rainbow of different colours. They were supposed to be a Sunday treat, but were much disliked. Yet they were made simply from milk, sugar and cornflour, the very same ingredients that my own children and others of their generation gobbled up happily in the form of Bird's Angel Delight; just a good way to get milk inside them without a fuss, really.

Even unpopular puddings have their aficionados. "Spotted Dick rolled in a tea towel was my absolute favourite, with real custard," said a rare fan. One family gave a rave review to their grandmother's "Chocolate Splodge," a form of the much-despised blancmange, but the point was that she could never get it to set, and the family preferred her splodgy version. Two people even stood up to be counted for junket. The rest of us ate it because we were told to, but were often nearly defeated by the texture, so slippery on the spoon, the whey so watery, and the dusting of nutmeg so, well, dusty.

Apart from stodge and splodge, there was plenty of fruit to be enjoyed, not only, as my brother reminds me, in the "vast amounts of fruit in the garden eaten in passing," but in the fools and mousses of summer and the tarts, pies and crumbles of autumn and winter. Although there were no home freezers for storing fruit, the harvest from gardens and local orchards was nevertheless preserved, bottled in syrup. By the end of September, rows of sealed glass Kilner jars stood on high larder shelves, glowing with ruby raspberries, purple and golden plums, green and yellow gages, pink rhubarb, green gooseberries, and pale, fat, grainy pears.

Apples appeared in so many guises they should have a chapter of their own. As well as the usual tarts, puddings and pies there were apple fritters, baked apples, apple dumplings, apple charlotte, brown betty, apple hat, and more. The only negative comment came from a grandmother who remembered with disgust the "toenails" in stewed apples. More positively, another granny told how much her family enjoy stewed apples cooked with honey instead of sugar. Apples were often being prepared when we visited the kitchen as children. As soon as we were safe with knives, we were allowed to peel one each. The idea was to carve off as long a strip of unbroken peel as possible. When you dropped it over your shoulder on to the floor it would take the form of your true love's initial. This custom gave rise to much teasing.

Blackberry and Apple Pudding.
Serves 6

*I must speak up for suet. The most glorious dish of all, the treat of treats,
was blackberry and apple suet pudding made I suppose like a steak and
kidney pudding but tipped out on to a dish so that it arrived in a steaming
volcano of mauve and black fruit sliding down the flanks of the suet.
When I was grown up I still used to come home for the weekend in the
hope that Kate, my grandmother's cook, would produce one.*
GUY HUNGERFORD

For the suet pastry:
225G/8OZ SELF-RAISING FLOUR
1 LEVEL TEASPOON SALT
115G/4OZ SUET, GRATED
COLD WATER

For the filling:
675G/1½ LB COOKING APPLES, PEELED, CORED AND SLICED
175G/6OZ BLACKBERRIES
115G/4OZ SUGAR
*Note: the proportion of apples to blackberries can be varied;
if you have plenty of blackberries, use fewer apples.*

Grease a 1.3 litre/2¼ pint pudding basin. Sift the flour and salt into a bowl,
add the suet and mix. Add cold water, a little at a time, until the dough holds
together. On a floured surface, roll it out into a big circle and use it to line the
pudding basin with a slight overlap, cutting out a wedge to make it fit. Squidge
up the surplus wedge and roll it out again to make the lid. Put the apples and
blackberries into the basin in layers, sprinkling each layer with sugar. Brush
the edges of the pastry with water, put on the lid and seal carefully. Cover the
top with greaseproof paper or foil, tying it down with string. Put the basin in
a saucepan and pour in boiling water to halfway up the sides. Boil for 2½
hours, topping up the water from the kettle if it becomes necessary.

When the pudding is cooked, to turn it out, remove the greaseproof paper or foil, ease a palette knife down the sides of the basin to loosen the pudding, put a deep plate or shallow dish over the top and up-end it. Be extremely careful as the filling is very hot and will burn if it leaks out. With luck, after a sharp tap or two, the basin will come away, leaving the pudding intact. Eat it with custard or thick cream and extra sugar if needed.

Variations: Fill the pudding with any fruit that happens to be in season.

Apple In and Out.

My parents always took separate holidays, my father's being a week for Epsom races, and my grandmother, mother and I going to the seaside somewhere. Dad was no great shakes in the kitchen but always cooked a meal for us to come home to at the end of our holiday, usually a roast, always followed by Apple In and Out, a Devonshire favourite.

JANICE PALMER

225G/8OZ SELF-RAISING FLOUR
115G/4OZ BEEF SUET, SHREDDED
3 LARGE COOKING APPLES, PEELED AND SLICED
3 TABLESPOONS CASTER SUGAR
ABOUT 300ML/$\frac{1}{2}$ PINT MILK

Set the oven at 175°C. Grease a baking tin.
Mix the flour, suet and sugar, add the apples and enough milk to bring the mixture to a dropping consistency. Put the mixture into the tin and bake it until it is brown and crunchy on top. Eat it with clotted cream.

Note: If the apples are very tart, you may need extra sugar.

Bramley Burnt Creams.

Serves 6 to 8

My Mum was the Queen of Crème Brulée (see the recipe on page 238), but when short of time, she sometimes made this instead. It is very simple and, in it's way, every bit as good. Start preparation at least a few hours before you are planning to eat the creams.

1 KG/2LB 4OZ BRAMLEY APPLES, PEELED, CORED AND SLICED
2 OR 3 TABLESPOONS CASTER SUGAR
330ML/11½ OZ DOUBLE CREAM
6-8 DESSERTSPOONS SOFT BROWN SUGAR

Put the apples in a saucepan with 2 tablespoons of caster sugar and just enough water to stop them sticking. Cook gently, stirring occasionally until the apples are soft and translucent. As they cool, stir them to make a smooth purée, adding more sugar if necessary, but the apple purée should taste a little sharp. Fill six to eight ramekins two-thirds full, and chill in the fridge. Whip the cream until stiff and spread it over each ramekin, leaving just enough space for a thin layer of sugar on top. Smooth the tops with a knife and refrigerate again for an hour or so, or overnight. If short of time, put them in the freezer for 15 minutes. Sprinkle a dessertspoon of soft brown sugar over each ramekin and smooth off with a knife. Put them under a very hot grill until the sugar is just melted. It doesn't matter if the cream bubbles up under the sugar and spills out a bit. Remove from the grill. After a few minutes the sugar will harden and the Bramley Burnt Creams are ready to eat.

Variations: If you haven't got ramekins, use one large gratin dish. The formula works well with other fruit too.

Castle Puddings with Homemade Jam.

Makes 6-8 castles

These light, cake-y little sponge puds topped with hot jam sauce came joint first with Queen of Puddings in the nostalgia ratings. Almost everyone of my generation has fond memories of them. They are baked in special little tins called dariole moulds, the shape of a small tumbler. I use the same moulds for Panna Cotta (Italy's highly desirable answer to Blancmange), or individual jellies.

100G/3½ OZ BUTTER, SOFTENED
100G/3½ OZ CASTER SUGAR
GRATED RIND AND JUICE OF ½ A LEMON
2 EGGS
100G/3½ OZ SELF-RAISING FLOUR, SIFTED
RASPBERRY JAM, PREFERABLY HOME-MADE

Set the oven at 175°C. Grease 6-8 dariole moulds with butter.

Whisk the butter and sugar together until pale and creamy. Add the lemon rind and beat in the eggs, one at a time. Fold in the flour. If necessary add a little water to bring the mixture to a dropping consistency. Put a heaped tea-spoon of jam in each mould, and fill the moulds three-quarters full with the sponge mixture. Bake for about 15-20 minutes until the mixture shrinks slight-ly away from the sides of the moulds, and the top bounces back when pushed with a finger.

Meanwhile, put 4 tablespoonfuls of jam in a small saucepan with 2 table-spoons of water, and heat, stirring, until the jam has melted. Cool a little and add lemon juice to taste (traditional puddings and sauces are sometimes too sweet for modern palates). To turn out, loosen the sides of each pudding with a flexible knife. Put a small plate or bowl over the top and up-end the pudding. Tap the top of the mould and ease it off. Pour the hot jam sauce around the bases of the castles and eat hot, with custard (see pages 242-3) or cream if you like.

Stodge.

Steamed or baked, suet puddings and sponge puddings used to be known generically as "stodge," and were invariably served with custard at school dinners and sometimes at home as well. Suet puddings were designed to make a little go a long way, especially when they were made properly, and boiled in a cloth. The word "stodge" was not used in a pejorative sense, it was simply descriptive. The element of stodge was provided by flour combined with fat, which could be suet, margarine, or butter, and sometimes by breadcrumbs. The most appealing were sponge puddings which included eggs and were the same texture as cake, topped, when turned out of the pudding basin on to a serving dish, with delicious hot sauce: syrup, chocolate, jam, marmalade, lemon curd or butterscotch.

Nowadays it is almost unheard of for anyone to boil a pudding in a tea cloth. Most cooks use pudding basins, and although I have sometimes described how to tie a foil or greaseproof paper cover on to a basin with string, the difficulty of doing it single-handed if nobody is around to put a thumb on the knot can be avoided by investing in a lidded basin.

Steaming is achieved by putting the basin in the top of a purpose-made steamer, a saucepan with holes in it which fits on top of another saucepan containing boiling water. The alternative is to rest the pudding bowl on an upturned saucer in a saucepan, and pour in boiling water to come between one-third and halfway up the side of the bowl. Cover and steam. The secret of success is to keep the water boiling merrily, and to be vigilant and top it up from the kettle before it boils dry.

When the pudding is cooked, it helps to leave it for a few moments before turning it out, as it will shrink a little and come out of the basin more easily. Help it on its way by easing a flexible knife between the basin and the pudding, put a deep plate or shallow dish over the top and up-end it. With a sharp tap it should come out intact.

Steamed Syrup Sponge (not stodgy).

Serves 6

At my boarding school, it was known as syrup stodge, although it is not at all stodgy, and was the favourite of the stodges. All puddings were served with custard but syrup stodge was served with extra syrup.

SANDRA SMITH-GORDON

4 TABLESPOONS GOLDEN SYRUP
3 MEDIUM EGGS
SOFTENED BUTTER THE WEIGHT OF THE 3 EGGS
CASTER SUGAR THE WEIGHT OF THE EGGS
SELF-RAISING FLOUR THE WEIGHT OF THE EGGS
1 TEASPOON BAKING POWDER
EXTRA SYRUP FOR THE SAUCE

Grease a 1.2 litre/2 pint pudding bowl with a lid. Put the syrup in the bottom of the bowl. Sift the flour with the baking powder. Cream the butter and sugar until pale and fluffy, then beat in the eggs one at a time. Fold in the flour. Put the mixture into the bowl on top of the syrup, leaving 2.5cm/1in space at the top for the sponge to rise. Cover the bowl with its lid or tie foil over the top. Boil or steam the pudding for 2 hours, checking from time to time that the water has not boiled away and topping it up with boiling water if necessary.

When it is cooked, let the pudding cool a little. It will shrink slightly making it easier to turn out. Remove the lid and run a palette knife round the sides of the bowl. Put a deep plate or shallow dish upside-down over the top and up-end the pudding on to the dish. Be extremely careful as the syrup is very hot. Serve with extra syrup, heated gently, or custard (recipe on page 242-3).

Variations: For chocolate sponge pudding, substitute a tablespoon of cocoa for a tablespoon of the flour, and serve with chocolate sauce. For ginger pudding, add a teaspoon of ground ginger, a tablespoon of treacle and some chopped stem ginger. Canary pudding has grated lemon rind added, and jam at the bottom of the bowl.

Guards Pudding.

Serves 6

A very special pudding, which used to be the delight of my boyhood...
I believe that strawberry jam may be used, but for me the authentic
flavour is of raspberries.
GOOD FOOD ON THE AGA BY AMBROSE HEATH

I have not been able to discover how this much-loved nursery dish, also known as Burbage pudding first got its name.

190G/6½OZ WHITE BREADCRUMBS
115G/4OZ CASTER SUGAR
115G/4OZ MELTED BUTTER
½ TEASPOON BICARBONATE OF SODA DISSOLVED IN 1 TEASPOON OF WATER
4 WELL-BEATEN EGGS
8 TABLESPOONS RASPBERRY JAM

Mix everything well together and put in a buttered pudding basin. Tie on a cover of buttered, greaseproof paper or foil with a pleat folded down the centre. Steam for 2 hours. Eat with cream.

Variation: For a modern take on a classic, try making it with fresh raspberries instead of jam.

Jam Roly Poly.
Serves 4-6

It was made at school in a huge long roll, with suet pastry and
known as dead man's leg.
SANDRA SMITH-GORDON

A classic in the nursery, at school and in gentlemen's clubs, roly poly pudding with it's shiny, suet pastry exterior, is also known to some as "Aunt's Leg", to others as "Washerwoman's Arm" and, in its saucepan-shaped variety, as "Haynes' Hat". Traditionally, roly poly pudding was wrapped in a cloth and boiled for 2 hours or more, ending up with the greyish, rather slimy outside that gave rise to the unflattering nicknames. It doesn't have to be like that. This version, in which the roll is baked in the oven, is much more appealing. It is adapted from Lady Jekyll's *Kitchen Essays*.

200G/7OZ PLAIN FLOUR

A PINCH OF SALT

1 TABLESPOON BAKING POWDER

115G/4OZ SUET

50G/1¾ OZ DEMERARA SUGAR

UP TO 150ML/¼ PINT COLD WATER

5 TABLESPOONS RED JAM

MILK TO GLAZE

Set the oven at 190°C. Lay a sheet of baking parchment on a baking tray.

Sift the flour and baking powder into a bowl, add the suet and salt and mix with enough water to make a workable dough. The less you handle the dough, the lighter it will be. On a floured surface, roll it into a rectangle about 5mm/ ¼ in thick. Spread jam generously over the pastry, stopping just short of the edges. Dampen the edges, roll up the pastry lightly and press the edges to seal them. Bake for 35 to 45 minutes, until golden brown. Serve with extra jam and custard.

Fruit Fools, Pies, Tarts, Cobblers and Crumbles.

The late Lord Dudley could not dine comfortably without an apple pie… Dining, when Foreign Secretary, at a grand dinner at Prince Esterhazy's, he was terribly put out on finding that his favourite delicacy was wanting, and kept on murmuring pretty audibly, in his absent way: "God bless my soul! No apple pie." *The Art of Dining*, P. Morton Shand, 1852

The allure of a fruit tart, pie or crumble lies in the contrast between the soft, sharp-sweet fruit and the crisp pastry or topping. Unctuous custard or cream provides a deeply satisfying third element, and, with stone fruits like apricots, plums and damsons, the opportunity to play "Tinker, tailor…" with the cast off stones, adds to the pleasure.

Fools are much preferred by most children and many adults to plain stewed rhubarb, gooseberries or plums. In the days when cream was not available, or was considered a great extravagance, fools were made by adding custard to fruit purée, but cream, whipped not too stiff, but to about the same texture as the fruit, is nicer. If you want to make a lighter confection, fold in a stiffly beaten egg white or a little plain yoghurt.

Whether fruit appears in a pie or tart, or stewed, or in a fool, its flavour can be enhanced by adding the companion. The best rhubarb crumble I ever ate was cooked by our friend Roz Paynter-Reece. She had added strawberries to the rhubarb, greatly reducing its sharpness. Orange zest and juice, or a little grated ginger, or both, also go well with rhubarb, as do cinnamon with plums and cloves with apples. Squeeze a little lemon juice over raspberries, or mix them with redcurrants. Prunes can be soaked in red wine or, better still, tea. My father swore by a turn or two of freshly ground black pepper on his strawberries, with no sugar or cream, and in time I grew to think he had a point.

Good, crunchy biscuits are essential companions for fools. Brandy snaps go well with rhubarb, and there are more good biscuit recipes in Chapter 8.

Plum Crumble.

Serves 6

Sharp fruits like cooking apples, rhubarb, damsons and plums, make excellent crumbles, their sharpness contrasting with the sweet topping. To prevent the fruit giving off too much juice and making the top go soggy, partly cook the fruit and pour off the surplus juice. A basic crumble is made with flour, butter and sugar, in the proportions 175g/6oz flour to 115g/4oz butter to 115g/4oz sugar. This makes enough topping to cover 650-900g/1½-2lb of fruit. Process the mixture until it is the consistency of breadcrumbs. You can add oats, chopped nuts and spices to the basic mixture. A good spice complement is 2 of teaspoons cinnamon, 1 teaspoon of ground ginger and a good shaving of fresh nutmeg. The crumble recipes below are made by a slightly different method, using oats and no flour, rather like a flapjack mixture.

700G/1LB 9OZ PLUMS
55G/2OZ CASTER SUGAR
85G/3OZ GOLDEN SYRUP AND 85G/3OZ BUTTER
175G/6OZ OATS
55G/2OZ SLIVERED ALMONDS
1 HEAPED TEASPOON CINNAMON

Set the oven at 175°C.

Put the plums (or other fruit) in a saucepan with the caster sugar and just enough water to prevent them sticking to the bottom of the pan. Cook gently until the juices run. Strain off the juice and put the plums into a pie dish. Boil the juice rapidly until it is reduced and syrupy, then pour it over the plums. Melt the golden syrup and butter together. Mix the oats, almonds and spice together and stir them into the syrup and butter. Spread the mixture gently over the fruit and bake for 20-30 minutes until the top is lightly browned.

Variation: Topping for rhubarb crumble – 85g/3oz butter, 85g/3oz jumbo oats, 85g/3oz porridge oats, 15g/½ oz sesame seeds, 30g/1oz chopped walnuts, 55g/2oz light muscovado sugar. Melt the butter and mix in the remaining ingredients.

Goosegog and Elderflower Fool.

I have never managed to walk through the looking glass into that illusory time when the flowering of elders coincides with the ripening of gooseberries. In our garden, by the time the gooseberries are ready, the elderflowers have shed their petals. So, to achieve that classic marriage of flavours, I freeze elderflower syrup until the gooseberries ripen. If you don't want to make your own elderflower syrup, a bottle of good cordial will do just as well.

500G/1LB 2OZ GOOSEBERRIES
150ML/¼ PINT ELDERFLOWER CORDIAL
A STRIP OF LEMON ZEST
CASTER SUGAR TO TASTE
300ML/½ PINT DOUBLE CREAM

Put the gooseberries, elderflower cordial and lemon zest in a pan, bring to the boil and simmer gently for about 15 minutes, until the gooseberries are very soft. Whiz them in a blender or food processor, then rub them through a sieve and taste for sweetness, adding sugar if necessary. Whip the cream lightly and fold it into the gooseberry purée. Pile the fool into a glass bowl and chill it until needed. Eat with Mary's Biscuits (see page 184).

Blackberry Cobbler.

Katherine Futers
Serves 4

This is a batter pudding in the style of a clafouti, and can be made with almost any fruit, notably cherries, blueberries, cranberries or raspberries, or a mixture of some of these.

100G/3½OZ BUTTER
200G/7OZ SUGAR
¼ TEASPOON SALT
1 TEASPOON BICARBONATE OF SODA
100G/3½OZ FLOUR
175ML/6 FL OZ MILK
350G/12OZ BLACKBERRIES

Set the oven at 175°C.

Melt the butter in an ovenproof dish of about 20cm/8in diameter. Mix the dry ingredients in a bowl and beat in the milk to make a smooth batter. Pour it into the hot, melted butter. Do not stir. Sprinkle the blackberries over the batter. Do not stir. Bake for 45 minutes or until golden.

Rum Baba.

Big Granny's Rum Babas were legendary.
Sophy F-W

For the baba dough:
175G/6OZ FLOUR
PINCH OF SALT
100ML/3½ FL OZ WARM MILK
55G/2OZ BUTTER, SOFTENED
20G/¾ OZ YEAST
2 EGGS, BEATEN
30G/1OZ SUGAR

For the syrup:
115G/4OZ SUGAR
4 TABLESPOONS WATER
4 TABLESPOONS RUM

Sift the flour and salt into a warm bowl. Dissolve the yeast in the milk. Add the yeast and the beaten eggs to the flour, mix and beat vigorously by hand for 3 minutes. Cover the bowl and leave it in a warm place for 30 minutes to 1 hour, until the dough has doubled in size.

Set the oven at 205°C. Butter some muffin or brioche tins.

Add the butter and sugar to the dough and beat by hand again for 5 minutes. (Talk about elbow grease!) Half fill the tins with the dough and leave to rise again, for 5-10 minutes. Bake for 10-15 minutes, until golden brown.

Meanwhile, make the syrup. Dissolve the sugar in the water and boil it for 10 minutes. Add the rum and allow the syrup to cool a little before dribbling it over the babas. Serve them hot or cold with whipped cream to which more rum has been added.

Cranachan.
Serves 6

Any fruit can be used in this easy-to-make and easy-to-eat Scottish pudding, but it is particularly good with raspberries.

115G/4OZ COARSE PINHEAD OATMEAL
115G/4OZ CHOPPED HAZELNUTS
450G/1LB RASPBERRIES
CASTER SUGAR
300ML/½ PINT DOUBLE CREAM
4 TABLESPOONS WHISKY
1 TABLESPOON HEATHER HONEY

Toast the oatmeal in a dry pan until it is golden and crisp. Mix the hazelnuts with the oatmeal. Divide the fruit among six large wine glasses, so that each glass is half full. Sprinkle with caster sugar: how much depends on how tart the raspberries are. Add just enough to stop them being too tart. If they were frozen they may need a dessertspoon of sugar for each glass, if freshly picked they may need no sugar at all. Lightly whip the cream and whisk in the honey and whisky. Sprinkle a layer of oatmeal and nuts over the fruit, then a layer of cream, then more oatmeal on top. Do not wait too long before serving, or the oatmeal will lose its crispness.

Crème Brulée.

Serves 8

This was my mother's star turn for dinner parties. My brother always chose it for his last meal before going back to boarding school, preceded by sausages. Some people bake the cream custard in the oven and some use brown sugar for the top. Crème brulée made by those methods tastes good but is not the real thing, the texture of baked custard being quite different from that of custard made by stirring and stirring it until it thickens. Molten caster sugar on the top hardens to a glassy smooth, pristine ice rink, more beautiful and more satisfying to tap through with your spoon than the rough surface produced by brown sugar. Start making crème brulée the day before, or at least the morning before you are going to eat it, setting aside half an hour when you will be uninterrupted.

850ML/1½ PINTS DOUBLE CREAM
1 VANILLA POD, SPLIT LENGTHWAYS
6 LARGE EGG YOLKS
ABOUT 150G/5½OZ CASTER SUGAR

Put the dish you are going to serve the crème brulée in into the fridge. It should be a shallow, heatproof dish that will be almost filled by the mixture, or use chilled ramekins.

Put the cream and vanilla pod into a thick saucepan and bring to boiling point. Remove from the heat and leave the mixture to infuse for 15 minutes. In a bowl, beat the eggs and 1 tablespoon of the sugar.

Remove the vanilla pod from the cream and pour the cream over the egg yolks, mixing it thoroughly. Put the mixture into the saucepan over a very low heat, and stir it contiuously with a wooden spoon. This is where you need patience. The cream will take longer to thicken than you think, but don't be tempted to turn up the heat, just keep at it. It may take half an hour. When the mixture is thick enough to coat the back of a spoon, it is done. Take it off the heat, still stirring until it has cooled a little. Pour it into the chilled serving dish. Don't worry that the cream is still quite liquid. It will set firmer as it cools. Refrigerate it for at least 8 hours.

Up to two hours before serving, turn the grill on high. Sprinkle caster sugar over the top of the cream so that it is completely, but not thickly, covered. Slide the dish under the grill, as close as you can get it to the heat. As soon as the sugar has melted, remove it. The surface should be glossy and marbled with brown and gold like polished tortoise-shell. It doesn't matter if the cream has bubbled out round the edges.

Tip: If you are really scared of the cream curdling (separating), add a scant teaspoon of cornflour to the yolks and sugar. If it does curdle, it can usually be rescued by tipping it straight into a blender and whizzing it up.

Norwegian Cream.
Serves 6

A delicious take on baked custard.

2 LARGE TABLESPOONS JAM (APRICOT IS BEST)
3 EGGS
1 TABLESPOON CASTER SUGAR
$\frac{1}{2}$ TEASPOON VANILLA EXTRACT
425ML/$\frac{3}{4}$ PINT HOT MILK
3 TABLESPOONS WHIPPED CREAM
GRATED DARK CHOCOLATE

Set the oven at 175°C.

Spread the jam over the bottom of a soufflé dish. Put 2 eggs and 1 yolk in a bowl and beat with the sugar and vanilla. Pour on the milk, stir and strain the mixture into the soufflé dish. Stand the dish in a baking tin half full of water, put a piece of foil over the top of the dish and bake until just set. Leave it to get cold. Grate the chocolate over the custard. Whip the remaining egg white, fold it into the whipped cream and spread it over the chocolate. Sprinkle a little more chocolate over the top.

Crème Caramel (Crème renversée).

Serves 4

225G/8OZ CASTER SUGAR
2 WHOLE EGGS AND 2 MORE YOLKS
600ML/1 PINT MILK
A VANILLA POD

Set the oven at 170°C. Warm a soufflé dish. Heat the milk with 2 tablespoons of the sugar and the vanilla pod. In a small saucepan, melt the rest of the sugar without stirring it. When it begins to change colour, stir it gently until it is golden brown, then pour it into the warm soufflé dish and turn the dish round and round till the bottom and sides are coated with caramel.

Beat the eggs and pour the hot milk over them, stirring all the time, and pour into the soufflé dish. Put the dish in a baking tin of hot water and bake in the oven for 40 minutes or until the custard is set so that it does not tremble in the centre when you give the dish a gentle shove. Let it get cold before turning it out; ease a knife round the wall of the soufflé dish, put a deep plate or shallow dish over the top, up-end it and give it a little shake to loosen the cream. Lift the dish off carefully, leaving the top and sides of the pudding coated in the caramel sauce.

Variations: Leave out the caramel and you have baked custard, which can be flavoured with vanilla, chocolate or coffee.

Plum Pudding.

This is the only Christmas pudding my daughter-in-law likes. The recipe was
given to me about 85 years ago by an Australian friend. It really is the best:
a revelation to anyone who thinks they hate Christmas pud.
SYBIL D'ALBIAC

It is traditional to make the Christmas pudding on "stir-up Sunday", the last
Sunday before Advent, everyone in the family giving it a stir. But it will keep
a couple of months in the fridge until Christmas Day, when it can be boiled
again for an hour or two.

225G/8OZ SUET
55G/2OZ FLOUR
225G/8OZ RAISINS
115G/4OZ MIXED PEEL
115G/4OZ CURRANTS
115G/4OZ SULTANAS
1/4 TEASPOON MIXED SPICE
225G/8OZ BREADCRUMBS
55G/2OZ SHREDDED ALMONDS
A PINCH OF SALT
150ML/1/4 PINT MILK
4 EGGS
1 WINE GLASS OF RUM OR BRANDY
GRATED RIND AND JUICE OF 1 LEMON

Note: "I am not very fond of a lot of peel so I use 1 1/4 lb Whitworth's mixed
fruit which has a little peel in it anyway." (Sybil D'Albiac)

Put all the dry ingredients in a basin, add the milk, stir in the eggs one at a
time, add the rum or brandy and the grated rind and strained juice of the
lemon. Put the mixture into a well-buttered basin or pudding cloth. Boil it for
4 hours.

Rhubarb and Custard.

Serves 4

This careful way of cooking rhubarb ensures that the pieces stay whole instead of dissolving into a mush. Oranges have an affinity with rhubarb, enhancing its flavour, and the custard is only very distantly related to the lumpy stuff with skin on top remembered from school dinners. If you are not yet convinced that properly made egg custard is delicious, think of it not as custard but as *crème à la vanille*, or *crème anglaise*.

For the rhubarb:
500G / 1LB 2OZ RHUBARB
GRATED RIND AND JUICE OF 2 ORANGES
3 TABLESPOONS GOLDEN SYRUP

For the custard:
600 ML / 1 PINT WHOLE MILK
1 VANILLA POD
4 EGG YOLKS
1 TABLESPOON CASTER SUGAR

Cook the rhubarb: Wash the rhubarb, string it if necessary and cut into 4cm / 1½ in lengths. Put an ovenproof dish in the oven (160°C) to get hot.

Using a spoon dipped in hot water to get the syrup out of the tin, put the golden syrup into a saucepan with the grated orange rind and juice. Stir it over a gentle heat, to melt the syrup. Pour the mixture into the hot dish and add the rhubarb, turning it gently so that it is coated with the syrup mixture. Cover the dish and cook in the oven for 15 minutes. By now the rhubarb should be giving off its juices. Take out and stir very gently to turn the rhubarb pieces without breaking them. Cook for another 20 or 30 minutes until the rhubarb is tender. Remove from the oven, take off the lid and leave to get cold.

Make the custard: Heat the milk with the vanilla pod. Beat the egg yolks and sugar. Take the vanilla pod out and pour the milk slowly on to the eggs, stirring constantly. Put the mixture into a double boiler or a thick-bottomed saucepan, and cook it over a very low heat, stirring it all the time. When it thickens to the consistency of double cream, remove it from the heat and pour it straight into a cold bowl to reduce the heat. The secret of success is not to be in a hurry. If the worst comes to the worst and the mixture starts to separate, pour it straight into a blender and whiz it up. The problem can be pre-empted by adding a small teaspoon of cornflour to the egg yolks before adding the milk.

Variations: Instead of, or as well as, the orange zest and juice, add a teaspoon of grated ginger root to the rhubarb. For a richer custard, use single cream instead of milk.

Mini Apple Tarts.
Roz Paynter-Reece

These doll-sized apple tarts are probably what the Queen of Hearts made and the Knave stole. They are a great success with children and grownups alike. Last time I made them our five grandchildren were visiting. I left a tray of 24 tarts on the kitchen shelf to cool and when I came back they had vanished.

A PACKET OF PUFF PASTRY
3 OR 4 EATING APPLES, PEELED AND THINLY SLICED
2 TEASPOONS OF HONEY

Set the oven at 200°C.

In a saucepan, cook the sliced apples gently with the honey until they are just soft. Taste and if they are not sweet enough, add a little more honey. Leave to cool.

Either use ready-rolled pastry or roll out the pastry on a floured surface. Cut out rounds 5cm/2in diameter to line tartlet tins. Put a few slices of apple in each tart. Cut narrow strips from the pastry trimmings and lay them criss-cross over the apple. Bake the tarts in the oven for 6-8 minutes until the pastry is golden.

Kaiserschmarrn.

Serves 4-6

This variation on a pancake theme is much enjoyed by our grandchildren when they visit Oma, their step-grandmother, in Austria. Tradition has it that the original dish was knocked together by a poor farmer's wife with the only ingredients she had in her kitchen, to offer Emperor Franz Josef when he called in unexpectedly while out hunting.

125ML/4 FL OZ MILK
1 TABLESPOON SOURED CREAM
4 EGGS, SEPARATED
4 TABLESPOONS SUGAR
125G/4OZ FLOUR
55G/2OZ RAISINS SOAKED FOR 30 MINUTES IN RUM
A LITTLE BUTTER FOR FRYING
ICING SUGAR
PLUM PRESERVE OR JAM

In a food processor or using an electric whisk, whiz the milk, soured cream, egg yolks, sugar and flour to make a smooth batter. Turn the mixture out into a large bowl and stir in the raisins. Whisk the egg whites until stiff and fold them in.

In a large frying pan, heat enough butter to grease the surface. Pour the batter in and cook it until it is brown on one side. Turn it over (it doesn't matter if it gets broken). After about 1 minute, use two forks to pull the pancake apart and break it up. Turn the pieces until they are brown all over. Sprinkle icing sugar over them and eat them hot. Traditional accompaniments are plum preserve, cooked apple, or a sprinkling of cinnamon.

Peach Melba.

Serves 6

In the 1950s, if we were taken to a posh restaurant for a birthday, I always chose this and was never disappointed. There is a world of difference between Auguste Escoffier's most famous pudding, created to honour the opera diva Dame Nellie Melba, and the travesty of it, made with tinned peaches, cream-free ice cream and cheap raspberry jam. Escoffier's version, given here, is a seasonal dish, to be eaten towards the end of the summer, when fresh peaches and raspberries coincide.

450G / 1LB FRESH RASPBERRIES

CASTER SUGAR

6 RIPE PEACHES

1 LEMON, HALVED

750ML / 1¼ PINTS OF VERY GOOD VANILLA ICE CREAM

You also need six shallow glass sundae dishes or bowls. But if such vessels are not available, the peaches can be arranged in a single glass bowl.

Whiz the raspberries in a food processor or blender to make a purée. Sieve the purée to remove the pips, and stir in sugar to sweeten it a little. However, it should be a little sharp.

Put the peaches in a bowl and pour boiling water over them. After a few seconds transfer them to a bowl of water containing ice cubes. Peel each peach and immediately rub the surface with a cut lemon half and sprinkle it lightly all over with sugar, to stop it discolouring. Put the peaches on a plate and cover them with cling-film until needed. At the last minute, put a layer of ice cream in each glass or bowl, then a peach. Spoon the raspberry purée over the peaches and eat at once.

Pineapple Upside-Down Pudding.

Serves 4-6

Tinned pineapple rings are excellent in this dish. It can be made in a cake tin of the old-fashioned kind, with its base integral with the sides – the juice would leak out of a tin with a push-out base. Or use a soufflé dish.

For the base:
2 TABLESPOONS BROWN SUGAR
50G/2OZ BUTTER
425G/15OZ TIN PINEAPPLE RINGS

For the cake:
125G/5OZ SELF-RAISING FLOUR
100G/4OZ SUGAR
1 EGG
100ML/3½ FL OZ MILK
50G/2OZ BUTTER, MELTED

Set the oven at 180°C. Grease an 18cm/7in cake tin or soufflé dish.
Make the base: In a saucepan, dissolve the brown sugar and the butter in 3 tablespoons of juice from the pineapple tin. Boil the mixture until it is a thick golden brown syrup and pour it over the base and sides of the tin or dish. Arrange the pineapple rings on the base in two layers, cutting the rings if necessary, to cover it.
Make the cake: Sift the flour and put it, with the sugar, into a food processor. Pulse to mix it. Whisk the egg, milk and melted butter together and pour them over the flour. Pulse just until the mixture is smooth. Pour it over the pineapple and bake in the oven for about 40 minutes. Turn it out on to a plate and serve either hot or cold, with custard or cream.

Variations: Other fruit can be used in the same way, plums or apricots for example.

Port Wine Jelly.

Lyla Harling
Serves 4

In the nursery jelly was a special treat, and I still get a thrill when the wobbly, translucent stuff appears on the table. Our friend Lyla's cooking is always original and delicious. Her vinous jelly is strictly for grown-ups and, in larger quantities, would be ideal for a sticky dinner party.

300ML/½ PINT WATER
75G/2¾ OZ SUGAR
1½ SACHETS OF GELATINE
300ML/½ PINT PORT
4 TABLESPOONS BRANDY
4 TABLESPOONS ORANGE JUICE

In a saucepan, bring the water to the boil. Remove it from the heat, add the sugar and stir until dissolved. Cool it slightly, sprinkle on the gelatine and stir until it has melted. Add the port, brandy and orange juice. Pour into a mould or into four wine glasses, and chill until it sets. Serve with Orange Jumbles (see page 183).

Variations: Jelly made with almost any fruit juice, freshly squeezed and sweetened to taste, is a refreshing treat for adults and children alike. At Easter we sometimes have lemon jelly with primroses embedded in it (one of Hugh's recipes).

Rice Pudding.

Serves 6-8

There are few people of my generation whose lives were untouched by rice pudding. Some loved and others loathed the crisp skin, burnt almost black, and the mushy, milky rice underneath. In general, how well rice pudding goes down depends on timing. If it is not cooked long enough, separate grains of rice float in liquid milk. If cooked too long the rice swells into a stodgy mass. When cooked just right it is the same texture as Ambrosia tinned creamed rice and as delicious. It may seem decadent to add cream to rice pudding, but it is the best way to ensure the Ambrosia effect.

In colonial days, Lady Bernard, wife of Sir Charles Bernard, Chief Commissioner of Burma, used to make a rice pudding every day for her husband's tiffin. No one, he said, could make it as well as she did. When I was first married I made rice pudding for Rob, not daily like Lady Bernard, but perhaps once a month, under the illusion that it was one of his favourite puddings. We had passed our third wedding anniversary before he explained that he really didn't like rice pudding much. He ate it out of politeness.

110G/4OZ SHORT-GRAIN RICE
450ML/¾ PINT MILK
450ML/¾ PINT SINGLE CREAM
55G/2OZ CASTER SUGAR
1 VANILLA POD OR 1 TEASPOON VANILLA EXTRACT
25G/1OZ HARD BUTTER, DICED
JAM OR SYRUP

Set the oven at 150°C. Butter a pie dish.

Put the rice, milk, cream, vanilla pod and sugar into the dish and give it a stir. Leave it for half an hour. Remove the vanilla pod, stir the mixture again and dot the butter over the top. Bake in the oven for about 3 hours, checking from time to time to make sure the top does not burn. Eat it hot or cold, with a spoonful of jam or syrup on each helping, or as an accompaniment to cooked fruit.

Variation: Use brown sugar instead of caster.

Tips: Milk puddings cannot be cooked too slowly. "If the milk boils the pudding spoils."

Short-grain pudding rice is essential. You cannot make a respectable rice pudding with the long-grain variety.

Hot Prune Soufflé.
Serves 4

In our childhood prunes were always served stewed, their wrinkles unappealingly intact. This soufflé is a revelation of how delicious they can be.

225G/8OZ PRUNES SOAKED OVERNIGHT IN TEA
GRATED RIND AND JUICE OF $\frac{1}{2}$ A LEMON
SUGAR TO TASTE
3 EGG YOLKS AND 4 EGG WHITES

Set the oven at 200°C. Grease a soufflé dish with butter.

In a saucepan, simmer the prunes in the tea they were soaked in, with the lemon rind and juice, until the prunes are soft. Put them in a food processor with some of the liquid in which they were cooked and whiz to purée them, adding more liquid if the purée seems too stiff. Taste the purée and sweeten it with caster sugar if necessary. Put the prune purée into a bowl and beat the egg yolks in. Whisk the whites until stiff and fold them into the purée. Pour the mixture into the soufflé dish and bake for 20 to 25 minutes.

Variation: Make the soufflé with dried apricots, soaked not in tea but in white wine, and using orange rind and juice instead of lemon.

Queen of Puddings.

Serves 6

Of all puddings, this meringue-topped mixture of jam, lemon, custard and breadcrumbs generates the most poignant nostalgia among my contemporaries.

600ML/1 PINT WHOLE MILK
15G/½ OZ BUTTER
GRATED RIND OF 2 LEMONS
200G/7OZ CASTER SUGAR
75G/3OZ FRESH WHITE BREADCRUMBS
2 EGG YOLKS, 3 EGG WHITES
2 TABLESPOONS RASPBERRY JAM

Set the oven at 180°C. Butter a 1.2 litre/2 pint pie dish.

In a saucepan, heat the milk, butter, lemon rind, and 25g/1oz of the sugar. Stir in the breadcrumbs and leave the mixture to cool. Beat in the egg yolks, one at a time; put the mixture into the pie dish and leave it for 30 minutes. Bake in the oven for 20 to 30 minutes, until set. Lower the oven to 150°C.

Warm the jam and spread it over the surface of the cooked mixture. Whip the egg whites until stiff, and fold in all but a teaspoon of the sugar. Pile the meringue on top of the pudding and sprinkle the remaining teaspoon of sugar over it. Leave it for 5 minutes then cook in the oven for about 15 minutes until the meringue is pale gold and set. Serve immediately.

Variation: If the pudding seems too sweet for modern palates, substitute a layer of fresh raspberries for the jam.

Stone Cream.

In the days before domestic refrigerators, creams, jellies and blancmanges were put to set on the coldest place in the house: the stone floor of the underground cellar – hence the phrase "stone cold" as in "stone cold sober", and hence the name of this messy but delicious pudding, included for the sheer fun of it. It comes from *Lady Maclean's Cookbook*, published in 1965, a mixture of Lady Maclean's own recipes and others contributed by her friends. The following instructions are as she gave them, with my suggestions added in italics.

This is a very old Lancashire dish. You need a stepladder in the kitchen to make it and a lot of newspaper on the floor.

600ML/1 PINT CREAM
25G/1 OZ/2 TABLESPOONS GRANULATED SUGAR
1 LEAF OR ½ SACHET GELATINE
A FEW DROPS VANILLA ESSENCE
3 TABLESPOONFULS APRICOT JAM
A WINE GLASS (50ML) OF MEDIUM DRY SHERRY
1 LEMON

Boil 1 pint of good cream for a few minutes with a little sugar, the melted gelatine and a few drops of vanilla or ratafia essence. *Stir the jam, sherry and grated rind and juice of the lemon together until well mixed, and until the jam has dissolved.* Have ready a deep glass dish, cover the bottom with the *jam, sherry and lemon* mixture. When the cream has cooled *transfer it into a jug, place the glass dish on the floor, or out of doors to minimize splashing, and* pour it into this dish from as high as you can. Let it stand overnight in a cool place before using. In the morning the cream will be all bubbly and aerated. (*You may need to wipe the splattered sides of the dish clean before chilling it, which can be done in the fridge instead of the cellar.*)

Treacle Tart.

Serves 6

In the days when families bought a fresh white loaf every day, treacle tart was one of many ways to use up yesterday's bread. It has become one of the all-time greats. "Treacle" really means golden syrup. The lion lying down on Lyle's golden syrup tin is not asleep, he is dead. The picture and the quotation, "Out of the strong came forth sweetness", refers to the Bible story (Judges 14:14) of Samson's riddle – a swarm of bees was discovered in a dead lion's body.

The secret of success lies in the proportion of syrup to bread crumbs: too much syrup, and the mixture is too sloppy; too much bread and it becomes too solid. The inclusion of a lemon is important to stop the tart being sickly sweet.

For the pastry:
85G/3OZ GROUND ALMONDS
85G/3OZ PLAIN FLOUR
85G/3OZ BUTTER

For the filling:
4 HEAPED TABLESPOONS OF FRESH WHITE BREADCRUMBS
5 TABLESPOONS GOLDEN SYRUP
GRATED RIND AND JUICE OF 1 LARGE LEMON

Whiz the pastry ingredients in a food processor, adding a little water if necessary to make a dough. Wrap it in cling-film and chill for half an hour. Set the oven at 190°C.

Roll out the pastry and line a 20cm/8in flan ring or tart tin. Using a spoon dipped in hot water, measure the golden syrup into a saucepan. Stir in the lemon rind and juice and warm the mixture until the syrup has melted. Stir in the breadcrumbs and leave the mixture to stand for 10 minutes, so the crumbs can soak up the syrup. If the mixture is too stiff, add a little more warmed syrup, if too sloppy add more crumbs.

Pour the mixture into the pastry case and bake in the oven for about 25 minutes. Check after 20 minutes to make sure the pastry is not burning, and if necessary cover loosely with foil. When the filling is golden brown, remove the tart from the oven. Let it stand for 15 to 30 minutes and serve it warm with clotted cream or crème fraiche.

Variation: I'm a purist about treacle tart, and don't like it messed with. For example, the school version with cornflakes instead of breadcrumbs always disappointed. But porridge oats and breadcrumbs half-and-half goes down well.

Tessa and Jane's Apple and Chestnut Layers.
Serves 6

When we were young and unmarried and working in London, Tessa and I shared a flat. When friends came to dinner we made this instant pudding and it was always a great success. Rather than cooking the apples, we used to buy several tins of apple purée baby food. Clement Faugier is still making tinned chestnut purée as a by-product of *marrons glacés*, and the design of the tin has not changed in 50 years. Be sure to get the sweetened version.

700G (1LB 9OZ) COOKING APPLES
3 OR 4 TABLESPOONS CASTER SUGAR
1 LARGE TIN SWEETENED CHESTNUT PURÉE
300ML/½ PINT DOUBLE CREAM
DARK CHOCOLATE

Peel and slice the apples. Cook them with 2 tablespoons of sugar until they are soft and mushy. Purée them in a food processor or blender, adding more sugar if necessary. They should remain quite tart as the chestnut mixture is very sweet. Leave the apple purée to get cold. Whip the cream.

In a glass bowl or in six large wine glasses, put a layer of apple, then a layer of chestnut purée, then a layer of whipped cream. Grate a little chocolate over the top.

Trifle.

Serves 6-8

*I remember very delicious trifle with everything homemade: sponge cake soaked in
sherry, strawberry jam, custard, thick layer of whipped cream; decorated with
ratafias and blanched almonds. If I made it, would anybody eat that now?*
MADELINE WILKS

Yes, please, I would, to exorcise the memory of a far less delicious version
that used to appear at children's parties. A layer of soggy stale cake lay at
the bottom of a glass dish, above which floated tinned fruit embedded in red
jelly like flies in amber, and above that, yellow custard thick with cornflour.
On top lay a blanket of what appeared to be shaving foam, dusted with multi-
coloured Hundreds and Thousands and decorated with glacé cherries and
angelica. Ugh.

The following recipe is all that a trifle should be, admittedly rich, but the
presence of fresh fruit prevents it being too sweet and cloying.

HALF A SPONGE CAKE OR 6 TRIFLE SPONGES
RASPBERRY OR STRAWBERRY JAM
150ML/¼ PINT SWEET SHERRY OR MARSALA
450G/1LB RASPBERRIES OR STRAWBERRIES (SLICED)
300ML/½ PINT DOUBLE CREAM
FLAKED ALMONDS, TOASTED

Break up the sponge cake, spread jam on the pieces and put them at the bottom of a glass bowl. Sprinkle the Marsala or sherry over the cake. When it has
soaked in, scatter the strawberries or raspberries over the cake.

Make the custard in the way described on page 242-3, using half milk, half
single cream. Leave it to get cold and pour it over the fruit. Whip the double
cream and spread it over the custard. Chill and, shortly before serving, scatter
toasted, flaked almonds over the top.

Granny's Foam Pudding with Granny's Custard.

Serves 6

My mother-in law used to make this for my children — they insisted on it on every visit to those grandparents and now my grandchildren HAVE to have it when they come here. I have to make double the amount of custard to serve separately as everyone loves it. Once I cheated and bought Tesco's finest but my 12-year-old granddaughter knew immediately and I was so ticked off I have never cheated again.

DIANA ROYDEN

300ML / ½ PINT HOT WATER
125G / 4½OZ SUGAR
JUICE AND RIND OF 1 LARGE LEMON
2 TABLESPOONS CORNFLOUR
2 EGG WHITES

Melt the sugar in the hot water, add the lemon rind, bring to the boil and leave to infuse for half an hour. Strain into a jug. Mix the cornflour with enough of the lemon syrup to make a thin cream, stirring until smooth. Add the rest of the syrup and bring the mixture to the boil, stirring all the time until it is smooth and thick. Boil for 6 or 7 minutes, stirring occasionally. Remove from the heat and leave to get cold.

In a large bowl, whisk the egg whites until stiff. Pour on the cornflour mixture and continue beating for 10 minutes or until the mixture has trebled in size. Fold in the lemon juice, then turn the foam into a large glass bowl.

Use the two egg yolks to make custard (see pages 242-3). When the custard is cold, pour it slowly, from a height, into the centre of the white foam, so that it sinks to the bottom of the bowl. Serve with extra custard.

Meringues.

My mother made the most wonderful meringues. The tips would just curl over and a crisp, crunchy outer shell would envelop a delightfully chewy interior – resistant yet melting, a medley of textures. As a child, I remember being stunned by the ease with which she transformed the viscous egg whites into airy, billowing clouds. By contrast I battled to hold the beater steady with my left hand while turning the handle laboriously and shakily with the right as it skittered around the bowl.
"When you're older you'll be able to do it," she reassured.
Still, the meringues I make have never come close to how I know they can be.
PRUE SALASKY, IN AN ARTICLE IN THE DAILY PRESS,
NEWPORT NEWS, VIRGINIA, USA

Meringues – confections of air trapped in sugar – have almost universal appeal, but only when properly made: "my hate as a child was shop-bought meringues, probably made of synthetic ingredients as rationing was still in place," a grandmother writes, "They were meant to be a treat but I really could not swallow them. But I love them now, with cream inside." I too remember those ersatz shop-bought meringues, made, it seemed, from sweetened blackboard chalk.

But home-made meringues were always a treat, appearing at birthdays, stuck together with whipped cream, chocolate or coffee cream, or vanilla ice cream. Meringues à la Suisse were piled in a dish with layers of melted chocolate and whipped cream, the top dusted with chopped, roasted almonds. Strawberry Mess, invented at Eton College, consisted of broken meringues, mashed strawberries and cream. Very simple and very delicious.

I used to have a problem with meringues. Either a pool of syrup oozed out of each meringue while they were cooking, or else they stuck so hard to the baking sheet that they shattered into a hundred shards when I tried to prize them off. It ended in tears.

Now I have finally got the hang of it. These rules are foolproof:

1. Never use less than 55g/2oz of sugar for each egg white.

2. Whisk the egg whites until you can turn the bowl upside-down without them falling out.

3. Whisk 2 large tablespoons of sugar into the egg whites before folding in the rest.

4. Set the mixture out on baking parchment rather than straight on to a metal sheet.

5. Leave the oven door open a crack to let the meringues dry out as they cook. Two hours in the bottom oven of an AGA (the temperature is 100°C in mine) does it.

There are two schools of thought as to what colour a meringue should be. One grandmother's pride was shattered by her grandson's reaction when her meringues emerged from the oven the perfect shade of pale café-au-lait: "My other granny makes white ones," he remarked.

Different meringue effects can be created by using soft brown sugar instead of caster, or by adding cocoa or ground hazelnuts (125g/4½ oz of cocoa or nuts to 4 egg whites and 8oz sugar) to the meringue mixture.

Gateau Diane.
Serves 8-10

Constance Spry's recipe was a very popular party pudding. Make it the day before you need it.

For the meringue (see page 257, using quantities below):
4 EGG WHITES
250G/9OZ CASTER SUGAR

For the filling:
2 EGG WHITES
115G/4OZ ICING SUGAR
225G/8OZ UNSALTED BUTTER, SOFTENED
100G/3⅓OZ GOOD DARK CHOCOLATE
CHOPPED TOASTED ALMONDS

Set the oven at 100°C. Cover 2 baking sheets with baking parchment.
Make the meringue: Whip the 4 egg whites until stiff, whisk in 2 tablespoons of the caster sugar, then fold in the rest. Spread the meringue into 4 discs about 6mm/¼ in thick, 2 on each baking sheet.

Cook in a slow oven until crisp, 1½ to 2 hours. Turn them over and put them back in the oven to dry out, for about 10 minutes with the oven door ajar.
Make the filling: Whip the 2 egg whites with the icing sugar over a gentle heat until thick. Cream the butter well, melt the chocolate and let it cool. Beat the egg white mixture into the butter and add the chocolate.

Use some of the chocolate cream to sandwich the meringue discs one above the other. Spread the rest over the sides and top, and cover with the toasted almonds. Chill the cake and serve it the next day.

Variations: Sandwich the meringue layers with coffee cream or whipped cream and strawberries or raspberries, but then it is no longer Gateau Diane.

Mont Blanc.

Serves 4

Another pudding remembered from birthday meals in restaurants.

450G/1LB CHESTNUTS OR A LARGE TIN OF SWEETENED CHESTNUT PURÉE
PINCH OF SALT
115G/4OZ ICING SUGAR, SIFTED
150ML/¼ PINT DOUBLE CREAM
8 MERINGUES (SEE PAGES 256-7)
MARRONS GLACÉS TO DECORATE (OPTIONAL)

If you are using whole, fresh chestnuts, make criss-cross slits on the skins of each chestnut with a sharp knife. Cover them with water and boil gently for 15 minutes. While they are still hot, remove the shells and inner skins. Cover the shelled chestnuts with water and simmer for 45 minutes to 1 hour, until they are very soft. Drain thoroughly, mash in a bowl, add the sugar and salt and beat until smooth. Leave the mixture to get cold.

Halve the meringues and form circles with the pieces on 4 small plates. If the chestnut purée is stiff enough, force it through a potato-ricer on to each meringue circle so that it forms a cone-shaped mound of chestnut vermicelli. If the purée is too soft, or you don't have a ricer, just heap it up with a spoon. Shortly before serving, whip the cream until thick and heap it over the chestnuts like snow on a mountain. Decorate the base with marrons glacés.

Hot Chocolate Soufflés.

From Entertaining on Ice by Tessa Hayward.
Serves 8

Aparty pud to prepare in advance for the freezer, and to cook from frozen at the last minute.

100G/3½ OZ BEST QUALITY PLAIN CHOCOLATE
25G/1OZ CORNFLOUR
300ML/½ PINT MILK
75G/2½ OZ SUGAR
5 EGG WHITES
3 EGG YOLKS
50G/2OZ PLAIN CHOCOLATE CHIPS
ICING SUGAR TO FINISH

Advance preparation: Generously grease 8 large (150ml/¼ pint capacity) ramekins with butter.

Melt the chocolate in a bowl set over a pan of boiling water, stir until it is smooth then set it aside. Mix the cornflour to a smooth paste with a little of the milk, then stir in 50g/1¾ oz of the sugar and the rest of the milk. Pour into a saucepan and, stirring constantly, bring the mixture to the boil. Let it bubble gently for a minute, remove from the heat and stir in the chocolate. Leave the mixture to cool until it is tepid, stirring occasionally to prevent a skin forming.

Whisk the egg whites stiff, add the remaining sugar and continue whisking for a few moments until you have a glossy meringue mixture. Stir the egg yolks into the chocolate mixture, then add the chocolate chips. Gradually fold in the meringue misture, and then spoon it into the ramekins. Cover with a double layer of cling-film and freeze.

Cooking and serving: Preheat the oven to 190°C.

Cook the frozen soufflés for 30 to 35 minutes until well risen and brown on the top. They should still be slightly liquid in the middle. Sieve a little icing sugar over each one and serve immediately. Hand round a jug of cream or, even better, cream laced with a little brandy, to pour into the centre of each.

Ice Creams, Sorbets and Toppings.

You could tell the story of my life in ice cream… the merest sniff of
chocolate ice cream has been known to bring back memories from 20, 30,
40 years ago with frightening clarity. Put that same ice cream on a little
wooden spoon and I can recall the cinema I was in when I ate it, the feel
of the (red) velvet seats on the back of my bare knees, the colour of
the ice cream attendant's overall (lemon, with green piping).
NIGEL SLATER

Nigel Slater's vivid description prompted memories of the ice creams of my own childhood. We bought cornets, wafers, or choc ices on the way home from school, once safely out of sight of the school gates, defying the school's "no eating in the streets" rule. We did, however, stick religiously to a parental rule which insisted we only buy ices made by Wall's or Lyons'; from less trustworthy brands, it was thought, one might catch polio. Satchels containing the Shortbread Eating Primer trailed from our shoulders and we wore our uniforms defiantly St Trinian's style, grey woollen socks concertina-ed and felt hats battered. Ice cream dripped from the bitten-off bottoms of cornets on to our ties.

Bought ice cream came in white ("vanilla"), pink ("strawberry") or brown ("chocolate"). All the colours tasted much the same, and were reputed to be made from whale blubber. At home we had, as an occasional treat, "real" ice cream, made with eggs and milk, and sometimes even cream, frozen in the ice trays of the fridge. Vanilla ice cream was eaten with hot puddings, or fruity ones, and sometimes came on its own with a hot sauce: chocolate, toffee, fudge, mincemeat, raspberry, melted Mars bars or Crunchies. Later, when we had children of our own, and their friends to feed, an ice cream machine was one of our best investments.

Ovaltine Ice Cream.

We are the Ovaltineys, little girls and boys…
Because we all drink Ovaltine, we're happy girls and boys.
RADIO LUXEMBOURG, 1935

This quick and easy recipe is a homage to Ovaltine, the malted milk drink we used to have for elevenses and, when suffering from colds or flu, as a bed-time drink. When nobody was looking, I used to eat the crunchy granules with a spoon, straight from the tin. Still do, actually. Ovaltine was also available in solid form, as small tablets which could be passed around under desks at school: crunch, crunch! And it was gone.

175G/6OZ SOFT BROWN SUGAR
85G/3OZ COCOA
150ML/¼ PINT BOILING WATER
150G/5½OZ OVALTINE
400ML/14 FL OZ WHOLE MILK
400ML/14 FL OZ SINGLE CREAM

Mix the sugar, cocoa and boiling water until smooth. Add the Ovaltine and stir it until smooth. Add the milk and cream and leave the mixture to get cold. Freeze it in an ice cream machine.

Rob's Damson Ice Cream.

Rob is the ice cream maker in our house. He grows the fruit or takes a picking party to the local fruit farm, prepares it and turns it into ice cream. After many years of making it the hard way, by adding fruit purée and whipped cream to an egg and sugar mousse, we held tasting tests and discovered that the easy way, simply mixing fruit purée with cream and freezing it, brings just as good results. Rob says the important thing is to keep on tasting: taste the fruit purée for sweetness before adding the cream, and taste during the final stage before freezing, holding back some of the cream if the flavour is in danger of becoming bland. His damson is best of all, but blackcurrant and raspberry (add the juice of ½ a lemon) are close contenders.

700G/1LB 9OZ DAMSONS
250G/9OZ SUGAR
450ML/16 FL OZ WHIPPING CREAM

Put the damsons into a saucepan with 200g of the sugar and enough water barely to cover the base of the pan. Cook them gently with the lid on until the juice runs. Stir to dissolve the sugar and continue to simmer until the fruit is soft.

Sieve the damsons, pressing the juice through the sieve but not pushing too much pulp through. Allow the purée to get quite cold, and taste, adding more sugar if it is not sweet enough. Stir in most of the cream and taste again. Add the rest of the cream little by little until the strength tastes right. Put the mixture into a jug and pour it into an ice-cream machine. If you don't have a machine, put it in a plastic bowl in the freezer. When it is partly frozen, take it out and beat with an electric whisk before returning it to the freezer.

Take the ice cream out of the freezer half an hour or so before you eat it.

Tip: Home-made ice cream is best eaten within a few weeks, so don't leave it in the freezer too long.

Black-Currant Leaf Water Ice.

*... Russian Ice, a recipe acquired from a Muscovite friend and useful to
those who can beg, borrow, or pluck from black-currant bushes a large handful
of their youngest leaves. ...It resembles lemon water ice in appearance,
but the flavour is a far more ethereal one and endued with the compelling
power of the Blarney Stone.*
KITCHEN ESSAYS BY LADY JEKYLL, DBE, 1922

My mother used to make this as a summer treat.

500G / 1LB 2OZ GRANULATED SUGAR
A LARGE HANDFUL OF YOUNG BLACKCURRANT LEAVES
JUICE OF 6 LEMONS

In a saucepan, dissolve the sugar in 600ml/1 pint of water. Bring to the boil
and boil rapidly for 5 minutes. Add the blackcurrant leaves, cover the pan
and leave to cool for 2 hours. Strain the syrup, stir in the lemon juice. Taste
and if the mixture is too strong, dilute with a little water. But remember that
freezing will reduce the strength and sweetness of the flavours. Freeze in an
ice cream machine.

Variations: Elderflowers instead of blackcurrant leaves make an intriguingly
aromatic and refreshing sorbet. This is also the basic technique for all fruit
sorbets. Most fruits benefit from the addition of one or two lemons to bring
out their flavour. Blackberry sorbet has a specially delicate taste, redcurrants
and raspberries mixed are excellent and exotic juices from the health food shop
are worth trying as sorbets.

Hugh's Vanilla Fudge Ice Cream.

One of our son Hugh's earliest commercial enterprises consisted of making his Special Vanilla Fudge Ice Cream in the school holidays and selling it to one of our closest friends for her dinner parties. It always went down a treat. The fudge recipe came off a condensed milk tin, and the ice cream is made by Constance Spry's classic egg mousse method, which we still swear by for vanilla ice cream.

For the fudge:
(SEE CHAPTER 11, TREATS AND SWEETS, PAGE 272.)

For the ice cream:
200G/7OZ SUGAR
300ML/½ PINT WATER
6 EGG YOLKS
1 LITRE/1¾ PINTS DOUBLE CREAM
1 TEASPOON VANILLA EXTRACT

Dissolve the sugar in the water and boil hard for 5 minutes or until the syrup forms a thread. In a bowl, whisk the egg yolks and slowly pour in the hot syrup, whisking all the time until the mixture is pale and mousse-like. Lightly whip the cream and fold it in, with the vanilla. Put the mixture in the freezer or churn it in an ice cream machine.

Break about 150g/5½ oz of the fudge into little pieces. When the ice cream is half frozen, or has finished churning but is still soft, stir in the fudge. Freeze.

London Granny's Fudge-y Gunge.

Modern cooks know this as the main ingredient in Banoffee Pie. It's bad for the teeth and bad for the figure, and for anyone who loves sweet treats, totally addictive. Granny served it with vanilla ice cream.

1 TIN OF SWEETENED CONDENSED MILK

Boil the tin, unopened, for 3 hours. Allow it to cool, then open it and spoon out the contents which will be like soft caramel toffee.

Granny Ray's Chocolate Sauce.
Serves 6

My cousin Prue Salasky sent me her mother's (my godmother's) recipe. It was first published in Prue's column in the *Daily Press*, Newport News, Virginia, USA.

40G / 1½ OZ BUTTER
9 TABLESPOONS SOFT BROWN SUGAR
9 TABLESPOONS BEST-QUALITY COCOA
3 TABLESPOONS BLACK COFFEE

Melt the butter over a low heat. Stir in the sugar, then the cocoa and black coffee. Mix well, stirring constantly. Serve the sauce immediately, while warm, over vanilla ice cream.

Big Granny's Butterscotch Sauce.

My mother used to make this, and I had forgotten all about it until my brother told me he and his family had kept it going and still loved it.

250G/8OZ GRANULATED SUGAR
50G/2OZ BUTTER
75ML/3 FL OZ DOUBLE CREAM

Put the sugar into a saucepan with 150ml (¼ pint) water, and stir until the sugar is dissolved. Heat it and boil rapidly until it forms a caramel syrup. Let it cool a little, then whisk in the butter followed by the cream. Serve it hot with vanilla ice cream.

Variation: Add chopped walnuts.

Chapter 11.

Treats and Sweets.

9 Recipes

I have always been against the "Bread-and-butter-before-cake" line of thought since, in my long-and-long-ago, an enlightened hostess excited a solemn children's tea-party to ecstasy by the magical words, "Now! Let's start with the strawberries and cream!"
MOLLY KEANE

Peppermint Creams.

No cooking involved

450G/1LB ICING SUGAR
1 EGG WHITE
50ML/2 FL OZ DOUBLE CREAM
OIL OF PEPPERMINT OR PEPPERMINT ESSENCE

Mix the sugar, egg white and cream together, adding the peppermint drop by drop until it tastes right. Dust a clean, dry surface with icing sugar and roll out the paste to about ½ cm/¼ in thick. If it is too sticky, keep adding icing sugar until it is the right consistency. Using a small cutter, stamp out rounds, set them on a wire rack and leave them to dry for about 12 hours.

Pecan Pralines.

My maternal grandmother came from New Orleans and used to make
Pecan Pralines as a special treat for us — the pecans having been
ordered fresh from Louisiana.
SALLIE COOLIDGE

900G/2LB GRANULATED SUGAR
1 TEASPOON SALT
500ML/18 FL OZ CREAM
700G/1LB 9OZ PECAN HALVES

Mix 700g/1lb 9oz of the sugar with the salt and cream, stirring until the sugar has dissolved. In a heavy-based saucepan, dissolve the rest of the sugar slowly over a low heat, stirring constantly until it forms a caramel-coloured syrup. Add the sugar and cream mixture all at once and stir vigorously. Boil without stirring until a little of the mixture dropped into cold water will form a soft ball. Stir in the pecan halves and drop teaspoonfuls on to a tin or board lined with baking parchment or greased foil.

Fudge.

My mother (Granny Babs) used to make this fudge every Christmas, right up until she died aged 79. The recipe has been passed on to all her children and grandchildren, and now her great-grandchildren are enjoying it too. It really is comfort food, and evokes memories of Christmasses sitting round the fire eating home-made sweeties and retelling family stories again and again with much enjoyment by the teller and the listeners.
LESLEY FLANNAGAN

It's the grainy texture that makes home-made fudge so special. Hugh F-W's recipe is much the same as Granny Babs', but he gives double the quantities, so, on the grounds that you can never have too much fudge even if it makes you feel sick, his is the version I give here.

300ML/½ PINT FRESH MILK
250G/9OZ BUTTER
1 KILO/2LB 4OZ GRANULATED SUGAR
2 TABLESPOONS GOLDEN SYRUP
1 LARGE TIN CONDENSED MILK
1 TEASPOON VANILLA EXTRACT

Lightly grease a shallow tin. Put the fresh milk, butter and sugar into a heavy based saucepan over a low heat and stir until the sugar has dissolved. Add the syrup and condensed milk and bring the mixture slowly to the boil. Simmer, stirring continuously, for up to 35 minutes, perhaps longer. To test for the setting point, drop a little of the mixture into cold water. If it will press into a soft ball, the fudge is ready.

Remove it from the heat and let it cool for five minutes. Add the vanilla essence and beat with a wooden spoon until the texture is thick and grainy. Pour it into the tin and leave until partially set. Mark into 2½ cm/1in squares with a sharp knife. When the fudge is cold, cut it into squares.

Melting Moments.
Makes 16

These little goodies are neither cakes nor biscuits nor sweets, but share the characteristics of all three.

115G/4OZ BUTTER, SOFTENED
75G/3OZ CASTER SUGAR
1 EGG YOLK
½ TEASPOON VANILLA EXTRACT
115G/4OZ SELF-RAISING FLOUR
ABOUT 55G/2OZ PORRIDGE OATS, CRUSHED WITH A ROLLING PIN

Line 2 baking trays with baking parchment. Put the oats on a plate or shallow dish.

Beat the butter and sugar together until light and fluffy; beat in the egg yolk and vanilla, and stir in the flour. Work the mixture together lightly with your hands. Then, using a teaspoon, form the dough into small balls and flatten them slightly with your palm. Put each little cake in the oats and coat it all over. Set them well apart on the trays as they will spread to more than double their original size. Refrigerate for 20 minutes. Meanwhile, set the oven at 180°C. Bake the Moments for about 15 minutes, then cool on a wire rack.

Ginger Beer.

A fizzy, non-alcoholic drink, chilled ginger beer is refreshing on a hot summer day. It makes children feel sophisticated, and the homemade version is less sweet than commercial kinds. Mixed half and half with ale, it makes a traditional shandy.

2 LEMONS

115G/4OZ ROOT GINGER

450G/1 LB GRANULATED SUGAR

25G/1OZ/2 TABLESPOONS CREAM OF TARTAR

5½ LITRES/10 PINTS BOILING WATER

1 TABLESPOON DRIED YEAST

Pare the lemon rind thinly. Squeeze and reserve the lemon juice. Bruise the ginger by crushing it with a hammer or pestle.

Put all the ingredients except the yeast and the lemon juice into a large crock and leave the mixture to cool until it is blood temperature. Cream the yeast and add it to the mixture. Leave it to stand for 12 hours.

Strain it, add the lemon juice, and pour it through a funnel into sterilized bottles. Seal the bottles and keep in a cool place for 2 or 3 days, by which time it should be ready to drink.

Damson Cheese.

The old-fashioned term "sweetmeats" best describes fruit cheeses, and they are well worth making at times of glut. The intensely flavoured jellied preserve is cut into cubes to eat with cheese or, instead of the more usual redcurrant jelly, with game and other meat. If cooked for a shorter time, their consistency will be softer, and they can be used as spreads on bread or toast.

1KG/2LB 4OZ DAMSONS
ABOUT 500G/1LB 2OZ GRANULATED SUGAR

Wash the fruit and put it in a heavy-based saucepan with 150ml/¼ pint of water. Bring to the boil and simmer gently until the fruit is very soft. This may take an hour or more.

Rub the fruit through a nylon sieve. Measure the purée and add 450g/1lb of sugar to each pint. Stir until the sugar is dissolved, bring to the boil and boil for 1 to 1½ hours, stirring and scraping the bottom of the pan to stop the mixture sticking. It is ready when the spoon leaves a clear line when scraped across the bottom of the pan.

Let the mixture cool a little, pour it into an oiled, shallow tin and, when cold, remove it from the tin, wrap it in cling-film and refrigerate it. Store in an airtight tin, and cut into cubes when needed.

Variations: Instead of damsons, use quinces (in Spain quince cheese is called *membrillo*), gooseberries, apples, specially crab apples, or a mixture of apples and pears.

Bilbrook Uncooked Raspberry Jam.

This recipe comes from my mother's old home, Bilbrook in Shropshire.
It was also very much part of my childhood in Dorset — jam sandwiches
and lemonade at teatime and for picnics.
SALT EDWARDS

Because the raspberries are not heated beyond boiling point, they retain their
fresh taste. The jam is delicious on bread or toast, and raspberry jam fea-
tures again and again in recipes for puddings and cakes, so it is hardly possible
to have too much of it.

1.8KG/4LB RASPBERRIES
2.25KG/5LB SUGAR

Put the raspberries in a large bowl and heat them in the oven. Put the sugar in
another bowl and heat it in the oven. When the raspberries are very hot but
not boiling, remove them and the sugar from the oven and beat the fruit, gradually adding the sugar and beating it in. Continue until the sugar has all dissolved. Put the jam into sterilized jars, seal and label.

Chocolate Cornflakes.
(or Rice Krispies or puffed wheat)
Makes about 15

100G/3½ OZ BEST-QUALITY PLAIN CHOCOLATE
4 TABLESPOONS GOLDEN SYRUP
50G/1¾ OZ BUTTER
75G/2½ OZ CORNFLAKES

B reak up the chocolate and put it in a bowl with the syrup and butter. Melt over a bowl of hot water, and stir to mix. Off the heat, stir in the cornflakes, spoon the mixture into paper cases and leave in a cool place to set.

Granny's Chocolate Sandwiches.

T o be eaten as a surprise treat at breakfast, elevenses, lunch or tea.

2 SLICES OF BREAD PER PERSON
BUTTER
A LARGE BAR OF DARK CHOCOLATE

Butter the bread and arrange squares of chocolate evenly over half the slices. Put them in the AGA for 30 seconds (optional) before squishing another slice of buttered bread on top.

Acknowledgements.

First I want to thank Victoria Merrill and my husband Rob, who separately and simultaneously came up with the idea for this book. Rob is the person who eats most of my cooking, when I am not eating his. He is my sternest but also my most appreciative critic, and has patiently put up with the occasional mood swing when things have not been going well on the kitchen front.

This book would not exist without the people who are no longer here to thank: my parents and grandparents, and their contemporaries, whose cooking is celebrated in this book.

I am lucky enough to have three professional food writers in the family, and I have picked their brains mercilessly: they have been very patient and creative in their advice, and generous in allowing me to use their recipes. So, very special thanks to our son Hugh Fearnley-Whittingstall, author of, among other food books, the *River Cottage* series; to my cousin Tessa Hayward, whose books include *The Magimix Cake Book* and *The Salmon Cookbook*. Tessa and I grew up together, eating the same food, so she has a unique personal understanding of the theme of this book. She has not only given permission to include some of her recipes, but has been generous with her time, testing other recipes and making very constructive suggestions. Further afield, my cousin Prue Salasky was, for 18 years, food editor of the *Daily Press* in Newport News, Virginia. She has prompted my memories of her mother Ray's wonderful cooking, and passed on Ray's recipes.

I would like to thank all those who have been guinea pigs: the friends who have come to stay, or just to lunch or dinner and have been subjected to recipe tests; also our children and grandchildren, Sophy and Nick with their sons, Max and Guy; and Hugh and Marie with Chloe, Oscar and Freddie. Fortunately, the guinea pigs' verdict has more often been "yummy" than "yucky".

I know some of the recipes so well that I did not need to test them, but of the rest, I have cooked as many of them as could. I am grateful to Sophy for taking on others. There are some recipes completely new to me which I could not have published with any confidence had Sallie Coolidge not tried them and given a favourable verdict. I am extremely lucky to have had her professional expertise and experience to rely on.

The book is based as much on other people's food memories and recipes as my own and my family's. Friends and acquaintances have been very generous with both their recollections and their recipes, and I wish I could have included all of them in the book. I now have more than enough on file for another book, should the occasion arise!

Thank you very much indeed, Shona Anderson, Janet Bagley, Gerda Barlow, Merle Barrington, Ruth Biddiss, Sue Bowen, Jill Carlisle, Pat Churchill, Teen Cooke, Carole Cox, Carole D'Albiac, Sybil D'Albiac, Jan Dalley, Amanda Edwards, April Edwards, Bonnie Etchell, Anne Fearnley-Whittingstall, Gail Fearnley-Whittingstall, Lesley Flanagan, the Frearson family, Caroline Fuglistaller, Katherine Futers, Victoria Gledhill, Carol Guise, Liz Hammond, Lyla Harling, Ann Harthill, Sczerina Hichens, Kay Holme, Amanda Hornby, Guy Hungerford, Caroline Jowett, Anne and Peter Lascelles, Val Marriott, Alison McMahon, Marlene Noble, Mira Osmond, Janice Palmer, Roz Paynter-Reece, Tom Roberts, Diana Royden, Julie Ryman, Prue Salasky, Colin Senior, Sarah Sharpe, Diana Shepherd, Elise Smith, Sandra Smith-Gordon, Mary Spyromilio, Cicely Taylor, Helen Thomas, Ruth Watson, Derek Webb, Tessa White, Madeline Wilks, Francine Yorke, Alyn Younie.

Special thanks to Catherine Corbett for lending me her copy of *The Times Cookbook* which Rex chewed up 30 years ago.

I also thank Josceline Dimbleby for kindly giving permission to use her recipe for Lamb Casserole with Cinnamon, to Virago Press for permission to use two recipes from *Fish, Flesh and Good Red Herring* by Alice Thomas Ellis and to HarperCollins for permission to quote from Lady Maclean's Cookbook.

I am very grateful to Alex Fox for his illustrations, which capture the spirit of the book so well and to Georgia Vaux for her elegant and evocative design. I would like to thank Aurea Carpenter and Rebecca Nicolson for their confidence in me, their enthusiasm for the book, and their imperturbable efficiency, and Emily Fox and Vanessa Webb for always being so cheerful and helpful.

Index.

A

All in one fruit cake 177
Anchovies
  Janssen's temptation 212,
  213
  salade Nicoise 150
Andrew's spinach supper 89
Angel cake USA 166, 167
Anne's beef stew 116, 117
Apples
  apple in and out 225
  blackberry and apple
  pudding 224
  Bramley apple and celeriac
  soup 190
  Bramley burnt creams 226
  Gloucestershire squab
  pie 80
  mini apple tarts 243
  nusskuchen 174, 175
  slow roasted pork belly
  with cider 124
  Somerset chicken 90
  Tessa and Jane's apple and
  chestnut layers 253
  uses of 223
Apricot soufflé 249
Armand 2001 marmalade
  32, 33
Aubergines
  cheesy baked aubergines
  140
  lamb with aubergines and
  cinnamon 128
  Mary's proper Greek
  moussaka 82

B

Bacon
  creamed sprouts with
  chestnuts and bacon 138
  devils on horseback 211
  greens with bacon and
  onion 134, 135
  leek and bacon tart 95
  Lord Melville 205
  pick and mix fry-up 27
  Rob's lunchtime salad 153
Barley salad 149
Barlow, Gerda 55
Beef
  Anne's beef stew 116, 117
  billabong stew 113
  bobotie 114, 115
  boeuf à la mode 48, 49
  boiled beef and carrots
  with Diana's dumplings 46
  Cornish pasties 84
  Hungarian goulash 88
  steak and kidney pudding
  52, 53
  stovies 70
Beetroot
  red flannel hash 68
Belgium shortbread 178
Big Granny's butterscotch
  sauce 267
Big Granny's chicken and
  ham pie 56, 57
Billabong stew 113
Biscuits
  Belgium shortbread 178
  brandy snaps 179

choc chip cookies 180
chocolate fork biscuits 184
Crow's nicky-nacky men
  182
devilled biscuits 218
flapjacks 184
fork biscuits 184
gipsy creams 181
Mary's biscuits 184
orange jumbles 183
Black pudding
  pick and mix fry-up 27
Black-currant leaf water ice
  264
Blackberries
  blackberry and apple
  pudding 224
  blackberry cobbler 235
Bobotie 114, 115
Boeuf à la mode 48, 49
Boiled eggs with Marmite
  soldiers 36
Borlotti beans
  pork and beans 64
Brandy snaps 179
Bread
  cinnamon toast 33
  eggy bread 37
  French toast 37
  garlic bread 204
  Marmite soldiers 36
  Potter's loaf 202, 203
Breakfast
  cooked dishes 24
  Edwardian 22
  fruit 24
  pick and mix fry-up 27
  recipes 25-37

Index

traditional dishes 23
Brussels sprouts
  creamed sprouts with
  chestnuts and bacon 138
Bubble and squeak 61
Butter beans
  tuna and bean salad 108
Butterscotch
  big Granny's butterscotch
  sauce 267

C

Cabbage
  braised red cabbage with
  spicy sausages 91
  bubble and squeak 61
  colcannon 61
Cakes
  all in one fruit cake 177
  angel cake USA 166, 167
  chocolate biscuit cake 171
  chocolate cake 168
  chocolate eclairs 170
  lemon drizzle cake 176
  London Granny's crusty
  sponge cake 173
  Loney's sticky ginger cake
  172
  madeleines 175
  nusskuchen 174, 175
  Swiss roll 176, 177
Canary pudding 229
Carrots
  carrot fritters 142
  carrots Vichy 136, 137
  potage Crécy 193
  three root mash 146
Castle puddings with home
  made jam 227
Cauliflower cheese 135
Celeriac

Bramley apple and celeriac
  soup 190
celeriac fritters 142
celeriac remoulade with
  walnuts 151
Cheese
  Andrew's spinach supper
  89
  cauliflower cheese 135
  cheese pudding 78
  cheesy baked aubergines
  140
  cheesy eggs 79
  courgette frittatas 137
  gardener's pie 139
  gougère 217
  London Granny's cheese
  straws 214
  macaroni cheese 83
  pan Haggerty 157, 158
  pork chops Auberge Saint
  Pierre 87
  Welsh rabbit 216
Chestnuts
  creamed sprouts with
  chestnuts and bacon 138
  Mont Blanc 259
  pheasant and chestnut
  casserole 126
  Tessa and Jane's apple and
  chestnut layers 253
Chicken
  Big Granny's chicken and
  ham pie 56, 57
  coq au vin 118, 119
  curried chicken 62
  devilled chicken 63
  Gerda's chicken 55
  head mistress chicken 96
  Hugh's TV chicken dinner
  65
  poulet Grand-Mère 125

savoury pancakes 69
Somerset chicken 90
tarragon-roasted chicken
  54
Chicken livers
  risotto with chicken livers
  86
  warm chicken liver salad
  207
Chicory and orange salad
  152
Chipolata casserole 81
Chocolate
  choc chip cookies 180
  chocolate biscuit cake 171
  chocolate cake 168
  chocolate cornflakes 277
  chocolate eclairs 170
  chocolate sponge pudding
  229
  gateau Diane 258
  gipsy creams 181
  Granny Ray's chocolate
  sauce 266
  Granny's chocolate sand
  wiches 277
  hot chocolate soufflés 260
  nusskuchen 174, 175
Cinnamon
  cinnamon toast 33
  lamb with aubergines and
  cinnamon 128
Colcannon 61
Cookery books 13, 14
Coq au vin 118, 119
Corned beef
  red flannel hash 68
Cornish pasties 84
Courgettes
  courgette frittatas 137
  courgette fritters 142
  courgette soufflé 141

Craig, Elizabeth 24
Cranachan 237
Crème brulée 238
Crème caramel 240
Crème renversée 240
Crow's nicky-nacky men 182
Crudités 206
Cullen skink 191
Curry
  curried chicken 62
  curried eggs 63
  curried lamb 62
  Gerda's chicken 55
Custard 242
Custard tarts 169

D

Damsons
  damson cheese 275
  Rob's damson ice cream 263
Devilled biscuits 218
Devilled chicken 63
Devilled kidneys 25
Devilled turkey 63
Devils on horseback 211
Drop/dropped scones 26

E

Eggs 34
  Andrew's spinach supper 89
  boiled, with Marmite soldiers 36
  cheese pudding 78
  cheesy eggs 79
  crudités 206
  curried eggs 63
  egg mousse 208
  egg sauce 45
  eggy bread 37
  French toast 37
  fried 35
  kedgeree 28
  Lord Melville 205
  oeufs en cocotte 35
  pick and mix fry-up 27
  poached 35
  red flannel hash 68
  salade Nicoise 150
  scrambled 36
  smoked haddock with poached eggs 109
  stuffed eggs 219
Elderflower
  goosegog and elderflower fool 234
  water ice 264
Elevenses 164, 165

F

Fish. See also Haddock, etc
  Friday, on 100
  Italian baked fish 103
  Mum's fish pie 104, 105
  very speedy fish pie 105
Fish cakes 102
Flapjacks 184
Fork biscuits 184
French beans
  salade Nicoise 150
French toast 37
Fried eggs 35
Fruit. See also Apples, etc
  breakfast, for 24
  fools, pies, part, cobblers and crumbles 232
  homegrown 132
  preserving 222
  variety of 133

Fudge 272
  Hugh's vanilla fudge ice cream 265

G

Gammon with parsley sauce 44, 45
Gardener's pie 139
Garlic
  beans with garlic and pine nuts 134
  garlic bread 204
  garlicky spinach soup 195
Gateau Diane 258
Gazpacho 192, 193
Gerda's chicken 55
Ginger
  ginger beer 274
  ginger sponge pudding 229
  Loney's sticky ginger cake 172
  parsnip soup with orange and ginger 194
Gipsy creams 181
Gloucestershire squab pie 80
Goosegog and elderflower fool 234
Gougère 217
Granny B's sausage rolls 215
Granny Ray's chocolate sauce 266
Granny's chocolate sandwiches 277
Granny's foam pudding with Granny's custard 255
Green beans
  beans with garlic and pine nuts 134
Guards pudding 230

Index

H

Haddock
  fish cakes 102
  smoked. See Smoked
  haddock
  stuffed haddock baked in
  foil 109
  very speedy fish pie 105
Ham
  Big Granny's chicken and
  ham pie 56, 57
  ham and leek parcels 72
  Rob's turkeyburgers 72
Hazelnuts
  cranachan 237
  nusskuchen 174, 175
Head mistress chicken 96
Heath, Ambrose 188, 205
Heinz tomato soup 194
Herb dumplings 47
Herby lamb chop
  gratin 97
Hot Cross Buns 30
Hugh's TV chicken dinner
  65
Hugh's vanilla fudge ice
  cream 265
Hungarian goulash 88

I

Ice cream 261
  Hugh's vanilla fudge ice
  cream 265
  Ovaltine ice cream 262
  Rob's damson ice cream
  263
Italian baked fish 103

J

Jam roly poly 231
Janssen's temptation 212,
  213
Jekyll, Lady 24
Jerusalem artichoke soufflé
  141

K

Kaiserschmarrn 244
Kedgeree 28
Kidneys
  devilled kidneys 25
  steak and kidney pudding
  52, 53
Kippers
  marinated kipper fillets 209

L

Lamb
  curried lamb 62
  Gloucestershire squab pie
  80
  herby lamb chop gratin 97
  lamb with aubergines and
  cinnamon 128
  Lancashire hot pot 120
  Mary's proper Greek
  moussaka 82
  Mira's rack of lamb with
  herby mustard crust 43
  navarin of lamb 121
  shepherd's pie 66
  shoulder or leg of lamb à
  la Boulangère 50, 51
  souvlaki 92
  stovies 70
  very slow shoulder of
  lamb 129

Lancashire hot pot 120
Leeks
  fish baked on a bed of
  leeks 101
  ham and leek parcels 72
  leek and bacon tart 95
  leek and potato soup 200
Lemon drizzle cake 176
Lentils
  bobotie 114, 115
  rabbit with lentil purée 122
Lettuce
  pea and lettuce risotto 143
London Granny's cheese
  straws 214
London Granny's crusty
  sponge cake 173
London Granny's fudgey
  gunge 266
Loney's Oatcakes 31
Loney's sticky ginger cake
  172
Lord Melville 205

M

Malone, Mrs (Loney) 12, 24,
  31, 172
Marmalade, Armand 2001
  32, 33
Marmite soldiers 36
Mary's biscuits 184
Mary's proper Greek
  moussaka 82
Meals, structure of 188
Melting moments 273
Meringues 256, 257
  gateau Diane 258
  Mont Blanc 259
  queen of puddings 250
Midweek meals
  dinners 77

recipes 78-97
weekday lunches 76, 77
Milly-Molly-Mandy
  potatoes 156
Minestrone 196
Mira's rack of lamb with
  herby mustard crust 43
Monday left-overs
  cold meat and salad 60
  recipes 61-73
Mont Blanc 259
Moules marinière 106
Moussaka
  Mary's proper Greek
  moussaka 82
Mum's fish pie 104, 105
Mushrooms
  head mistress chicken 96
  mushrooms on toast 213
  pick and mix fry-up 27
Mussels
  moules marinière 106

N

Navarin of lamb 121
Norwegian cream 239
Nusskuchen 174, 175

O

Oats/Oatmeal
  cranachan 237
  cullen skink 191
  flapjacks 184
  Loney's Oatcakes 31
  melting moments 273
  Porridge 23
Oeufs en cocotte 35
Onions
  Gloucestershire squab

pie 80
greens with bacon and
  onion 134, 135
onion boys' soup 201
onion sauce 45
veloute Johnny 201
Oranges
  chicory and orange salad
  152
  orange jumbles 183
  parsnip soup with orange
  and ginger 194
Ovaltine ice cream 262
Oxtail stew 123

P

Pancakes 29
  Kaiserschmarrn 244
  savoury pancakes 69
  Scotch pancakes 26
Parsley
  parsley sauce 45
  parsley soup 198
Parsnips
  parsnip fritters 142
  parsnip soup with orange
  and ginger 194
  three root mash 146
Pasta
  Hugh's TV chicken dinner
  65
  macaroni cheese 83
  spag. Bol. 127
  tomato sauce for 93
Peach Melba 245
Peas
  green pea soup 197
  pea and lettuce risotto 143
Pease pudding 144
Pecan pralines 271

Peppermint creams 270
Peppers
  gazpacho 192, 193
  stuffed peppers 145
Pheasant and chestnut
  casserole 126
Picnics 85
Pies
  Big Granny's chicken and
  ham pie 56, 57
  gardener's pie 139
  Gloucestershire squab pie
  80
  Mum's fish pie 104, 105
  shepherd's pie 66
  steak and kidney pie 53
  very speedy fish pie 105
Pineapple upside-down
  pudding 246
Plaice rolls 108
Plum crumble 233
Plum pudding 241
Poached eggs 35
  red flannel hash 68
  smoked haddock with
  poached eggs 109
Pork
  crackling 42
  pork and beans 64
  pork chops Auberge Saint
Pierre 87
  slow roasted pork belly
  with cider 124
Porridge 23
Port wine jelly 247
Potatoes 154
  best ever mash 155
  best ever roast potatoes
  154
  bubble and squeak 61
  champ 159

colcannon 61
cullen skink 191
gardener's pie 139
Janssen's temptation 212,
213
leek and potato soup 200
Mary's proper Greek
moussaka 82
Milly-Molly-Mandy
potatoes 156
Mum's fish pie 104, 105
mustard potatoes 158
pan Haggerty 157, 158
pick and mix fry-up 27
potato gratins 157
potato salad 156
red flannel hash 68
rissoles 67
shepherd's pie 66
stovies 70
three root mash 146
Potter's loaf, The 202, 203
Poulet Grand-Mère 125
Prawns
Mum's fish pie 104, 105
Prunes
devils on horseback 211
hot prune soufflé 249
Puddings
old-fashioned 222
school 222

Q

Queen of puddings 250

R

Rabbit with lentil purée 122
Raspberries
Bilbrook uncooked

raspberry jam 276
cranachan 237
peach Melba 245
Rationing 11
Red flannel hash 68
Remembrance of Things
Past 10
Rhubarb
rhubarb and custard 242
rhubarb crumble 233
Rice
bobotie 114, 115
kedgeree 28
pea and lettuce risotto 143
rice pudding 248
risotto with chicken livers
86
Risotto
pea and lettuce risotto 143
risotto with chicken livers
86
variations 87
Rissoles 67
Rob's damson ice cream 263
Rob's lunchtime salad 153
Rob's seduction sole 107
Rob's turkeyburgers 72
Rob's veg soup 199
Rum baba 236

S

Salad 148
barley salad 149
celeriac remoulade with
walnuts 151
chicory and orange salad
152
potato salad 156
Rob's lunchtime salad 153
salade Niçoise 150

tomato salad 148
tuna and bean salad 108
warm chicken liver salad
207
Salmon
Mum's fish pie 104, 105
shredded sorrel, on bed of
101
Salsa verde 51
Sandwiches 163
Sardines on toast 212
Sauces
big Granny's butterscotch
sauce 267
egg sauce 45
Granny Ray's chocolate
sauce 266
onion sauce 45
parsley sauce 45
salsa verde 51
tomato sauce for pasta 93
Sausages
braised red cabbage with
spicy sausages 91
chipolata casserole 81
Granny B's sausage rolls
215
pick and mix fry-up 27
toad in the hole 94
Savouries 188
Savoury pancakes 69
Scotch pancakes 26
Scrambled eggs 36
Seasonal cooking 16
Shallots
upside-down shallot tart
147
Shepherd's pie 66
Shrimps, potted 210
Smoked haddock
cullen skink 191

fish cakes 102
kedgeree 28
smoked haddock with poached eggs 109
Soft herring roes on toast 218
Sole
  Rob's seduction sole 107
Somerset chicken 90
Sorbet 261
  black-currant leaf water ice 264
Soufflés
  apricot soufflé 249
  courgette soufflé 141
  hot chocolate soufflés 260
  hot prune soufflé 249
  Jerusalem artichoke soufflé 141
Soup 189
  Bramley apple and celeriac soup 190
  cullen skink 191
  garlicky spinach soup 195
  garnish 189
  gazpacho 192, 193
  green pea soup 197
  Heinz tomato soup 194
  leek and potato soup 200
  minestrone 196
  onion boys' soup 201
  parsley soup 198
  parsnip with orange and ginger 194
  potage Crécy 193
  Rob's veg soup 199
  veloute Johnny 201
Souvlaki 92
Spaghetti Bolognese 127
Spinach
  Andrew's spinach

supper 89
creamed spinach 136
garlicky spinach soup 195
Split peas
  pease pudding 144
Steamed syrup pudding 229
Stews 112
  Anne's beef stew 116, 117
  billabong stew 113
  bobotie 114, 115
  coq au vin 118, 119
  lamb with aubergines and cinnamon 128
  Lancashire hot pot 120
  navarin of lamb 121
  oxtail stew 123
  pheasant and chestnut casserole 126
  poulet Grand-Mère 125
  rabbit with lentil purée 122
  slow roasted pork belly with cider 124
  spag. Bol 127
  very slow shoulder of lamb 129
Stodge 222, 228
Stone cream 251
Stovies 70
Suet
  apple in and out 225
  blackberry and apple pudding 224
  plum pudding 241
  steak and kidney pudding 52, 53
  suet crust 53
Summer Pudding 14
Sunday lunch
  recipes 42-57
  ritual 41
  variety in 40

Swedes
  three root mash 146
Swiss roll 176, 177

T

Tarragon-roasted chicken 54
Tea 164
Teacakes 31
Teatime
  afternoon tea, institution of 162
  biscuits. See Biscuits
  cakes. See Cakes
  country, in 163
  perfect cup of tea 164
  sandwiches 163
  tea shops 162
  toast and crumpets 163, 164
Tessa and Jane's apple and chestnut layers 253
Toad in the hole 94
Tomatoes
  gazpacho 192, 193
  Heinz tomato soup 194
  pick and mix fry-up | 27
  pork and beans 64
  tomato salad 148
  tomato sauce for pasta 93
Treacle tart 252
Trifle 254
Tuna
  salade Nicoise 150
  tuna and bean salad 108
  turkey tonnato 71
Turkey
  devilled turkey 63
  Rob's turkeyburgers 72

turkey tonnato 71

V

Vegetables 132, 133. See also
  Carrots, etc
  crudités 206
  gardener's pie 139
  greens with bacon and
  onion 134, 135
  gussied up 133
  homegrown 132
  minestrone 196
  Rob's veg soup 199
  variety of 133

W

Walnuts
  celeriac remoulade with
  walnuts 151
Welsh rabbit 216

Y

Yorkshire pudding 42

Jane Fearnley-Whittingstall, bestselling author of The Good Granny Guide, has written many other books on plants and gardening, including Gardening Made Easy and Peonies – The Imperial Flower. A grandmother of five, and the mother of TV chef Hugh, she lives with her husband in Gloucestershire.